PROBLEMS IN FOCUS SERIES

Each volume in the 'Problems in Focus' series is designed to make available to students important work on key historical problems and periods that they encounter in their courses. Each volume is devoted to a central topic or theme, and the most important aspects of this are dealt with by specially commissioned essays from scholars in the relevant field. The editorial introduction reviews the problem or period as a whole, and each essay provides an assessment of the particular aspect, pointing out the areas of development and controversy, and indicating where conclusions can be drawn or where further work is necessary. An annotated bibliography serves as a guide for further reading.

TITLES IN PRINT

European Warfare 1450–1815
  edited by Jeremy Black
European Warfare 1815–2000
  edited by Jeremy Black
The Wars of the Roses
  edited by A. J. Pollard
The Reign of Henry VIII
  edited by Diarmaid MacCulloch
The Mid-Tudor Polity c. 1540–1560
  edited by Jennifer Loach and Robert Tittler
The British Problem, c. 1534–1707
  edited by Brendan Bradshaw and John Morrill
Culture and Politics in Early Stuart England
  edited by Kevin Sharpe and Peter Lake
The Origins of the English Civil War
  edited by Conrad Russell
Reactions to the English Civil War 1642–1649
  edited by John Morrill
The Reigns of Charles II and James VII & II
  edited by Lionel K. J. Glassey
Absolutism in the Seventeenth Century
  edited by John Miller

D0162515

Britain in the Age of Walpole
  edited by Jeremy Black
Enlightened Absolutism
  edited by H. M. Scott
Popular Movements, c. 1830–1850
  edited by J. T. Ward

Problems in Focus
Series Standing Order
ISBN 0–333–71704–X hardcover
ISBN 0–333–69348–5 paperback
(*outside North America only*)

You can receive future titles in this series as they are
published. To place a standing order please contact your
bookseller or, in the case of difficulty, write to us at the
address below with your name and address, the title of the
series and an ISBN quoted above.

Customer Services Department, Macmillan Distribution Ltd,
Houndmills, Basingstoke, Hampshire RG21 6XS, England

European Warfare
1815–2000

Edited by

JEREMY BLACK

palgrave

First published 2002 by
PALGRAVE
Houndmills, Basingstoke, Hampshire RG21 6XS and
175 Fifth Avenue, New York, N.Y. 10010
Companies and representatives throughout the world

PALGRAVE is the new global academic imprint of
St. Martin's Press LLC Scholarly and Reference Division and
Palgrave Publishers Ltd (formerly Macmillan Press Ltd).

ISBN 0–333–78667–X hardback
ISBN 0–333–78668–8 paperback

This book is printed on paper suitable for recycling and
made from fully managed and sustained forest sources.

A catalogue record for this book is available
from the British Library.

Library of Congress Cataloging-in-Publication Data
European warfare, 1815–2000 / edited by Jeremy Black.
    p. cm. — (Problems in focus series)
    Includes bibliographical references and index.
    Contents: Europe's way of war, 1815–1864 / Dennis Showalter —
European warfare, 1864–1914 / Jeremy Black — The First World War /
Spencer Tucker — The European civil war: Reds versus Whites in Russia
and Spain, 1917–1939 / Francisco J. Romero Salvadó — The Second World
War / S.P. MacKenzie — Colonial wars / Bruce Vandervort — Naval power
and warfare / Lawrence Sondhaus — The transformation of war in Europe,
1945–2000 / Warren Chin.
    ISBN 0–333–78667–X — ISBN 0–333–78668–8 (pbk.)
    1. Europe—History, Military—19th century. 2. Europe—History,
Military—20th century. 3. War and society—History. I. Black, Jeremy.
II. Problems in focus series (Palgrave (Firm))
D361 .E97 2001
355'.0094—dc21   2001046010

10   9   8   7   6   5   4   3   2   1
11   10 09 08 07 06 05 04 03 02

Transferred to digital printing in 2006.

*For **Mark Overton***
a much respected colleague and a good friend

Contents

Introduction

JEREMY BLACK*

This is a book about the ideas and practices of the military and of military force over the past two centuries. It is also about the writing of military history. A reconsideration of both of these fields is needed in light of the great changes in the 1990s resulting from the collapse of the Soviet Union and the return of warfare in the Balkans.

> Official accounts reported that the attack would remain in history as a classic masterpiece of efficiency, organization, power, courage, and political sense. Colonel Emilio Canevari, the best known of the military commentators, reported the brilliant attack of non-existent motorized formations in close contact with the air force.[1]

Contemporary misleading descriptions of the successful Italian invasion of Albania in 1939 are a testimony to the teleological character of military commentary and history, more specifically the focus, for any one period, on a form of warfare believed to be appropriate and progressive, and the related habit of judging military organisation and activity in this light. Both global and European military history (and accounts of state development) have long suffered from this approach. A particular military form, or state organisation, is assumed to represent progress. It is the focus of attention, and other forms suffer from neglect and/or comparison. In short, military history is affected by a 'meta-narrative', or grand overarching synoptic account, that is linear, uni-directional and Whiggish; and at a time when Whiggish approaches have been discarded in most spheres of serious historical work.

This is linked to the paradigmatic quality of the analysis. In any one period, there is held to be a paradigm of effective military

* I would like to thank Gerry Bryant, Christopher Duffy, Paul Mackenzie, Dennis Showalter and Spencer Tucker for their comments on an earlier draft.

1

power. Capability can apparently be assessed in terms of this paradigm, while change occurs as a consequence of the transition from one paradigm to another. The stages are related to civil–military relations and to the more general issue of state-building. The notion of a paradigmatic means of warfare and individual military power, and the teleological and linear account of development employ diffusion and action/reaction models of development. These play a central role, albeit not generally an explicit one, in the discussion of military history.

This is a subject in which explicit theorisation plays a minor role, in part because of the ambiguous attitude of the military to such an approach and, in part, because of the lack of commercial 'market' interest and the focus of the latter on operational accounts and, thus, explanations. Most popular military history is operational, specifically the direction of a campaign in a particular theatre, in other words an analysis of individual campaigns and battles, of strategy and tactics in specifics. There is very little overall analysis of war in such accounts, and most of it is derived from a chronological organisation of operational detail. Such an approach seems to offer nothing to other fields of historical research. That, however, does not trouble the practitioners or publishers of books on military history, the vast majority of whom are not academics.

If the practice of military history appeared to have little to do with developments in the profession in the 1950s and 1960s, the situation was, in part, to change with what was termed the 'new military history'. This essentially translated the intellectual trends of anthropology, psychology and sociology to the military, and employed them in order to analyse its structure and culture. Issues such as recruitment and desertion were scrutinised. The 'new military history' reflected trends elsewhere in the profession. Thus it broadened out in the 1990s to include not only discussion of gender issues, but also of the body, as in studies of face-to-face killing.[2]

Such work was valuable, but not without its drawbacks. Much of the 'new military history' demilitarised the subject. In particular, it was apt to lose sight of war. Furthermore, there was a static quality to much of the analysis of structure and culture. Issues of respective quality and comparative capability tended to be omitted or treated in a simplistic fashion.

The teleological character of military history ensures, for example, that the history of European warfare in the nineteenth century is dominated by two periods, the Napoleonic Wars of the first fifteen years and the conflicts of 1854–71: the Crimean War and the Wars of German and Italian Unification. This is understandable. Each of these periods was one of important struggle and also affected ideas about warfare in the following decades. Yet such a focus risks underrating events and developments in the intervening period.

Furthermore, a concentration on paradigmatic conflict between the regular forces of European states is unhelpful as an account both of the variety of warfare within Europe and of Europe's military position in the wider world; both themes treated in this book. Thus Prussia's success in the Wars of German Unification (1864–71) made the Prussian army a model for developments elsewhere, most obviously in the creation of General Staffs. Yet the treatment of the Prussian/German military as a paradigm neglects the extent to which other armies, especially those of Britain, France, Portugal, Russia and Spain had to devote much of their attention to operations outside Europe. Their armies had broader-spectrum missions than that of Germany and required a correspondingly flexible – or at least differentiated – organisation and ethos. It was suggested, with much reason, that the British army would have made a more successful job than the Germans in suppressing opposition in south-west Africa in 1904–5.[3] More generally, any taxonomy and analysis of military style has to be able to comprehend symmetrical as well as asymmetrical warfare. The latter involved not only conflict outside Europe, but also the operations against irregular forces within Europe that are apt to be underrated in synoptic accounts of European military history.

These theoretical points can both be given greater weight and be 'located' by considering them, in part, in terms of the 'dialogue' between offensive and defensive deployments and tactics. In essence, paradigmatic models are apt to focus on the offensive. Thus, the paradigm moves from the Prussians, under Frederick the Great (1740–86), to the French army of the Revolution and Napoleon, the Prussians in the Wars of German Unification, and the Wehrmacht (German army) in the World Wars, especially in the *blitzkrieg* campaigns early in World War

Two. The 'offensive' is a concept that has to be handled with some care as the strategic offensive could be combined with the tactical defensive to deadly effect, as by the Prussians against the French at Sedan in 1870. Nevertheless, the advantage of attacking as opposed to defending was debated throughout the period and, in general, the attack was seen as spiritually superior as well as being militarily necessary in order to defeat the enemy and capture territory. Thus, for example, in the warfare of the 1820s to 1850s, there was a determination to fix and then overcome opponents, and a conviction that defensive firepower could be overcome by manoeuvre, before and during the battle, and by the élan of a well-directed shock attack. Military planners for the remainder of our period were to try to recover this confidence.

All the paradigmatic forces listed above were important and influential, rightly deserving of study, but a focus on them has had a number of adverse effects. These include a failure to devote sufficient attention to their opponents and a frequently limited understanding of the campaigns themselves. In short, established assumptions tend to guide operational accounts, especially their underlying suppositions, and these in turn sustain the meta-narrative. This can be considered first by focusing on the major conflicts that attract most attention and then by looking at the range of warfare in the period.

In the first case, there have been important re-evaluations of both world wars, although their impact on the popular literature has been limited. Thus the popular image of World War One remains that of total futility and mindless slaughter, and this is more generally significant for military history as it reflects a disenchantment with war understood both as pursuit of state interest and as fighting. However, the scholarly focus, as Spencer Tucker shows, has instead been on the development of new fighting techniques in the war. For example, there has been an emphasis on the development of successful new offensive tactics in 1916–18, especially by the Germans, as well as on the success of the British army in overcoming earlier limitations in order to produce a war-winning operational doctrine and force structure later in 1918. The Allied offensive of that year saw systematic co-ordination, reflecting more effective control of both infantry and massive artillery support, and improved communications.[4]

The possibility of reconsidering World War One in light of the campaigns in Eastern Europe can be placed in the wider context of the need for the re-evaluation of the military history of Eastern Europe, not only for its own sake, but also in order to use the discussion of warfare there in order to reconsider the general assessment of European military development. On the whole, the linear, teleological and paradigmatic approach to military history has focused on Western Europe (stretching to include Prussia), while Eastern Europe has been made to appear less important, if not primitive, in comparison. This geographical emphasis characterised discussion of medieval and early-modern military history, although the latter has been questioned in some of the work on the so-called Military Revolution of the sixteenth century. As far as 1815–2000 is concerned, there has been a focus on a given 'core' of struggles. Thus, for the nineteenth century, the Wars of German and Italian Unification attract attention, but not the Russo–Polish struggles of 1830–1 and 1863–4 or the Hungarian rising of 1848–9. Similarly, the Carlist Wars in Spain, and other conflicts in Iberia, are neglected.

This failure is not simply limited to historians. For example, Richard Hall, in his study of the Balkan Wars of 1912–13, in which he sought to explain the inability of military attachés to appreciate many of the tactical lessons that would become very important during World War One, particularly the role of field fortifications, suggests that one reason 'was the assumption that events in regions of lesser development such as the Balkans could do little to instruct the Great Powers'.[5] Similar assumptions affected the response to the tactical and other lessons offered by the Boer War of 1899–1902 in South Africa.

Comments about the nature of war in World War One based on the Western Front are misleading, as warfare in Eastern Europe was more fluid. Individual campaigns could be decisive. Austrian, German and Bulgarian forces conquered Serbia in 1915 and Romania in 1916. Furthermore, as success was translated into conquest, so attitudes towards the conflict changed. For example, German successes, particularly in 1915, led to the development by the Germans of new categories of viewing Eastern Europe and to the attempt to create a new-model society under military direction that better fits the definition of total war than the more static conflict and objectives on the Western Front: 'Seizing on the ideology of German Work, the army prepared to build a military utopia which would change the place. The most durable product of the venture, however, would be the transformation which took place within individual soldiers, creating a specific way of viewing and treating the lands and peoples of the East'. As later, under the Nazis, 'overreaching ambitions in Ober Ost's utopian vision sanctioned a brutal, arbitrary, and violent rule which undercut its own goals'.[6]

The Eastern Front also provides opportunities for the re-evaluation of World War Two, not least because until recently disproportionate attention has been devoted to conflict involving Britain and the USA for a host of reasons, including limited access to Soviet archives, linguistic problems[7] and the impact of political pressures on the presentation of history during the Soviet period. As a consequence, it is possible to direct attention to operations that have been neglected.[8] In particular, the Soviet portrayal of a continuous march to victory from late 1942 encouraged successive oversights of less successful campaigns. There is a need both for detailed re-evaluation and for the incorporation of the resulting insights into the overall account of the war in the East.

For a long time, German failure there was attributed to the size of the Soviet Union, the winter, Soviet numbers, and Hitler's maladroit interventions. It is apparent, however, that these interpretations, which drew heavily on German sources, have to be re-examined. In particular, it is necessary to re-evaluate positively the quality of the Red Army and its command, both in defence and attack. Soviet doctrine, with its emphasis on defence in depth, and its stress on artillery in defence and attack, proved effective once the initial shock and surprise of the German attack had been absorbed. It proved possible to thwart tank attacks and to block *blitzkrieg*. Furthermore, Soviet operational art towards the end of the war stressed firepower, but also effectively employed mobile tank warfare. In less than two-and-a-half years' fighting, the Soviets drove the Germans from the Volga to the Elbe, a distance greater than that achieved by any European force for over a century, and one secured despite the strength and determination of the defenders.

The re-evaluations of both world wars have, as their common

core, an emphasis not on new weaponry, but on fighting quality involving the effective use of established weaponry. In short, this is an account not about a paradigm shift resulting from the introduction of aircraft and tanks (and, later, the numbers of each available), but rather it is about the need also to consider the continued value of artillery and infantry and also of more effective tactical co-ordination of arms and better communications. In place of a fascination with the machine and the modern, we have an awareness of the importance of effectiveness and change within established military traditions and practice. Planning and command skills and, more generally, the ability to articulate and integrate different arms, a long-established aspect of effectiveness, became more important with the greater range of available technology. Thus it became necessary to integrate infantry, artillery and armour successfully in battle (and not just in peacetime planning), as well as air and land, air and sea, and sea and land forces. These were necessary not only to achieve success in the attack but also in defence, and in all dimensions of war, including sea and air. In February 1943, Admiral Sir Dudley Pound, First Sea Lord in the British Admiralty, noted

> At the moment we are doing all we can to produce super long-range aircraft so that we can cover the whole of the Atlantic from one side to the other, as there is no question but that if you can put aircraft over the U-boats during the day, it prevents them getting into position for their night attacks. I am hoping very much that we shall be able to blast them out of their operational bases in the Bay of Biscay

by air attack.[9] More generally, a stress on the campaigns in both world wars, especially on fighting qualities and command skills, ensures that there is due attention to the defeat of Germany on the battlefield; and that this is not treated simply as an aspect of superior Allied resources (which can indeed be stressed for both world wars) or of a collapse of the German Home Front and alliance system (World War One).

Moving away from machinisation and fascination with the new as an explanation for battlefield success has an impact not only in our understanding of the two world wars but also, more generally, in terms of the content and character of the linear approach to Western military history. If it becomes less clear that the availability of quantities of new weapons was crucial to victory, then a hierarchy of military capability, based on their possession, is rendered uncertain.

Furthermore, the habit of judging inter-war periods in terms of an account of weapons development and acquisition is rendered problematic. Indeed, consideration of such periods on their own terms clarifies and explains contemporary uncertainty about appropriate force structures and doctrines. This can be seen in naval thought in the late nineteenth century, in which, as Lawrence Sondhaus shows, there was considerable uncertainty about the respective merits of battleships, cruisers, and anti-battleship weaponry, principally torpedo boats but also, later, submarines. In 1885, General Roberts, commander of the Madras Army, part of the British army in India, pressed for 'swift steamers with long range guns' in order to protect ports against opponents capable of deploying the latter.[10]

Similarly, in the 'inter-war' period (the years between World Wars One and Two) there was uncertainty not only about the relationships between surface ships and submarines and between tanks, and infantry and artillery, but also in the air between long-range bombers, ground-support bombers (particularly dive-bombers), and fighters. To use the subsequent conflict, in this case World War Two, to assess the correctness of particular inter-war policies is not helpful because it presupposes that the military tasking that the war was to present had been clear earlier, and thus underrates the political context that determined tasking.

For example, for most of the period the British armed forces were principally concerned with preparing for war outside Europe, either with resistance to rebellion in colonies or with protecting them from attack by other major powers, a tasking that meant planning responses to Russian threats to India and, in the 1930s, Japanese threats to British positions in the Far East. Such tasks required a force structure centred on local garrisons and a fleet able to move rapidly in order to secure naval superiority and cover the movement of reinforcements from units based in Britain. As far as land warfare was concerned, the emphasis was not on tanks, which were not well suited to many tasks in imperial protection and were also cumbersome to move. Thus the argument, both at the time and subsequently, that the British should have developed more mechanised forces, including more tanks and ground support planes (with the tactical doctrine which went with them), in order better to counter the German *blitzkrieg* they unsuccessfully faced in France in 1940, neglects the circumstances that prevailed in the inter-war period. As a reminder of the difficulty of judging developments, it is instructive to turn for example to the papers of the British committee of 1926 on the reorganisation of the cavalry. It was uncertain whether the likeliest opponent of Britain in a future war would be the Soviet Union or Turkey. Colonel Lindsay, the Inspector of the Royal Tanks Corps, was in no doubt that cavalry was too vulnerable to modern small arms:

> All civil evolution is towards the elimination of manpower and animal power, and the substitution of mechanical power. History shows that the military mind has usually lagged behind in its appreciation of civil evolution and its possibilities . . . in the Army we must substitute machine and weapon power for man and animal power in every possible way, and that to do this we must carefully watch, and where necessary foster, those trends of civil evolution that will help us to this end . . . We are the nation above all others who can develop the mobile mechanical and weapon-power Army, for we have long service soldiers and a vast industrial organisation.

Other respondents were less happy about the wisdom of dispensing with cavalry and, instead, urged its combination with mechanised forces.

It was also unclear which vehicles would be most appropriate. Thus in 1927, General Milne, the Chief of the Imperial General Staff, told the officers of the experimental Mechanised Force, that it was necessary to have vehicles that would be immune to poison gas, and also claimed 'in a very few years the petrol engine itself will have to give way to something else'.[11]

Sir Philip Chetwode, Deputy Chief of the Imperial General Staff, suggested in 1921 that 'the tank would not prove to be such a formidable engine of war as people think and that before long it will have lost much of its terror', but he was more convinced of the threat of air attack on ground formations and emphasised that cavalry officers needed to think 'of the war of the future', not least in developing co-operation with tanks and planes.[12] Chetwode also argued that tank specifications and tactics ought to focus on colonial commitments. Thus he pressed for tanks to be armed with a machine gun, not a heavier gun, and for training in the use of tanks against opponents equipped with artillery and machine guns, but not tanks.[13]

There was also the question of allocating roles and resources between land and air forces. Thus in 1922, General Rawlinson, Commander-in-Chief in India, opposed the proposal of the government of India to abolish a division in order to add two more air squadrons.[14] Milne offered a far broader critique of air power, in which he linked doctrine to organisational structures and politics. He wrote of

the highly organised and unscrupulous propaganda of the Air Staff . . . the separation of the Air Staff from the General Staff which prevents problems of defence being considered as a whole, and with a proper sense of proportion as to their cost . . . the Air Staff have found it necessary, in order to find support for their separate and independent existence . . . to devise a special form of so called air strategy . . . there appear to be two principles or catch words upon which it is based . . . attack against the nerve centres of an enemy nation . . . and the moral effect of the air arm. In dealing with problems of war on a large scale against civilized countries the former term is usually employed. The objectives of such strategy are the centres of production-nominally of munitions, which, be it marked, is a term of very wide significance. In effect this new form of strategy takes the form of attack against civilian workers, including their women and children.

The hitherto accepted objectives of land and sea warfare have been the armed forces of the enemy, and whether or no we as a nation are justified morally in adopting a military policy which is so totally at variance with the accepted dictates of humanity, there is no doubt that we should be the first to suffer if the next war were to be waged on such principles.[15]

In 1936, when he resigned the post of Chief of the Imperial General Staff, Sir Archibald Montgomery-Massingberd wrote:

> I feel that the biggest battle that I have had to fight in the last three years is against the idea that on account of the arrival of Air Forces as a new arm, the Low Countries are of little value to us and that, therefore, we need not maintain a military force to assist in holding them . . . the elimination of any Army commitment on the Continent sounds such a comfortable and cheap policy . . . especially amongst the air mad . . . It has often been stated that we have yet to realise the extent to which the advent in large numbers of high-performance aeroplanes will affect the conduct of war. I agree, and it is because of this uncertainty as to the effect that air forces will have that we must go carefully and avoid jumping to false conclusions. So far as we know, the French are still prepared to risk the movement of troops on a large scale by land on the outbreak of war, and so I believe are the Germans. If there are any lessons to be drawn from the present war in Abyssinia, it seems to be that even against savages with no air force and no anti-aircraft weapons of any value, a strong air force is unable to bring about an early decision.
>
> Another thing that is often entirely ignored is the question of weather and atmosphere which would very definitely affect the success of bombing operations.

Mongomery-Massingberd claimed that a war on the Continent would still be decided on land, and he also drew attention to the political consequences of particular force doctrines and structures when he claimed that if the British focused on air power at the expense of a Continental commitment they would lose their allies.[16]

The role of political factors indeed emerges clearly in the subsequent chapters. It can be seen, for example, in World War Two, with the shift from the relatively fluid international situation in 1939–41 to the subsequent fight to the finish between Germany and a more stable opposing bloc. As Francisco Romero Salvadó shows, politics was even more important in the course of the civil wars in Russia (1917–21) and Spain (1936–9). He links both by presenting them in terms of a struggle between

Left and Right that he sees as the central theme throughout the period. Not all readers will agree with his emphasis, but it is clear that both wars were about far more than clashes in the field. This is supported by other work. For example, Geoffrey Swain's *Russia's Civil War* (Stroud, 2000) provides an essentially political account of the conflict that emphasises the autonomous role of the peasantry and the failure of the Whites to win peasant support. The brutality of the Bolsheviks emerges clearly, but also the eventual willingness to 'drop their socialist offensive and introduce a pro-peasant policy in order to win a measure of peasant support. The Green [peasant] rebels had fought the Bolsheviks to a sort of stalemate'.[17]

Subsequently, Stalin was to turn on the peasantry, using force to wage the internal warfare that totalitarian regimes particularly endorsed. This internal warfare is a major fact of military history, but one that has been relatively underplayed due to the focus on state-to-state conflict. Thus, as Dennis Showalter indicates, nineteenth-century governments used force to tackle urban uprisings and rural insurrection. The major powers also used their armies to suppress uprisings in the territories of allies and clients. For example, Habsburg (Austrian) forces crushed rebel forces in Naples and the Piedmontese part of the Kingdom of Sardinia in 1821. The forces deployed in such operations could be considerable. In 1831, the Russians deployed over 100 000 troops in a successful attempt to suppress a Polish rising for independence, while in 1832 a 62 000-strong French army besieged the Dutch-held citadel of Antwerp in the conflict that had begun when Belgium rose against Dutch rule in 1830.

These conflicts are an important reminder of the diversity of combat situations, as well as the political circumstances, facing armies. Thus on 23 September 1830, after 10 000 Dutch troops entered Brussels, they met determined opponents who employed the cover of barricades and fire from windows and housetops. The troops withdrew on the 26th.

The conflicts of this period prefigured the Bosnian war of 1992–5, discussed by Warren Chin, in a number of respects. Aside from the limited role of 'grand battle', there was also a political complexity with multiple players that made 'peacemaking' very difficult. More generally, the conflicts of the 1990s – Bosnia and Kosovo (1999) – can be seen as a return to the 'limited' warfare of 1816–63 after an intervening period of 'total' warfare. This approach begs the question of definition: there were, for example, within Europe few anticipations in the Wars of German Unification or World War One of the slaughter of civilians that was to be seen in Bosnia and Kosovo.

In addition, the implication is that in the age of 'total warfare' conflict was somehow left to the generals, and they were able to focus on defeating opposing armies rather than in engaging in counter-insurgency and other policing tasks. This is less than a complete account because it neglects the role of counter-insurgency in warfare. In the former case it is, for example, possible to focus on the major commitment of German military resources during World War Two to the suppression of opposition in occupied territories. This did not conform to the model of war as the clash between regular forces, but such an account has its limitations, especially for lengthy conflicts. The role of the Resistance is a reminder of the mistake of considering military strength in terms of regular forces, and also testifies to the character of total war. Just as the occupation of territory and the use of its resources were not enough for the Germans, especially in Eastern Europe, so their opponents were not prepared to accept the verdict of battle: after the defending regulars had been defeated, irregulars could still play a role in resisting occupying forces.

The better-armed Germans were generally able to defeat partisans in open conflict, as when they suppressed risings in Warsaw, Slovakia and the Vercors plateau in France in 1944. Furthermore, many areas remained under partisan control because the Germans chose not to deploy troops to occupy them. However, the resistance still achieved much. In Poland, the Balkans and occupied areas of the Soviet Union, there was particularly extensive partisan activity, helped by the vastness of the area in question, the nature of the terrain – for example the Yugoslav mountains and the Pripet Marshes – and the harshness of German rule. Most important, as with the Allied air offensive, was the diversion of large amounts of German resources to deal with the threat, as well as the need to adopt anti-partisan policies that affected the efficiency of German rule and economic and transport activities. In addition, considerable damage and disruption was inflicted by sabotage and guerrilla attacks, while the Allies benefited from large quantities of crucial intelligence, for example on defences, troop movements, bomb damage, and the development of German rocketry. Counter-insurgency operations on this scale were not seen in any other state-to-state conflict in this period and can thus be presented as a bridge between World War Two and the civil wars in which conflict of this type played a major role, for example the Carlist Wars.

Throughout the period 1864–1945, armies were involved in a full range of 'policing' tasks, including the suppression of insurrections, riots, strikes and political movements, and the maintenance or replacement of governments. In 1871 the French army suppressed the very radical Paris Commune, a striking example for other governments, and for the propertied as a whole, of the need for powerful armies. In 1931 artillery was deployed against anarchist strikers in Seville, while, in 1934, strikes in Portugal led to the deployment of troops and the army suppressed a miners' rising in the Asturias region of Spain; the ability of the miners to unite, seize weapons and defeat the local police led to a brutal military response. After the rebellion had been defeated there was widespread killing of prisoners as well as civilians. In January 1941 the Romanian army suppressed the powerful Iron Guards, a fascist movement.

This process was not restricted to autocratic regimes. Their democratic counterparts also felt challenged by labour unrest. In Britain 12 000 troops were deployed in Glasgow in 1919, as were tanks. Two years later strikes led the General Staff to think of bringing in troops 'from all over Europe' (i.e., from foreign postings) and to consider calling out reservists.[18] There were extensive movements of troops at the time of the General Strike in 1926 (although no use of force),[19] while in France they were used to try to keep order at the time of the Stavisky riots in 1934. The need to have forces able to confront labour unrest encouraged an emphasis on the value of regular troops, which were seen as more reliable than conscripts or reservists.

These and other episodes might suggest that the military has fundamentally stood for order and stability and there is much to say for this intuitive point. The relationship between the military and society can in large part be written around a bond of conservatism. The military has tended to be dominated by conservative forces in society and has generally acted to maintain conservative structures.

Yet it is also necessary to note limitations with this equation before moving on to consider the related, but separate, issue of war and society. The first obvious limitation is the role of the military in revolutionary situations, both the active role of revolutionary units and the more passive, but still important, role of others being unwilling to suppress revolution. This can be seen with the Russian Revolution in 1917, but, in the previous century, there was also a series of risings by radical army units, for example in Portugal in 1820, in Piedmont in 1821 and in Russia in 1825. Related to this was the importance in liberal circles, especially in France and Italy, of the idea of the citizen soldier. Secondly, there is the extent to which the military acted as the agent of states with transforming agendas. This was true for example of the process of state building in the nineteenth century and of totalitarian regimes in the twentieth century.

Thirdly (and these categories can overlap), there was the role in military structures of professionalism and of new developments, a situation accentuated in wartime by the pressures of conflict, and the extent to which existing structures seemed defective.[20] The net effect, both in peace and war, was to encourage a desire to improve on existing arrangements. This owed much to changes in weaponry and force structure, which encouraged a degree of volatility in military life greater in the nineteenth than in the eighteenth century, and even greater in the twentieth. Commenting on the need to develop vehicle tracks able to withstand the rocky terrain of India, Montgomery-Massingberd wrote in 1929 'things advance so quickly now that things which seemed impossible a year or two ago are already practically accomplished.'[21]

However, other factors that can be more securely located in the political sphere were also at play. As professionalism was defined in terms of meritocratic considerations that focused on what was presented as modernisation, so a potential rift developed between the military understood as an efficient force and the military understood as a force to maintain order, let alone a conservative force. This helped provide a tension in state–military relations, although the configuration of this tension varied greatly. Lieutenant-General Hamilton, then General Officer Commanding

Southern Command in Britain, in his observations on the Austrian and German manoeuvres in 1906, captured the contrast between the social politics and military habits of an army that was not responding rapidly to the possibilities of change, and one that was:

> From the purely professional standpoint, the Austrian officers resemble the British officer of the nineteenth century. I mean they look on their military career rather as an exciting game than as the most deadly earnest work any mortal man may dare to put his hand to . . . stand very far apart from their men.

Hamilton thought the Austrian infantry 'evinced but small appreciation of the power of modern artillery or rifles, or of the necessity these new factors involve for quick movement and concealment'. In contrast with the Germans 'the system; the machine; has become more and more irresistibly perfect in every department of the state'.[22]

War and society was a relationship expressed in a radical bond. However much the political forces that instigated and supported the decision to fight intended to maintain social and political stability and, in part, backed war for precisely that reason, major conflicts tended to have a very different impact. Aside from the massive strains caused by casualties and suffering, wartime allocation of resources and manpower, the cost of conflict, the resulting taxation and inflation and the destruction of buildings and infrastructure, there was also the experience of conflict by much of the young male population. Whereas the wars of 1816–63 had been waged by relatively small forces of professional regular troops, thereafter there was a greater emphasis on conscription and reservists drawing in a large proportion of a country's fit young men; this emphasis has only ebbed over the last three decades.

The acceptance across much of the West that universal male military service was a requirement the state could expect and enforce had a number of roots. It sprung from authoritarian (especially serf) societies, particularly Russia, but also from the notion of the people in arms developed in the American and French Revolutions. The radical nature of the latter encouraged a preference for regulars in Europe after the fall of

Napoleon in 1815, but the emphasis shifted in the second half of the nineteenth century as the need for large forces was driven, in part, by the increased prospect of a major power war and, in part, by the need to respond to developments by rivals. In addition, conscription seemed a necessary response to a society made more volatile by mass urbanisation, industrialisation and secularisation, by the extension of the franchise to most or all men and by the growth of worker activism. In response, young men at an impressionistic age were exposed to state-directed military organisation and discipline. In addition, state direction was centralised: the sub-contracting of military functions to entrepreneurs and the autonomy of aristocratic officers had both ended, or, at least, greatly eroded. Conscription was less expensive than hiring soldiers, but it required a structure of training and authority that was under government control. Conscripts served for about two or three years and then entered the reserves, ensuring that substantial forces of trained men could be mobilised in the event of war and that the state did not have to pay them in peace. Combined with demographic and economic growth, this dramatically increased the potential size of armies. Conscription helped in the militarisation of society and was seen as important to the ideological and political programme of modernisation, so that the major social changes did not lead to more pacific societies. Thanks to conscription, nationalism and the increase in the scale of mobilisation of resources, it became more apparent that war was a struggle between societies, rather than simply military forces.

The world wars saw a mobilisation of societies for war, with conscription introduced in hitherto exempt countries (Britain 1916, 1939), with large sections of their economies placed under government control, and with both society and politics regulated. For all combatants, the mass management of resources, the economy and society became more important. War gave the states power and enabled them to circumvent many of the constraints and exigencies of pre-war politics. As such, it was a catalyst for modernisation. The political, social and economic privileges and status of established elites and middle classes alike were qualified or challenged, and the stability of a number of countries was made more precarious. Gender and social roles were re-examined.

In World War Two, economic regulation and conscription were introduced more rapidly and comprehensively in states that did not already have them than had been the case in World War One. It was not only for this reason that the war was more 'total' than the earlier war. The Nazification of the Germans played a major role in ensuring that World War Two was different. Once the Soviet Union had been invaded in 1941, the conflict was presented by Hitler in millenarian terms as a fight for racial mastery and a conflict of wills. This helped ensure that Nazi ideology was at the centre of the struggle and also influenced the way in which the war was waged, particularly the brutality shown to Russians and in occupied areas in Eastern Europe, and how the Allies, with their insistence on unconditional German surrender, reacted to it. The genocidal treatment of the Jews from 1941 was not an exception, but rather the culmination of a totalising ideological militarism although the extremism of Nazi anti-Semitism gave this policy a particular ferocity.

Although different in design, another aspect of the assault on opposing peoples was provided by the bombing of civilian targets, a practice begun on a large scale by the German *Luftwaffe* with the terror bombing of undefended cities, especially Warsaw (1939), Rotterdam (1940) and Belgrade (1941), done deliberately in order to create panic and to cause heavy civilian casualties: 17 000 people were killed in Belgrade. In these cases, bombing was an adjunct of ground invasions. Strategic air campaigns intended as long-term preparation for ground attack (and seen by the protagonists of air power as a substitute for it) began in 1940 with the unsuccessful German attempt to prepare for an invasion of Britain, and then became an unsuccessful campaign to reduce Britain to submission by bombing. This failed in part because of a lack of sufficient trained pilots, and the limitations of their planes and tactics.

The British, joined later by the Americans, in turn launched a strategic bombing campaign against Germany. Despite the limited precision of bombing by high-flying aeroplanes dropping free-fall bombs, German logistics, communications and weapons production were increasingly disrupted, so that the rise in weapons production was less than it would otherwise have been. The Germans diverted massive resources to anti-aircraft defence that might otherwise have had an impact on the front line. The area bombing that was increasingly adopted as an objective, with the hope that it would devastate urban life and bring an end to the war by increasing civilian misery, caused heavy civilian casualties, but did not break German civilian morale.[23] The direct consequences, nevertheless, were far more devastating than the Allied blockade of Germany in World War One or the attempted German aerial riposte in 1944–5: the launching of V1 pilotless planes and V2 ground-to-ground rockets, which ushered in the age of strategic rocket warfare.[24]

The notion of war bridging the foreign and domestic spheres was not only true for the Nazi state. The brutality shown to those judged unacceptable within states, and the harsh treatment of dissidents, were regarded not only as a necessary by-product of policy goals but also as part of the Nazi and Communist missions. Thus the fall of Nazi Germany in 1945 did not bring the end of concentration camps (as the Soviet gulags testified) or, more generally, the end of the use of force in an attempt to remould society. In the post-war decades, right-wing authoritarian regimes in Portugal (–1974), Spain (–1975) and Greece (1967–74) relied on force. The military played an important role in their creation, with Franco's regime in Spain resting on victory in the Civil War, and that in Greece stemming from a coup. Conversely, a military rising overthrew the dictatorial regime in Portugal.

Although each of these regimes relied on force they were less brutal or durable than their counterparts in the Communist bloc of Eastern Europe, which did not collapse until 1989–90. Force had played a major role in the extension of Communist control in, and after, the closing stage of World War Two and was important thereafter. Anti-Communist activity, reformist movements and demonstrations against aspects of government policy were all suppressed, frequently brutally. This was most apparent with the suppression of risings in East Germany in 1953 and Hungary in 1956, and with an invasion of Czechoslovakia in 1968 that brought down a reformist Communist government. In addition, force was used in Poland, particularly in response to labour unrest in 1956 and 1976, and again in 1981 when martial law was declared. The scale of some of this activity was massive. The determined use of Soviet armour, supported by air attacks and helicopters, crushed popular opposition in Hungary in 1956.

In 1968 about 250 000 Soviet troops, backed by Polish, Hungarian
and Bulgarian forces, were sent into Czechoslovakia. This was
not a war: the Czech government decided not to offer armed
resistance as it feared the consequences for the civilian population
and knew that there was no prospect of Western support. Dem-
onstrators relied on non-violent protest, for example throwing
paint against tanks, which had a major impact on international
opinion, but failed to dislodge the Soviets. Although not war,
this invasion was important in the military history of Europe. It
underlined the extent to which Eastern European Communism
relied on force, and could do so.

Force also played a role in democratic states. In France in
1961, dissident elements in the army unsuccessfully sought to
prevent the government under de Gaulle, a former general,
from negotiating independence for Algeria. Seven years later,
the government was driven to seek military backing when confronted with serious student and worker demonstrations. The
promise of such support helped stiffen the government. The
following year, the British government deployed troops in an
unsuccessful attempt to maintain order in Northern Ireland where
rioting had broken out the previous year. This deployment was
intended as a short-term measure, but instead the very presence
of troops became an issue and led to violence. In 1971, the
Provisional Irish Republican Army (IRA) launched its first major
offensive and, amidst widespread shooting and bombings the
following year, the Catholic population and the army increasingly
saw each other as enemies. As paramilitary-led violence spread,
the British government reacted with a determined attempt to
re-impose control. In Operation Motorman, the IRA's 'no-go'
areas in Belfast and Londonderry were reopened for military
and police patrols, leading the IRA to abandon attempts to stage
a revolutionary war and, instead, to turn to terrorism. The number
of troops deployed in Northern Ireland rose from 6000 in 1969
to 20 000 by 1972. The British army acquired considerable experience in anti-terrorist policing, but the difficulty of ending terrorism
in the absence of widespread civilian support became readily
apparent. Furthermore, the nature of the political context was
such that the army could not use much of its weaponry. Instead
of tanks or bombing, military proficiency was measured in traditional
infantry skills such as patrolling and the use of cover.

There was an echo of accounts of colonial operations against opponents who made good use of cover. Thus a British officer at the Boer victory at Majuba Hill in 1881 recorded the problems caused by 'bullets from an enemy we could not see' and, as a result, that 'the Boer fire so completely dominated ours'.[25]

Soviet military ascendancy in Eastern Europe helped lead to an essential territorial stability within Europe during the 'Cold War': the confrontation between Communist and non-Communist systems and militaries that followed World War Two. This both provided a background to the division of Europe into two armed camps and also, arguably, prevented the volatility that might have led to a full-scale conflict. The latter could have become nuclear either as a result of the attempt by one or both sides to gain advantage at the outset of a war, or, subsequently, in the event of Soviet attack, as the Western powers sought to respond to Soviet numerical superiority in Europe. Furthermore, the Soviets built up a formidable naval presence. The six Typhoons, the largest ballistic missile submarines built, entered service in the Soviet navy from 1980 and their most impressive surface warships, including the *Kuznetsov*, their only big carrier, also entered service in the 1980s.

The inhibiting effect of the destructive potential of nuclear weaponry served as much to increase interest in defining a sphere for tactical nuclear weapons and in planning an effective strategic nuclear first strike as it did to lessen the chance of a great power war, or to increase the probability that such a conflict would be essentially conventional. During the Cold War, the crucial strategic zone was defined as the North European Plain, and the Soviet Union had a major superiority in conventional forces there. This led to a series of responses in NATO planning, each of which focused on the degree to which nuclear weaponry would be involved and when. The essential stages were that of an immediate nuclear response to a conventional Soviet assault; massive nuclear retaliation; flexible response, a theory capable of many interpretations; and, eventually, an American stress on an enhanced conventional response.[26] The prospect of retaliation by American nuclear strength, both tactical (e.g., one-mile range atomic bazookas) and strategic, served to lessen the Soviet threat in Europe, but, in the 1970s, the Soviet Union was able to make major advances in comparative nuclear potency, producing a situation in which war was seen as likely to lead to MAD (mutually assured destruction). As a consequence, MAD-based strategies of deterrence and of graduated response were developed. The nuclear programme helped seriously exacerbate a very high level of military expenditure that distorted the Soviet economy and created serious social strains.

Although atomic weaponry was not used after 1945, it played a major role in the military history of Europe, not least in strategic planning and force structures. The Americans used the atom bomb in 1945; the Soviet Union had such bombs from 1949, Britain from 1952 and France from 1960. The destructive power of nuclear weaponry increased when the atom bomb was followed by the hydrogen bomb, first exploded by the USA in 1951. The Soviet Union followed in 1953, Britain in 1957 and France in 1968. The hydrogen bomb employed a nuclear explosion to heat hydrogen isotopes sufficiently to fuse them into helium atoms, a transformation that released an enormous amount of destructive energy. Nuclear weaponry led to a major shift in the share of resources from the army towards, first, the air force, and then to submarines and land-based intercontinental missiles capable of delivering atomic warheads.

This contributed greatly to the sense of volatility in military structures and doctrines that can be seen in the decades following World War Two, for it was far from clear how best to integrate nuclear weaponry with both. Experimentation with tactical nuclear weapons began in 1953.

At one level, the weapons and weapons systems of 1945 were still dominant in 1975, suggesting a degree of continuity not apparent when contrasting say 1900 and 1930. Tanks, field artillery, aircraft carriers and other weapons all suggested considerable continuity. Yet there were also major developments, especially in the enhancement of existing weapons systems. The technology of warfare became more sophisticated, in part as weapons and techniques developed in the latter stages of World War Two, such as jet aircraft, rockets and the underwater recharging of submarine batteries, were refined. In submarines, there were major advances in design, construction techniques, propulsion, communications, weaponry and surveillance. Competition hastened the development and acquisition of weapons such as jet fighters in the late 1940s and 1950s.

More generally, weaponry in which machinery played a major role, including, for example, complex automatic systems for sighting, ensured that skill rather than physical strength became more important for soldiering. Computers transformed operational horizons and command and control options from the 1960s. The notion that 'the navy mans equipment, while the army equips men', became an increasingly limited description of modern armies. The premium on skill led to greater military concern about the quality of both troops and training, and encouraged military support for a professional volunteer force rather than conscripts.

The dissemination of advanced weaponry to ordinary units was a major feature of postwar upgrading. In particular, armies became fully motorised and mechanised as the character of infantry changed. This permitted the development of infantry doctrine that focused on mobility, rather than on essentially static position warfare. Thus the Red Army replaced advances on foot and, in 1967, introduced the high-speed Boevaya Mashina Pekhoty infantry vehicle capable of carrying eight men as well as a crew of three, protected by an air filtration system and armed with a gun, a machine gun, an anti-tank guided missile and rifle ports. This was designed to give bite to the expansion in the number of Soviet motor vehicle divisions.[27]

The same process also characterised logistics. Horses, still used extensively in World War Two on the Eastern Front, were replaced, but the role of rail was also minimised as the lorry came to dominate the supply system. Mobility was seen as essential by both sides, as it was assumed that any war touched off by a Warsaw Pact invasion of Western Europe would be decided by superior speed and manoeuvrability. A flexible defence was called for, not least to use tactical nuclear weapons in counter-attacks.

Furthermore, only a flexible defence would allow the Western forces to regain and exploit the initiative. The skill of the Israelis against Arab defensive positions in the Six-Day War of 1967 and, eventually, after initial Arab successes, in the Yom Kippur War of 1973, demonstrated the vulnerability of forces with a low rate of activity. Conversely, but also putting an emphasis on mobility and tempo, the Soviets sought a rapid advance into NATO rear areas, which would compromise the use of Western nuclear weaponry. Essentially building on the operational policy of their advance in the latter stage of World War Two, with its penetration between German defensive hedgehogs, the Red Army put a premium on a rapid advance.

The qualitative range of weaponry increased. For example, weapons such as defoliation chemicals and infra-red viewing devices were able to alter the physical environment of conflicts. Nevertheless, it is important not to forget what has also been termed 'low-end high-tech' weaponry. This has had a major impact on small-scale and unconventional wars. The assault rifle, the shoulder-fired missile, the light mortar and the land mine have all combined to revolutionise low-intensity conflict, revolutionary war and wars of national liberation.

Sophisticated weaponry was expensive, in both nominal and real terms. Advanced industrial mass-production capacity and the ability to fund it were crucial. Metal-bashing processes remained important, but a greater role than hitherto was played by advanced electronic engineering. The high costs of the Cold War placed a crippling burden on the Soviet Union and helped limit the appeal of Communism to its citizens.

By 1990, and arguably by the mid-1980s when pressure for change became dominant in Soviet governmental circles, the Cold War clearly had been lost by the Soviet Union. This was less clear in the mid-1970s as the Western colonial empires finally crumbled and the Vietnam conflict closed with the fall of Saigon to the Communists in 1975. At that time the economic strength of the West seemed compromised by the economic strains following the oil price hike after the 1973 Arab–Israel war. Simultaneously, the West appeared to be suffering from poor leadership. The Watergate Crisis in the USA had led not only to the fall of President Nixon in 1974, but also to a crisis of confidence in American leadership. Of the other Western powers, Britain was faced by a political crisis in 1974 linked to a miners' strike, and then by a more general crisis in the mid-1970s, as high inflation and trade union power contributed to an acute sense of economic malaise and weakness.

These problems were not registered in a major world conflict, although the Cold War heated up in Angola in Africa in 1975 with the USA supplying anti-Communist forces in the civil war there. Instead, the mid-1970s saw a number of treaties, especially the Helsinki Treaty of 1975, which, in recognising the position and interests of the Eastern Bloc, appeared to consolidate its position. This *détente* was not the irritable harmony of allies, but a truce between rivals and, in so far as it suggested that the Cold War had cooled down, it did not do so by marking any victory of the West. Whereas in 1990 it would be clear that a major struggle had ended with the victory of the West, this was not apparent in 1975. Instead, it seemed that both East and West still had all to play for in a world adapting to the end of the European colonial empires.

Furthermore, a process of revision in military thought that was to put a premium on deep-space operations was about to begin. Far from being wedded to particular force structures, strategies and tactics, military thinkers in both NATO and the Warsaw Pact were to devote the following fifteen years to rethinking how to best fight war. The Soviets developed earlier concepts of deep battle under Marshal N.V. Ogarkov, who became Chief of the General Staff in 1977, while the Americans advanced the doctrine of Air Land Battle as their military reformulated its thinking and practice after the Vietnam War.[28] Although these forces did not wage war, had they done so it would have been a different conflict to any conducted prior to the mid-1970s.

If the history of modern warfare has an overarching lesson, it is that what works with one force structure in a particular time and place may not work in another. It is a mistake to read from the success of the American-led coalition in conflict with Iraq in the Gulf War in 1991 to the likely result had NATO ground forces attacked the Serbs in Kosovo in 1999. Instead, it is apparent that the Allied air offensive inflicted only limited damage on Serbian forces not least because of the height at which planes flew in order to avoid ground fire and hence air crew casualties. It is likely that a ground assault would only have succeeded after heavy casualties. The symbiosis of strength of a defending force operating in its own familiar environment is apparent whether in Northern Ireland or in the Balkans. Attacking doctrines are more likely to succeed against comparable regular forces rather than in such a situation.

Communist regimes and Soviet power collapsed in 1989–91 without any major conflict outside the former Yugoslavia and the Caucasus. The decision of the Soviet authorities not to use the forces at their disposal was one of the most important episodes in the military history of the last fifty years. Similarly, the decision of Britain and France, the leading Western imperial states, to abandon most of their colonies without conflict, especially in the 1960s, was important both in military and in global history. Already in 1922 Rawlinson warned from India, 'Once you get the people of England definitely at variance with educated public opinion in this country, I do not see how you can get out of it without a good deal of bloodshed and returning to our previous autocratic method of ruling India by the sword.'[29]

In both cases, a range of factors pertained, but one that stands out was a growing hesitation in the use of force that, in part, reflected a sense of an altered social politics of force. Put simply, war depends on a willingness to risk death, as well as the readiness to kill, which is less difficult to inculcate. This has become much less widespread in Europe and the USA (since Vietnam) in recent decades, as societies have become more individualistic and hedonistic and less deferential; this is the key military revolution of that period, not changes in weaponry or force structures. This revolution continues and it is one with which states and their militaries have to come to terms.

Conflict in 1864–1945 or 1914–45 between regular armed forces does not wholly define modern war, and that becomes increasingly clear as either period recedes from today. It is also necessary, in considering the 'modern', to look on the global scale to the insurrectionary and counter-insurgency warfare that followed 1945, beginning with the anti-colonial struggles, and to the ideological conflicts of the Cold War, many of which were civil wars. These can be prefigured in the nineteenth century, not least with the interventionist episodes of the 1820s, 1830s and 1840s. An understanding of the multiplicity and diversity of conflict both in the nineteenth century and in the first half of the twentieth opens our eyes to the very varied character of military modernity and to the diverse nature of the military history of more recent times.

1. Europe's Way of War, 1815–64

DENNIS SHOWALTER

Military history is arguably the last stronghold of what histori-ographers call the 'Whig interpretation'. Reduced to its simplest terms, this approach sees the development of warfare as pro-gressive. From the Macedonian phalanx, through the legions of Rome and the grenadiers of Frederick the Great, to the panzers of Nazi Germany and the information-age warfare currently touted in US military circles, the conduct of conflict is presented as becoming more sophisticated and more effective.

The process has not been simplistically linear. Dead ends and false starts abound. Rulers and generals make bad decisions. Societies lose touch with their militaries. Armed forces develop wrong doctrines or remain mired in allegiance to a constructed past. Nor are these flaws overlooked. A case can be made, indeed, that armed forces and military historians alike devote more energy to interpreting failure than to celebrating success. For soldiers, who spend far more time analysing their craft than practising it, focusing on past defects and present shortcomings is a counter-point to the lethargy and triumphalism that tends to infuse all institutions that do not face consistent accountability.[1] For histo-rians, the usual pleasures of hindsight are commonly reinforced by a certain antagonism to the people and the institutions that wage war. No body of literature along the lines of Norman Dixon's *On the Psychology of Military Incompetence* addresses law, medicine, or education with a view to demonstrating endemic, enduring deficiencies in perspective, flexibility, and emotional maturity.[2]

These intellectual patterns have essentially defined the nature of Europe's military experience in the half-century between the fall of Napoleon and the Wars of German Unification. The years from 1815 to 1864 appear in most general military histories as not merely a time of stagnation, but as a retrograde era, when states and armies turned away from the experiences of the Revolutionary/

Napoleonic Era, seeking instead to retame Bellona and return the genie of mass war to its bottle.[3] Intellectually and institutionally, in this model, armed forces stagnate. Often consciously, they overlook the weapons systems that would give conflict new dimensions on both sides of the Atlantic in the 1860s. The patriots of 1793 and the *grognards* of 1805 give way to conscripted automata, whose regimental officers in some cases cannot even speak their language and whose generals are far more concerned with gold mulcted from public funds than with laurels won on the battlefield.[4] Things come right again only when a Prussian army reborn under the eyes and in the spirit of its General Staff sweep away Austrian sawdust and French tinsel, setting Europe and the world on course for the trenches of World War One.[5]

The story is coherent, if not particularly inspiring. It is also sufficiently familiar to have discouraged large-scale, synergistic research. Closer examination, however, suggests a more complicated picture – one best expressed in terms of six dialectics that engaged and shaped Europe's armed forces in the years between Napoleon I and Moltke the Elder.

INTERNAL SECURITY/POWER PROJECTION

Prior to the French Revolution, internal security had a low priority for Europe's armies. Societies tolerated high levels of disorder and private safeguarding of life and property was normative. Large-scale brigandage, usually directed against internal customs regulations, was dealt with ad hoc by specific assignment of soldiers or warships or by the creation of constabulary forces like the French *marechaussée*.[6] Disaffection in territories that changed hands as a consequence of war or diplomacy was not unknown. Its scale and nature, however, usually responded to cooption and control by what a later generation would call constabulary methods. Even Scotland, while scarcely subject to conciliatory treatment after 1745, was policed rather than ruled by a garrison including the locally raised independent companies that became the Black Watch.[7] Prussia's absorption of western Poland is another useful example of the limited role military forces usually played in the process of 'socialising' new territories.[8]

The Revolutionary/Napoleonic Era changed that situation by introducing the forces of liberalism and nationalism – changed it in two ways. First, governments now believed their populations could become seriously dangerous, again in two ways. One, essentially urban, involved uprisings of the urban 'crowds' structured by discontented elements of the professional classes and facilitated by disaffected elements of the armed forces.[9] The other involved rural insurrection based on local grievances, along lines made familiar in Spain and southern Italy, and in the part of Poland that passed under Russian rule in the late eighteenth century. Experience strongly suggested that armies had neither the numbers nor the techniques to make a decisive end of such rebellions, save at the price of concession or repression at levels unacceptable to state authorities. There was, in other words, no rural counterpart to Bonaparte's famous 'whiff of grapeshot' that put paid to the Paris insurrection of 1795.[10]

The other consequence of liberalism and nationalism for public order involved an exponential expansion of government involvement in maintaining 'domestic tranquility', Deviance became a public problem, publicly defined. After 1815, more and more states organised police forces and *gendarmerie*. They rationalised legal systems and punishments.[11] Javert, the police official of Victor Hugo's *Les Miserables*, transformed to a negative archetype by the world-famous contemporary musical, was in his historical version a symbol of progress. His duty was to the law, rather than to any particular individual no matter his wealth or rank. When he informs Jean Valjean: 'Monsieur le Maire, you'll wear a *different* chain' than that of office, he asserts an equality of legal rights that was central to the French and American Revolutions, persisted in their aftermath, and depended on public enforcement.

Riots and insurrections were better overawed than put down in blood, and better deterred than suppressed. That meant keeping forces on the spot. Even with post-1815 improvements, roads were poor and rates of march were correspondingly slow. Not until the 1840s could railways do what helicopters would later do in Vietnam, and shift relatively limited forces from trouble spot to trouble spot. Instead the barracks complexes which states began building in their larger cities were the equivalent of water towers for a fire brigade. Their occupants were a highly visible presence. The evolution of uniforms to costumes had begun

during the Napoleonic Wars, when bright, even garish, colours
helped distinguish who was who on a black-powder battlefield.
Certain uniforms or accessories, like the bearskins of the Emperor's
Old Guard, sent even more explicit messages across the lines.
After 1815 military spectacle, parades and reviews by elegantly
uniformed, precisely drilled formations provided both entertain-
ment and warning to spectators.[12] At mid-century Napoleon III
sought the impact of realism, parading veteran regiments of the
Crimea and Italy through Paris in their ragged active-service
uniforms, wounded survivors at the head of the marching columns.
Ostensibly presented as a gesture of reconciliation, such spec-
tacles had an intimidating effect as well, conveying the power
and the will to power of the new Empire.[13]

   States also distributed garrisons systematically in rural areas,
sometimes by companies and squadrons. This constabulary model
of deployment had predictable negative effects on collective training and unit cohesion.[14] The latter problem was important from
a security perspective as well as an operational one. Units kept
too long in the same place developed formal and informal networks with local civilians. Girlfriends could be a more subversive
influence than pamphlets, as government after government discovered in 1848 when urban garrisons proved more loyal to
their neighbours than to their colours.[15] The problem was particularly acute for artillery and engineer units, whose technical
requirements made them difficult to assign outside urban areas.[16]

   An obvious solution was periodic transfer. France and Austria
in particular witnessed the regular movement of regiments from
place to place – a process complicated in Austria by a desire to
post formations away from their ethnic and linguistic recruitment areas.[17] Relevant as well for the eastern empires, and often
overlooked, was the problem they faced moving significant forces
anywhere. Austria's rail network lagged significantly behind those
of western Europe throughout this period, in part because of
geographic obstacles to high-capacity rail lines.[18] Russia was even
worse off for railways, and since its population and industrial
centres were far from its frontiers, a cadre/reserve army on the
model that became general after 1871 was almost certain to be
late anywhere it was required. Russia did not face anything like
the same internal security problem as its Western counterparts:
the 1825 Decembrist uprising was a coup, not an insurrection.

Yet as early as 1830 even the largest and most stable army in Europe was significantly overstretched by overlapping, at times contradictory, strategic requirements.[19]

Regimental transfers also facilitated another major role of armies in the period under discussion. That role was power projection. The Concert of Europe may have existed in its developed form for no more than a decade. As a deterrent to great-power war, however, it survived throughout the era.[20] While states continued to develop plans and theories for general conflicts, the normal pattern of actual engagement involved sending expeditionary forces into regions threatened by disorder or insurrection: what a later generation calls 'peacemaking' and 'peacekeeping.'

Ostensibly undertaken under Concert auspices or the equivalent, as opposed to unilaterally, these operations were nevertheless generally understood as opportunities to show the qualities of one's own armed forces. French troops, for example, went into Spain in 1823; Belgium in 1832; the Papal States in 1849. Habsburg task forces were regularly dispatched to the empire's Italian clients in the Age of Metternich. Russia sent entire armies into Persia and Turkey in the 1820s and Poland in 1831. The Caucasus was a consistently active – and highly expensive – theatre of war throughout the period.

Navies could play a similar role. An international naval force suppressed the Algerian corsairs in 1816 and maintained an antislavery patrol off West Africa for decades. France, Britain and Russia sent squadrons to support Greek rebels in the late 1820s. In the next decade the Ottoman sultan requested British naval help against Egypt's Mehemet Ali. That the request was not promptly answered reflected the lack of deployable heavy ships, as opposed to any reluctance to become involved.[21]

These expeditions, by no means all of them under Concert auspices, established patterns followed in larger-scale conflicts: the Crimea in 1854–5 and Italy in 1859. By their nature they were 'come-as-you-are' operations, undertaken from standing starts in response to particular contingencies and putting corresponding burdens on operational readiness. They also stood in opposition to an internal-security paradigm fostering dispersion and entropy, and thus discouraged the evolution of armies along constabulary lines.[22]

The tension between the two missions was resolved at the

expense of structure. Austria had permanent army corps, and
maintained a combination garrison and reaction force in Lombardy.
France had 'camps of instruction' that incorporated several regiments at a time. In both countries, however, the composition of
these institutions and organisations was so unstable that for practical purposes any structure above regimental level was improvised
for particular operations. These higher formations existing on
paper or as abstractions were too ephemeral to inspire or command heroic loyalty in their subordinate units.[23] The Russian
army maintained permanent army corps as operational units,
but also tended to accept regimental identity as a benchmark –
in good part because the impossibility of returning to civil life,
given the length of the term of service, led soldiers to turn to
their comrades as a substitute family.[24]

The result was a general devolution of 'fighting power'.
Napoleon had lifted its focus upwards, from the divisions of the
revolutionary armies to the corps, whose identity – often based
on a charismatic commander like Ney or Davout – was sufficiently stable to absorb regiments transferred in, and survive
the transfer of others elsewhere.[25] Now it was back to the regiment,
with corresponding negative impact on the potential of armies
to achieve decision in a large-scale battle.[26]

QUALITY/NUMBERS

On the surface, the revolutionary/Napoleonic Wars seemed to
herald the triumph of the mass army and the citizen soldier.
Present in ever-larger numbers, volunteer or conscript, motivated by universal ideals or nationalist patriotism, but knowing
what he fought for and fighting for what he knew, the citizen in
uniform continues to hold a certain pride of moral place, above
both the eighteenth-century mercenary and the contemporary
professional technowarrior.[27]

Experience, however, suggested an alternate perspective – even
in France, home of the *levée en masse*. The wars of the Napoleonic
era had shown an increasing tendency for armies to outgrow
their nervous systems. Even under Napoleon's master hand the
conscript masses of Borodino and Leipzig proved significantly
less effective than the lean strike forces of Lodi, Marengo and

Austerlitz. In the post-Waterloo years, not a few of Napoleon's former marshals advocated developing a quality army, smaller than its predecessors but susceptible to the kind of precise operational control that would avoid the costly gridlock characteristic of modern large-scale battles.

That force structure suited France's self-defined role as the fulcrum of Europe – a position sought alike by the Bourbon and Orléans monarchies and the Second Empire of Napoleon III. Achieving it, however, did not depend on replicating a quarter-century of general war waged by armed masses inspired by a revolution and an imperium. The new France sought aggrandizement by persuasion and example. Force was a last resort. Its application must correspondingly be surgical: the kind of deep, clean cut that inspired in the victim sober second thoughts about pursuing the dispute in arms, without generating fear of annihilation as a consequence of submission.[28]

The kind of soldiers best able to deliver such cuts were seen as the heirs of Napoleon's 'grumblers', the veterans who had carried the tricolor from Madrid to Moscow and died in their ranks at Waterloo. But how were such paladins to be mass-produced in peacetime? Bourbon, Orléans and Bonapartist governments alike rejected the concept of a nation in arms, and the accompanying principle that all fit males owe the state a term of military service. The possible political unreliability of such a force was less important than the burdens it was considered to impose on a population whose loyalty was ipso facto suspect. On the other hand, France possessed neither the surplus population nor the discretionary wealth to recruit an entire army of 'true volunteers'. Instead the army was sustained by a form of selective service based on a national lottery. A 'bad number' could condemn a man of twenty to seven years' active service – making him at discharge too old for an apprenticeship and out of the social networks that determined marriage into a farm.

Conscription legislation, however, required furnishing military service, not performing it. In other words, it allowed substitution. The funds thus raised provided re-enlistment bonuses for veterans and bounties for enlistees. Critics, then and now, described substitution as an obscene trafficking in human lives. To contemporaries at all social levels, substitution seemed no more than a logical application of an economic system in which people took their skins to market daily and accepted high physical risks in the process, whether in mill, mine or barrack. Viewed from a proper perspective, indeed, substitution was a form of capitalism, in which a man ventured his body against calculable risk for a calculable profit. That fundamental departure from peasant values may have been by itself a contributor to the often-documented alienation between army and countryside.[29]

The French soldier, then, whether conscript, substitute or re-enlisted veteran, was in uniform for the *longue durée*, preferably in the same regiment and among the same comrades. In his ideal form he was simultaneously a warrior and a craftsman. Able to outmarch, outfight and outthink his enemies, he could act on his own initiative in camp and battle, but effortlessly meld into a team when cooperation was required. He was correspond-ingly expected to be a go-anywhere, do-anything fighting man, a work tool in the hands of his officers, at the government's dis-posal for 'policy wars' anywhere in Europe or the world.

The French soldier benefited heavily from what a later gen-eration would call 'combat multipliers'. The French army was quick to introduce rifled small arms for its infantry, culminating in the *chassepot*, the ultimate paper-cartridge breechloader, in-troduced in 1866. The French artillery adopted rifled cannon in the early 1850s.[30] Nor was the soldier expected to develop endurance and expertise from experience alone. One of the conclusions most commonly drawn from the Napoleonic Wars was that under operational conditions drill regulations regu-larly went by the board. What was done in the field involved as a rule highly simplified versions of what the manuals required. As proportions of newly raised levies increased during the era's later years, the ability to shift from line to column to square was about the level of complication most regiments could achieve under fire. Yet time and again, from the Iberian Peninsula to central Europe to the field of Waterloo, superior training pro-duced tactical results.[31]

After 1815, all armies favoured increasing the amount of time spent on drill, as much to instill patterns of discipline and response as to inculcate specific movements. The improvised regiments of the American Civil War, so often held up as arche-types of common-sense soldiering, understood the value of prolonged drill – if not from the beginning, usually after their first serious action.[32] And in France as well, the *élan* and *cran* that were the essence of the modern professional soldier were believed to require cultivation. In 1839 the army created its first battalion of *chasseurs à pied*, light infantry armed with rifles and given special training in skirmishing and marksmanship. The Zouave regiments raised by the French in Algeria were also held up as an example for the rest of the army because of their fieldcraft and their spirit. Both were seen as functions of the expertise in drill movements that so attracted pre-Civil War American observers.[33] No less significant were their colourful and exotic uniforms, the baggy red trousers, the short jacket and sash, the whole ensemble topped by a red fez and indicating the increasing impact of 'hinterland' military cultures on metro-politan armies.[34]

The French soldier of the post-Napoleonic era increasingly became not quite the model, but certainly the justification for his counterparts in Austria and Russia. Neither of the eastern empires replicated French emphasis on armament and training as force multipliers. Their 'rifle' battalions and regiments, for example, had nothing like the specialised character of the *chasseurs*. Nor did either army emphasise re-enlistment to the French extent – in the case of Russia, a twenty-five year term of active service made the question moot. What was similar was the commitment to long terms of service, intended to replace any civilian ties with loyalty to regiment, army and state. Accompanying that was a belief that experience focused by training was a better predictor of operational effectiveness than enthusiasm: pro-fessionalism would trump patriotism every time.[35]

The major challenge to the French model of a quality army existed in Prussia.[36] Arguably more than any of the great powers, Prussia in the half-century after Napoleon was committed to maintaining itself in the stable continental and regional environ-ments shaped by the Concert of Europe and the German Confederation. That position was generally recognised as in principle best sustained by an army on the French model: a work tool in state hands, a professional force large enough to under-write great-power status, deter most policy wars and undertake the others from a standing start. Instead the Reform Movement of the Napoleonic Era had left a legacy of a mass army raised by conscription and depending on popular enthusiasm to generate military effectiveness. Even if the Prussian economy had been able to support an army on the French model, the Prussian government was unwilling to accept the domestic risks of creating one.

The result was a growing paradox. Essentially the Prussian army was a cadre force, depending on men recalled from civilian life. The kingdom was divided into districts, each responsible for producing an army corps on mobilisation. In its definitive form a corps consisted of two divisions. Each division had two brigades; each brigade had two regiments. One of these was an active unit whose peacetime mission was training successive intakes of conscripts. The other belonged to the *Landwehr*, a citizen militia improvised in 1813 and placed on equal footing with the army of the line by the Defence Act of 1814. Since even the active regiments required large infusions of reservists to take the field at effective strength, Prussia's military structure made it virtually impossible for Prussia to wage anything but all-out war. This was just the opposite of the flexible system Prussian policy and interests seemed to require.

After 1815, moreover, population growth made it impossible to finance a full term of active service for every eligible Prussian male. As a result, increasing numbers of conscripts were assigned directly to the *Landwehr*. This meant they received no formal training at all. The defense legislation of 1814–15, and the military reformers like Hermann von Boyen who inspired it, expected these '*Landwehr* recruits' to learn the craft of soldiering by osmosis – because they would want to learn it as part of their new position as citizens rather than subjects. That projected zeal proved increasingly difficult to sustain in the context of an authoritarian monarchical system suspicious of public enthusiasm in any context. It was also diminished by the lack of any clear purpose justifying the effort, since by definition and practice Prussian foreign policy was risk-averse and denied the existence of 'eternal enemies'.

By the 1850s Prussia's army had the worst of two worlds. Its operational effectiveness was open to serious doubt because of a dependence on men neither trained nor motivated. Its annual manoeuvers were described as 'compromising the profession of arms' by one French observer with a wit as sharp as his eyes were clear. As for loyalty, the revolutions of 1848 and subsequent lesser crises produced more sullen compliance than patriotic enthusiasm among reservists summoned to active duty for reasons they did not understand and causes they did not support – usually involving the use of force against fellow Prussians or other Germans. Morale was much higher in the brief encounter with Denmark in 1848–9 over Schleswig-Holstein's place in the German Confederation.[37]

The need for reform was obvious across virtually the entire political and administrative spectrum. In 1858, war minister Albrecht von Roon called for authorisation to double not the active army's strength but its size. As implemented by the reform authorised in 1860, most of the *Landwehr* regiments were converted into active units. Their ranks were filled by extending conscription. The annual draft call rose from 40 000 to slightly over 60 000. The term of active service was increased from two to three years – a step in the French and Austrian direction. Once discharged the conscript passed for four years into an active reserve that would be used to bring field units to strength on mobilisation. From there, by then in his late twenties, he would pass into a *Landwehr* reconfigured as a source of replacements and second-line garrison formations.

The result was a Prussian army whose peace strength increased by over 65 000 men, but whose new initial wartime total of 211 000 did not seriously challenge existing military balances. Critics as late as the mid-1860s dismissed the army's larger numbers as no more than increasing the runaways and prisoners that would be the consequence of an encounter with the professionalised army of a rival continental power. Nevertheless a general staff, a war ministry and a monarch stubborn enough to challenge Prussia's legislature in a war to the knife over control of the restructured army eventually took Prussia down a path of conquest unexpected anywhere else in Europe.

EXPERIENCE/THEORY

Prussia found itself in a minority position on another central issue as well. Since the Renaissance at least, war had been considered a craft whose mastery was best acquired by experience and apprenticeship. The pattern, as in Britain's Royal Navy, of sending pre-teen children to sea as midshipmen epitomised the principle that seamanship and command alike were skills best acquired by practice. The Navies with almost no ships, such as those of Austria and Prussia, similarly did their best to provide as much sea time as possible for officer cadets. The French navy had been too thoroughly humiliated in the Revolutionary/ Napoleonic wars to serve as a model for anyone else. Prior to 1789 it had concentrated heavily on theoretical training. After 1815 France's own senior naval officers tended to favour something along British lines for developing midshipmen. Not until mid-century was continued emphasis on theoretical and technical education perceived as giving France a certain advantage in naval matters.[38]

Armies were not indifferent to professional education. France had St. Cyr and the Ecole Polytechnique, the latter militarised under Napoleon. Britain's Royal Military College emerged from the Napoleonic Wars alongside the Royal Military Academy at Woolwich as a source of regimental officers. Austria and Prussia had their cadet schools, primarily for the sons of impecunious officers. Generally considered, however, these facilities served in the period under consideration as sources of technical instruction on the one hand and institutions of socialisation on the other. The US Military Academy as a developed institution, for example, emphasised engineering in its curriculum and discipline in its routines. Tactics and command played secondary, arguably tertiary, roles. Junior officers were expected to master their craft at its sharp end.[39]

To a degree that mind-set was the heritage of a quarter of a century of general war, when experience had been at the fingertips of any man seeking it. Napoleon's marshals and other senior officers, while by no means as innocent collectively of professional military education as their myth would have it, nevertheless took pains to present images as rough-hewn field soldiers. And nowhere was this mentality stronger than in a French army whose officers at all ranks were expected to be warriors, not bookworms or clerks. An officer's ability to impress women, hold liquor and lead men far outweighed any attendance at fancy schools.

The ethic of leading from the front, in battle or boudoir, was fostered by the fact that about two-thirds of the army's officers began their service in the ranks and won their commissions through some form of performance – albeit not always by valour in the face of the enemy. With their own formal educations significantly limited, such officers were unlikely to be impressed with any system focused on study of any kind. Junior officers in any army are unlikely to be attracted to book learning for its own sake – particularly when more immediately enticing alternatives are available, and those alternatives are valued by the superiors on whom one's own advancement heavily depends.[40] The result? As late as 1870 a French cavalry general allegedly dismissed geography and topography as 'a pile of shit'. Intelligence, he declared, meant telling a peasant: 'son, you're going to take us where we want to go, and then we'll give you a little drink and a pretty coin. If you steer us wrong, here are two guys with pistols who'll blow your head off!'[41]

This rough-and-ready style was replicated throughout Europe. Austrian regimental officers dismissed the rank and file as 'an army of pigs', Instead of learning the domestic speech of their men, many officers depended on the few dozen 'official' words of command in German that every soldier was supposed to know, supplemented as necessary by NCOs drawn from the regiment's ethnic community. Events from 1848 to 1859 showed this to be a recipe for neither loyalty nor fighting power.[42] Britain's complex system of purchasing military commissions contributed to a high turnover among junior officers in an army that continued to stress 'gentlemanly' over 'professional' qualities. By no means every British officer matched the familiar caricature of an aristocrat interested in nothing beyond drinking, womanising and field sports. Nevertheless, at company levels no more than a modicum of knowledge was necessary for officers able to display 'character' – the 'right stuff' of junior leadership that conveniently continues to defy precise definition.[43]

Romanticism, with its emphasis on inspiration as opposed to the eighteenth century's emphasis on reason and order, also facilitated seeking the spark of genius presumed to inhabit every successful great captain. Antoine-Henri Jomini, the Swiss-born staff officer whose analysis of warfare sought to bring order from what seemed to its participants a near-random process, repeatedly used the Emperor as his *deus ex machina*, explaining events in terms of Napoleon's specific gifts and then presenting those gifts as qualities to which others could aspire, approach and perhaps attain. In that sense his *Précis sur l'art de la Guerre* was well suited as a handbook for the ambitious officer who did not wish to overstrain himself by attention to specifics.[44]

The anti-intellectual aspects of Europe's officer corps should not be exaggerated. A developing public interest in practical science and technology did not stop at the doors of regimental messes.[45] Intellectual activity, moreover, can take many forms. Officers of the larger European armies had ample experience in warmaking over a broad spectrum of circumstances. From Paris and Lyons to Spain, Greece and the Levant, Bourbon white and Imperial tricolour were carried in every possible military environment. Russian troops waged large-scale counterinsurrection in Poland and fought against the Ottoman Empire in Turkey. They matched wit and will with formidable enemies in the Caucasus. They bested a Hungarian people's army with a Habsburg-trained core in 1849. Austrian armies fought all over Italy, measured themselves against the army of Piedmont in 1848, reconquered a crumbling empire in 1849, put down small-scale riots and insurgencies sparked in a dozen different cultures. The British army of the post-Napoleonic era became a global institution, its regiments deployed wherever the Union Jack flew even temporarily.

Experience does not exclude reflection. But reflection showed that what these particular military experiences had in common was that they had nothing in common. Context and common sense were the keys to survival and victory. Europe's enemies in this period were usually unable to challenge European armies directly with any prospect of success. But they possessed cultures and fighting traditions whose overcoming called for high levels of situational awareness, flexibility and ruthlessness.[46] The French army's famous – or infamous – System D (*se débrouiller*), or 'muddling through', was by no means a manifestation of insouciant indifference to anything but straightforward throat-slitting. It reflected instead a conviction that modern warmaking depended on adaptability, on throwing away the book and relying on one's own response to circumstances that were constantly changing from campaign to campaign, and within campaigns as well.

Abstraction and theory dulled a soldier's cutting edge, making him prone to indulge in what the first Napoleon called 'making pictures'. Plans of campaign could never be anything but guidelines, inapplicable after the first contact with the enemy. Good judgment and a good digestion, the qualities of character summed up under the vague, but well understood term *coup d'oeil*, were what was needed above all under the protean conditions of modern warfare. Military cartography, for example, was still in its early stages even in Europe. The Prussian General Staff itself devoted much of its initial efforts to producing accurate maps of its own country.[47] In that context, the definition of operational intelligence mentioned earlier loses much of its fecklessness. Rather than trusting a 'military science' that might well not exist, it was sheer good judgement to rely on cultivating local sources – by whatever means were appropriate, including those of the French cavalryman discussed above.

The pragmatists reinforced their case against theory by arguing that war could not be micro-managed from capital cities or geographically remote headquarters. During the 1850s the electric telegraph provided direct links between governments and their generals. But did the course of events in the Crimea go any smoother or more favourably than those in the spectacularly underreported Indian campaign that concluded, according to *Punch*, with Sir Charles's Napier's one-word dispatch 'peccavi!' ('I have sinned' – or in this case Sind)?[48]

Nor was concern for overcontrol confined to operational issues. The Austrian military command in Lombardy–Venetia expressed consistent frustration with a Vienna-based administration that seemed unable or unwilling to take account of the specific political and strategic issues in the empire's Italian provinces.[49] For over half a century the British parliament and the West Indian planters resisted the establishment of high-altitude garrisons, on the grounds of cost in one case and from a desire to have troops immediately present in the other. The result was a consistent heavy drain of men lost to tropical diseases and corresponding diminution of British operational effectiveness. Not until 1841, under heavy pressure from a new lieutenant governor, did London finally sanction a high-altitude station in Jamaica. By that time the strategic issue had long been moot.[50]

Again it was the Prussian army that stood on the other side of the education issue. Even its emphasis on theory grew out of the generally accepted European matrix of privileging experience – in this case by supplementing it. At the century's turn Johann von Scharnhorst and his fellow reformers had sought to develop an officer corps informed less by formal technical instruction than by the cultivation of individual understanding through open, systematic exchange of ideas and information. This approach was not intended to replace the existing command system. It was instead supposed to provide senior officers with amanuenses able to supplement experience with doctrine and pragmatism with principle. Ideally the relationship between a commanding general and his chief of staff resembled a conventionally 'good marriage' with companionate respect flowering into admiration and affection as the relationship matured.[51]

Nor were staff officers conceived as a privileged community. The Prussian War Academy, established in 1810, was intended to institutionalise the development of both staff officers and field commanders, offering a programme intended to combine general and professional study, emphasising students' independent work and thought. Both the General Staff and the War Ministry developed as organisations whose main purpose was providing for the most effective use of Prussia's limited resources in the greatest number of contingencies. The General Staff's specific evolution into a long-range planning body after 1815 reflected in good part the limited immediate demands placed on that institution by Prussia's limited foreign policy. It was also a consequence of a military system depending for effectiveness on systematic preparation and smooth mobilisation.[52]

That approach reached its summit in the career of Helmuth von Moltke. His long career as a staff planner convinced him that Austerlitz and Jena/Auerstaedt were not accidents. Decisive victories were in fact possible in a war's early stage. Moltke also accepted the dominant conventional wisdom that no plan survived initial contact with an enemy, but also came to believe that a well-prepared, comprehensive plan could make the first contact decisive. Given Prussia's weakness relative to the other great powers, limited wars with prompt results were the only kind of conflicts that made sense. And since the structure of the Prussian army was better suited to absolute wars of long duration, the dissonance was best resolved by high-level staff work.[53]

Prussia was not the only state that sought to compensate for perceived weakness by systematic administration. Russia faced an arguably more difficult problem than its western neighbour: how best to tap the country's theoretically available human and material resources in a strategic environment increasingly favouring come-as-you-are conflicts. Finding soldiers was difficult because of the limitations serfdom imposed on conscription.[54] Paying for them was difficult given the inflexible nature of Russia's tax system and the limits of its tax base. Equipping them to international standards became difficult as Russia fell behind the curve of nineteenth-century industrialisation. In the 1830s Tsar Nicholas I and his advisors abandoned as too narrowly focused a general staff system that was developing along Prussian lines. Power was instead transferred to a higher level: a war ministry that presided over a unified structure of military administration and planning. Results were mixed – but recent research makes an increasingly strong case that Russia's defeat in the Crimean War was due more to its strategic situation than to defects in its military organisation.[55]

TECHNOLOGY/TEMPO

Conventional wisdom asserts that after 1815 Europe's armed forces ignored or denigrated the militarily applicable technologies spun off by the Industrial Revolution, persisting in their indifference until the mid-century shocks imposed by Prussia. In fact, European armies and navies were generally well aware of the nature of technical developments after Waterloo – and of their applicability in warmaking.

The French navy was the most obvious example, as it sought to overcome Britain's lead in traditional categories of sea power by taking advantage of its own intellectualised, technically trained officer corps and introducing such innovations as shell guns, steam-powered warships and eventually armoured fighting vessels. The Royal Navy responded to a degree, generating a major naval race between the two powers that began in the 1840s. It was, however, a naval race with a difference, emphasising technological innovation at rates that generated obsolescence to degrees previously unknown.[56]

Another consequence of the Anglo–French competition was

the relegation of the rest of Europe to a generally acknowledged noncompetitive status.[57] States with the technical capacity,
such as Holland, lacked the financial resources to support effective
numbers of the new-model steam frigates and ships of the line.
States like Russia, with at least the theoretical budget capacity
to afford the ships, lacked the ability to build them – at least
initially.[58]

The concept of neutralising enemies through technological
superiority was not lost on armies. Seen from present-day perspectives, some of the lead times seem remarkable. As late as
1840 the French infantry was still carrying a musket whose basic
design dated to the 1770s. The Prussian artillery was armed
with guns so inaccurate that during target practice sentries were
posted to warn away passers-by: no one had any clear idea where
the shots would fall. These and similar circumstances were in
part a consequence of the presence of large numbers of service-
able weapons surplus to existing requirements, correspondingly
cheap to repair and replace by cannibalising. They also reflected
priorities reflecting limited budgets. For example, exponential
increases in army size discussed above absorbed a disproportionate amount of funds in feeding, clothing and sheltering
the larger numbers. The movement away from quartering troops
on the local populations in favour of concentrating them in
barracks required not merely building the facilities themselves,
but also acquiring land, often at premium prices in rapidly-
expanding urban communities.

Such 'macro' considerations took second place to the increasingly
lively debates surrounding such apparently minor technicalities
as percussion locks for muskets and such apparently minor design
questions as the appropriate weight of artillery pieces. These
discussions reflected the Industrial Revolution's growing interest
in practical science. They incorporated synergies of technical
and practical considerations to an extent previously unknown
in the age of gunpowder. And they reflected the fact that the
costs accompanying the adoption of new weapons systems made
being first less important than having the best.[59]

Thus there was no need to rush innovation. Nor was the question of what system was best always easily resolved. The
breech-loading, bolt-action Prussian needle gun, adopted in 1841,
is usually and accurately described as the first 'modern' infan-

try rifle. Its technical superiority to the smoothbore percussion muskets it replaced was obvious at all levels of the Prussian army, and to most foreign critics as well. But the new weapon's range was relatively short. Its breech leaked gas badly with sustained use. Its rate of fire was so high that keeping men supplied with ammunition in combat was considered difficult, if not dubious. Lest that last point be dismissed as absurd, it is worth noting that the US Army, epitome of a high-tech institution, modified its infantry rifle after the Vietnam War, replacing full automatic fire with a three-round burst capacity. On the other hand the Minie rifle, developed in the same time frame as the needle gun, possessed with its conical expanding bullet a longer range than its counterpart. It was simpler and more reliable than the breechloader. Its rate of fire was slower. It had the final advantage of looking and handling like infantry weapons for a century and a half – a combination of technology and aesthetics that proved difficult for war ministries and regimental officers to resist.[60]

Similar patterns of choice confusion existed in artillery design. The introduction of long range rifles led in turn to a gradual thinning out of infantry formations. As mass targets in the pattern of Friedland or Waterloo became less likely, artilleryman differed on whether the field piece of the future should be rifled, so as to hit particular targets at long range, or smoothbores designed to annihilate skirmishers and assault lines with point-blank shell and shrapnel fire – the 'Napoleons' of the American Civil War. The traditional gun metals, bronze and cast iron, were challenged by cast steel. But relative to the demands made on it by black-powder rounds, steel seemed in many quarters *too* high quality, and correspondingly too expensive, to be used for cannon barrels. Practical breechloading designs emerged in the 1850s, but as long as guns had fixed carriages the crucial factor in rate of fire was the time required to return the piece to 'battery': its original position. By then, a reasonably efficient crew could have the piece reloaded from either end.[61]

The improved range and lethality of firearms brought with them the enlargement of battlefield killing zones. Britain retained its traditional linear deployment. Both armies in the American Civil War also favoured linear formations. In theory at least, linear formations maximised the potential of aimed fire at long

range that was the Minie rifle's strong point. They offered a
difficult target at the new longer ranges. Infantry lines were
also difficult to control and focus in the advance, and required
high levels of training and experience to develop their potential. At the other end of the tactical spectrum, the Russian army
relied on mass formations with minimal numbers of skirmishers, and on attacks, delivered at bayonet point by closed columns.
In the tactical middle were the strong skirmish lines supplemented by company-and battalion-strength columns that became
the basis of French tactics and were widely credited with the
Second Empire's victories in 1859. Austria, loser in that conflict,
responded to defeat by abandoning its poorly developed fire
tactics for bayonet charges delivered at the double by shallow
battalion columns. Prussia increasingly turned to skirmish lines
supported closely by company-strength columns, but depended
on its needle guns to carry the attack.[62]

Even this cursory overview shows that there was no clear choice
between the principles of 'shock' and 'fire'. What armies had in
common was something else: tempo. On both sides of the Atlantic the concern of generals and regimental officers alike was
setting and forcing the pace of battles that would otherwise be
gridlocked by modern rifles and artillery. Clausewitz was only
one among many veterans of the Napoleonic Wars who noted the
entropic tendency of Napoleonic battles: 'burn[ing] slowly away
like wet powder' until both sides were exhausted.[63] The whole
thrust of post-Napoleonic war, by contrast, was towards speed, at
all levels. The railway, originally conceived as a means of defence
by facilitating concentration in an invader's path, increasingly
became an instrument for bringing force to bear on an enemy's
frontier. Tempo in turn was expected to produce decision: both
fire and shock were its subsets, a means to this wider end.

As yet, Europe's armies and those of the American Civil War
were not committed to the vitalist concepts that by the turn of the
century were to infuse armies with an 'offensive spirit' that arguably defied material realities. Instead their purpose was to integrate
the new technologies into the professionalised strike forces that
were a mid-century norm, for the purpose of forcing the general
pace of warmaking and in the long run sparing demands on state
systems. Seen in that context, the recently-questioned tactics of
Robert E. Lee from the Peninsular Campaign of 1862 through

Antietam and Gettysburg invite consideration not as a throwback to the first Napoleon, but as part of a common Atlantic-world military culture.[64] That, however, is another story for another volume.

EUROPE/OVERSEAS

Prior to 1815 the focus of Europe's armed forces had been the European continent. Overseas expeditions were difficult to sustain at any significant levels of strength. Even in the West Indies, perceived as economically and strategically vital by those powers with possessions in the area, strategic sweeps as opposed to permanent presence were the dominant form of engagement until the end of the period.[65] European troops and warships were a minority presence in India and North America, compared to local forces. The Revolutionary/Napoleonic Wars further encouraged concentration on Europe. Britain did not perceive its fate as ultimately being decided in, for example, North America by the War of 1812. Until Napoleon's first abdication, it fought that war with resources it felt able to spare from the Peninsular and Mediterranean theatres that were the state's primary strategic focus.[66]

The years immediately after Waterloo saw only limited variation from that pattern. A British army increasingly deployed overseas, in part as the Duke of Wellington suggested, to keep it out of sight of cost-conscious politicians hostile to standing armies, found ample work conquering empires in southern Africa and India. Overseas regimental service in remote colonies was thus anything but routine. Its lessons helped spark a genuine, wide-scale reform movement – especially as fear of a lightning French invasion based on railways and steamships developed in the 1850s.

Hew Strachan makes the point that the army's very adjustment to the demands of imperial expansion and home defence ironically tended to distract attention from the large-scale great-power force projection mission that emerged with the Crimean War.[67] Nevertheless much of the groundwork for coping with the administrative and operational shortcomings manifested in the Crimea had been laid a generation earlier, in colonial contexts.

Similarly the 'gunboat diplomacy' that opened China depended on a Royal Navy able to deliver overwhelming force, by surprise, against specifically targeted life lines.[68]

In the emerging 'second British Empire', redcoat regulars were the core of operations campaigns against adversaries regarded as taxing to the limit the mettle of the locally raised elements that had borne the brunt of eighteenth-century expansion. By the 1820s at least it was conventional wisdom in India that only British troops could be counted on to decide a battle or storm a fortress.[69] The Kaffir Wars in South Africa and the Sikh Wars of the 1840s were understood as depending for their outcomes on a strong ethnic British presence. Nor did British strategic thought during this period take seriously the prospect of using Imperial forces in anything but regional contexts of power projection, Ceylon, Burma, China in the Opium Wars and again in 1860, and usually accompanied by a strong British element. Select units of the Indian Army might be able to engage European forces under special circumstances. The notion of systematically involving them in 'European' war seemed absurd in a developing context of postulated racial hierarchy in an imperial system increasingly recognising that its rule was based on force.[70]

It was France that began the process of direct linking of imperial and European warmaking. On one level the process began with the expansion of the numbers and responsibilities of the *troupes de la marine* in the 1830s. Previously the responsibility for securing what remained of France's overseas possessions rested with a generally indifferent line army. The *troupes de la marine*, by contrast, were administered by the navy, and correspondingly available for expeditionary as well as garrison duty. Marines served in a half-dozen minor expeditions in Africa and the Pacific islands, in the landings at Mogador and Vera Cruz. A provisional regiment went to China in 1860, another to Mexico with Maximilian. Marines accompanied the Crimean expedition, and did so well that the line army saw no reason not to employ their services in Italy five years later.[71]

Instead the army began asserting responsibility for the operations the Second Republic and Second Empire undertook in the eastern Mediterranean, seeking to build French influence under the camouflage of protecting Christian interests. French regulars served in Lebanon and carried the weight of Napoleon III's Chinese and Mexican expeditions. It was Algeria, however, that established the first modern symbiosis between European and Imperial warfare. The original plan for a quick conquest, implemented in 1830, evolved into a permanent war. Over half the French army's infantry regiments, a significant proportion of the cavalry and artillery, and a high proportion of senior officers, rotated through North Africa in the next three decades. Algeria evolved into a proving ground for officers and men: a military environment below the level of European war but far above 'manoeuvers with live ammunition'. The experience of active service that was constantly available in Algeria was considered a major advantage by France's military neighbours. At the same time Algeria increasingly acquired patriotic and national significance, engaging popular emotion as a symbol of French power to a degree no earlier – and no later – colony could claim.[72] Worth noting as well was Algeria's role as a place of exile for revolutionaries and activists: near enough and large enough to absorb 'dangerous elements' without the drawbacks of ignoring them on one hand, imprisoning or executing them on the other.[73]

To France's advantage as well were the elite fighting units that emerged from Algeria's deserts and mountains. The Zouaves, originally locally recruited, were later composed of metropolitan Frenchmen, hard cases and bold adventurers. Their stablemates of the *Tirailleurs Algériens*, the Turcos, enlisted from among ethnic North Africans. Initially reluctant to use the latter in European campaigns, French authorities changed their minds in face of their performance in the Crimea. Another Turco regiment fought in Italy, doing so well than no subsequent French plans for *grande guerre* failed to include the Turcos alongside the Zouaves.[74] They would be the thin end of a wedge that in the next century would see hundreds of thousands of Asian and African soldiers deployed in Europe.

CONCLUSION

The half century from Waterloo to the Wars of German Unification, far from being a period of stagnation and reaction in military affairs, was characterised by broad-spectrum concern with change. Perhaps the most remarkable feature of that concern was that it was internally generated. The great powers avoided not only large-scale wars, but arms races as well. Extra-European ventures were much fewer and far less systematic than in the second half of the century. Nor did they have the publicity that meant a disaster in some colonial outpost could destabilise a government. European states correspondingly established military systems according to particular definitions of vital interest, relative to particular domestic capacities for military mobilisation. While there were significant areas of overlapping, in weapons systems for example, and significant interfacing of theories and doctrines, European armed forces between 1815 and 1864 developed along asymmetrical lines to an extent that would be replicated only after the Great War, when a comprehensive change again posed general challenge.

2. European Warfare 1864–1913

JEREMY BLACK*

As Dennis Showalter showed in the previous chapter,[1] the years from 1815 to 1864 were not a period of stagnation. Nor were they a period of uniform development. Instead, armies changed in response to a range of factors among which were their particular mission requirements and the political parameters that affected military mobilisation. Both remained important in the second half of the century, and this serves to qualify, if not subvert, any account of military change that focuses on a unitary pattern. The latter is indeed a method that is frequently used. It focuses on two related approaches: first, an emphasis on technology, more specifically weaponry, and the use of this indicator to provide a ranking of capability and, also, both narrative and explanation of change. Second, the notion of the paradigm military method and paradigm power is employed in order to explain both contemporary ranking and the emulation/diffusion processes by which developments in a particular period are supposed to have moved in step.

For 1864–1913, an essential unity is provided by the argument that Prussian (from 1871 German) techniques provided the paradigm. The Wars of German Unification (1864–71), the term sometimes employed to describe the conflicts between Prussia and Denmark (1864), Austria (1866) and France (1870–1), serve as marking the beginning of the period, as they saw the emergence of a great German state and the establishment of the superiority of her military methods. Thereafter, until World War One (1914–18), other Continental strategic planners considered how best to respond to German power and techniques, how far to emulate them, and how best to devise appropriate

* I would like to thank Ian Beckett, Gerry Bryant, Christopher Duffy, Dennis Showalter and Spencer Tucker for their comments on an earlier draft.

counter-strategies and counter-tactics. In World War One Germany's opponents succeeded in doing so, at least on the Western Front. The 'Allies' (principally France and Britain) managed to contain German offensives – in 1914, 1916, and in 1918 – and to launch a final offensive that led to the defeat of the German army in 1918. Although subsequently there were to be claims by the military that the German army had been 'stabbed in the back' by collapse on the Home Front, in fact the military–political strategies of the German state had been defeated.

If German power appears to provide a unity to the period, with its latter years discussed in terms of anticipations of World War One, such an account is misleading as it underrates the importance and diversity of developments in the wider world. This raises complex issues of tasking (the goals set for the military) and the accompanying requirements in force structure and doctrine. As Bruce Vandervort points out, this was a period of major European power projection, not only the 'Scramble for Africa', but also territorial aggrandisement in Central, South and South East Asia and in Oceania. With the exception of Austria, which sought expansion only in the Balkans, all major and several lesser European powers took part in this expansion. At the same time, their militaries were not equally committed or affected. Thus the Germans, who were involved in conquering and suppressing rebellion in South-West and East Africa, were less affected than Britain, Russia, Italy, France, Spain, Portugal and the Netherlands, who faced a greater diversity of problems and threats.

Multiple tasking did not only involve force projection outside Europe. There was also the important task of maintaining civil order, if not political control, within European territories. Again, this varied in importance and, again, was relatively less important for the Germans. Rebellions were also less serious in most states than they had been in 1815–63. Thus there was no recurrence of the major uprisings in Hungary and Poland. Yet there were serious problems of civil disorder with a political dimension, in a number of countries, as well as particular uprisings. For example, the French army suppressed the Paris Commune in 1871, its Spanish counterpart faced Carlist opponents in the Second Carlist War (1873–6) and also had to suppress the Cantonist uprising in 1873–4, and the Italian army was used to enforce the authority of the new Italian state in southern Italy, especially in Sicily in 1866. In Russia, in 1905, troops were used against those demanding change. Armies also played a prominent role in supporting or resisting coups. Thus army units played a key role in the successful coup that led to the overthrow of the Portuguese monarchy in 1910. The military also played an important part in resisting worker activism, particularly by breaking strikes. In 1910 sabotage by striking miners in South Wales led to the deployment of troops, while, in 1911, a general rail strike in Britain led to the deployment of troops who killed two strikers in Liverpool.

It would be misleading to focus exclusively on Prussian models of army organisation and ways of war, even in the case of conflict between European states. Thus the Greeks sent irregulars into Thessaly, Epirus and Macedonia in 1877–8 to attack the Turks. Nevertheless, accepting these variations, it was still the case that Prussian success played a major role in changing the culture of state warfare in Europe (which is not the same as the totality of military history). In particular, the focus on staff planning before and during a war and on staff generalship and officers in the Prussian army marked a shift from an earlier practice of command that had placed less emphasis on sequential planning and prior organisation and, instead, more emphasis on boldness and flair, such as the ethos of the *ancien régime* and of French Revolutionary and Napoleonic generalship. In the Franco-Prussian War, command positions were given to members of the Prussian royal family, but they were subordinated to the system run by the General Staff of the brightest professional officers in the army.

System was the key word. Napoleon's method was the model for this, but he did not institutionalise it in the French army. The Prussians planned for war and sought to control conflict as a process, in which the systematised application of planned pressure led to predicted results. Helmuth von Moltke, the Chief of the Prussian General Staff, adapted Napoleonic ideas of the continuous offensive to the practicalities of the industrial age, including railways. In place of frontal attack, he sought to envelop opposing forces and to oblige them to mount such attacks themselves in an effort to regain freedom of manoeuvre. Thus he sought by strategic manoeuvre to counter the benefits that rifled weapons and the scale of conflict had given the defence.

In battle, the Prussians benefited from the adaptability with which they responded to new weaponry. The Dreyse breech-loading 'needle' rifle could be loaded lying down and fired four to seven times a minute: in practice, it was often fired from the hip because of the problem of escaping gases. The Prussians used these rifles to deadly effect against Denmark in 1864 and Austria in 1866.

Prussia's success against the outnumbered Danes had less of an impact on contemporaries than the defeat of Austria two years later. Domestic problems encouraged both Wilhelm I of Prussia and Franz Joseph of Austria to press for war in 1866, although the unsettled nature both of the Austro-Prussian con-dominium of Schleswig–Holstein and of the political situation within Germany were themselves a cause of serious dispute.

The Seven Weeks' War (June–August 1866) saw a speedy triumph over the Austrians and their German allies: Hanover, Hesse-Cassel and Saxony were overrun. Prussia and Austria faced each other with comparable numbers, providing an opportunity for Prussia to demonstrate the superior quality of her army. The Prussians gained the initiative thanks in part to their more effective mobilisation and deployment plans. They were able to benefit from their rail system, which was better and also better organised for wartime deployment. The Prussians also benefited from the low morale of much of the multi-ethnic Austrian army: Hungarian, Italian, Czech, Polish and Croat support for the Habsburgs was limited, as could be seen in the numbers who surrendered unwounded.

Each side deployed a quarter of a million men at Sadowa, the decisive battle on 3 July 1866. Benedek, the Austrian commander, held a reasonable defensive position, had better artillery and the possibility of using interior lines to defeat the separate Prussian armies in detail, but, partly due to irresolution, was unable to take advantage of his interior position. Prior to the battle he had been outmanoeuvred by three Prussian armies which were operating Moltke's strategy of exterior lines. Whereas Napoleon I had used separately operating corps within his army, Moltke employed independently operating armies, that is, much larger forces. Furthermore, unlike Napoleon, who concentrated his forces prior to the battle, Moltke aimed for a concentration of his armies in the battle.

At Sadowa, Moltke failed to realise his ideal aim of closing the trap by driving in the Austrian flanks completely, but the Prussians had shown themselves superior not only in manoeuvre but also on the battlefield. Prussian units in attack possessed a flexibility their opponents lacked, ensuring that the Austrian positions were caught in the flank and hit by crossfire. Prussian companies, which had been trained to move independently, albeit within the confines of a plan, proved more flexible than the massed Austrian columns. Attacks by the latter led to heavy losses. The Austrians did best with their artillery, which outshot the Prussians and hit Prussian infantry advances, although the dispersed small-unit character of the latter minimised casualties.

Sadowa ended with the flight of the Austrians and the loss of their army's coherence, morale and artillery. The Prussians pressed on towards Vienna, but there was no final battle: the Prussians sought and needed a short war. Austrian civilian determination collapsed and Franz Joseph sued for peace. The two-power system in Germany, with Austria the senior, was replaced, with Prussia annexing Austria's North German allies.

The Seven Weeks' War led other powers to adopt or seek to better Prussian weaponry and tactical formations. Breech-loading rifles were now seen as far better than the slower muzzle-loaders: the Austrians were still armed with the muzzle-loading Lorenz rifle of 1854. In 1866, the French adopted the *chassepot* rifle which had a more gas-tight breech and a far greater range than the Prussian needle rifle, which no longer represented cutting-edge military technology. The Prussian tactic of concentrating strength on the skirmishing line, and adopting more extended formations that were less dense than columns or lines, and thus less exposed to fire, commanded attention. The redundancy of cavalry on the battlefield was another lesson from the recent war, but one that many cavalry officers were reluctant to accept. Reliance on more effective firepower also decreased the frequency with which units clashed in hand-to-hand fighting and ensured there was less need for the bayonet.

Relations between France and Prussia were tense in the late 1860s. Napoleon III was fearful of Prussian strength and determined to prevent Prussia from leading the southern German states into the Prussian-dominated North German Confederation created in 1867. The German Chancellor, Otto von Bismarck, sought war with France as necessary to secure such a union. The French were poorly prepared as they had no equivalent to the reservists in the Prussian *Landwehr*, in part because political opposition in the *Corps Législatif* had hamstrung the attempt in the 1868 Military Law to create a 400 000 strong reserve of *Garde Nationale Mobiles*. Distrustful of his adventurism, republican opponents of Napoleon III were dubious about the value of a larger army. The army was not keen on expansion because it feared that a large number of conscripts would dilute military quality. This exacerbated a numerical imbalance that reflected the larger German population and its higher growth rate; a contrast that underlined the damage done to France's strategic position by Prussia's success in partially unifying Germany in 1866.

There was no adequate French war plan. The improvisation that had worked against the Russians in 1854 and Austrians in 1859 was no longer appropriate. French operations in Algeria, Mexico and the Papal States in the 1860s did not provide experience in mass mobilisation or in manoeuvring against large numbers of well-trained, led, equipped and gunned forces.

Although the French declared war, Moltke rapidly deployed, regained the initiative and took the war into France. Rail mobilisation worked as never before, and the Prussians benefited from superior artillery: breech-loading steel guns manufactured by Krupp. The Prussians had also improved their artillery tactics and organisation, and pushed their guns to the front to make them more effective. In the *mitrailleuse*, the French had the first effective machine gun, a hand-cranked ring of 37 barrels of 10 shot magazines each, that could fire 100 to 150 rounds per minute, but they were used neither extensively nor intelligently: a failure to develop an appropriate tactical doctrine reduced the impact of new technology. The guns also weighed a ton and so were not very mobile.

On 6 August 1870, the Prussian Third Army invaded Alsace and defeated the greatly outnumbered I Corps at Fröschwiller and Wörth. The *chassepot* showed its value against frontal attacks, but the Prussians benefited from greater numbers, which also enabled them to outflank the defenders, and from their superior artillery. This critical victory encouraged Moltke to continue with the offensive and further to gain the initiative. Napoleon III lost confidence and his ill-chosen commander of the Army of the Rhine, Marshal Achille Bazaine, retreated into the Metz fortification system, thus surrendering both mobility and an opportunity first to block the Prussians and later to prevent envelopment. At Gravelotte-Saint Privat on 18 August, 188 000 Prussians under Moltke attacked 113 000 French troops under Bazaine in good defensive positions. With their effective *chassepots* and some use of the *mitrailleuse*, the French inflicted heavy casualties, but they failed to mount counterattacks. Instead, the initiative was retained by the Prussians, who used their more numerous and superior artillery with great effect. Repeated pressure finally led Bazaine to fall back on Metz (where it was soon besieged), which gave Moltke an opportunity to destroy the Army of Châlons being assembled under MacMahon. This was a victory of manoeuvre in which Moltke successfully grasped the options offered by the possible moves of Bazaine and MacMahon and defeated them separately. MacMahon retreated before Moltke's attempted encirclement but was trapped at Sedan by the rapidly-advancing Prussians. Forced marches, day and night, was one key to Moltke's victory. Moltke seized the hills around Sedan and used his artillery to drive back French attempts to seize them with heavy losses. Napoleon III surrendered on 2 September, with 83 000 troops; Metz followed on 28 October.

The Prussian use of dispersed forces with greater speed (ironically in the style of Napoleon I) had enabled them to outmanoeuvre the more concentrated and slower-moving French armies. In part, this reflected Prussian superiority in command and control, but a fixity of purpose and a clearly-planned strategy were also important, as were tactical differences. The French had responded to the Austro-Prussian War by adopting tight defensive formations designed to shoot down Prussian attackers. However, the resulting positions were vulnerable to flank attack and the more dispersed formations favoured by the Prussians reduced the target for the French. In an essay of 1864, 'Remarks on the Influence of Improved Rifles on the Attack', Moltke had decried closely-packed frontal assaults. Open-order deployment and small-unit fire tactics proved a more effective response to modern firearms.

The Prussians had also developed a system of General Staff work and training at a General Staff Academy that was given much of the credit for victory in 1866 and 1870. Training of

staff officers gave the Prussian army a coherence its opponents
lacked. Prussian staff officers were given an assured place in a
co-ordinated command system. Officers from the General Staff
were expected to advise commanders, and the latter were also
expected to heed their chiefs of staff. This led to a system of
joint responsibility in which either the commander or his first
general staff officer could issue orders. Such a system rested on
the reputation of the staff system. It also made predictable planning possible, which encouraged forward planning. There was
an emphasis on preparing for an entire campaign, rather than
simply for battle, and this led to a stress on strategic plans.
Preparedness and staff work ensured that large numbers of troops
and reservists could be mobilised and deployed successfully.

The Prussian command system was not without problems; it
could not prevent Prince Frederick Charles (nephew of Wilhelm
I), an army commander, from failing to observe strategic and
tactical plans in 1866, while in 1870 Steinmetz, commander of
the First Army, also disobeyed the strategic plan. Aside from
straightforward departure from plans, there was also a range of
factors causing the 'friction' Clausewitz had seen as the prime
inhibitor of plans. Even so, the effective General Staff system
ensured that the Prussians were better able than before to fight
major battles, with their attendant casualties and disruption, and
to press on to new tasks.

The Prussians were also more effective at the micro-level.
Thanks both to an ethos of commitment and to training, there
was an emphasis on a professionalism on the part of officers,
NCOs and soldiers that was more consistent than in the French
army. More particularly, the Prussians trained officers to take
their own decisions at all levels within the constraints of the
command plan. This was important, as defensive firepower, by
encouraging a 'lower density' battlefield with spread-out units
and dispersed formations, accentuated problems of command
and communication, which put a premium on coordination and
morale. The use of *Aufträgs*, orders that explained the situation
and goal of a force and left a degree of flexibility to the local
commanders, was particularly important, ensuring a dynamic
interaction, mediated by training, between hierarchy and de-
volved decision-making which facilitated small-unit operations
supporting and harmonising with those of large forces.

The uncertainty of war contributed to Prussian success, rather than undermining it, because of their superior ability to cope with it through better staff work. Partly as a consequence, Moltke's 1866 and 1870 campaigns worked out very differently to Napoleon I's of 1815. Like Napoleon I, Moltke encountered problems with opponents failing to move as anticipated, but, in the circumstances of 1866 and 1870, was better able to understand, think through and control the consequences. His nephew was to be far less successful in 1914, a reminder of the need to keep relative capability in mind (especially the contingent relative abilities of opposing generals) and to avoid assuming progressive or linear improvement. Prussia's victory in 1870–1 led to its gaining Alsace-Lorraine and an indemnity of five billion francs from France. It also enabled it to transform its hegemony within Germany into a German empire ruled from Berlin. Prussian success led to the conclusion that offensive operations that were carefully planned by an effective and professional general staff and drew on the logistical possibilities provided by railways could, indeed would, lead to swift and decisive victories; although there were serious logistical problems in 1870 with chaos on the railways and a dependence on horses.

Moltke himself later warned of the hazards of extrapolating from his victories. While arguing that it was preferable to fight on the territory of one's opponent, he was increasingly sceptical about the potential of the strategic offensive, because of increases in defensive firepower and the size of armies. Furthermore, in 1866 and 1870, deficiencies in leadership and strategy on the part of Austria and France had enabled the Prussians to outmanoeuvre their opponents. Benedek failed to make adequate preparations for attack or defence, and responded incompetently to the Prussian advance into Bohemia. No help was offered to Austria's German allies. French failures include Napoleon III's command decisions, a reluctance to benefit from the strategic possibilities of a rail system considerably better than Austria's, and an unwillingness to strengthen the defensive by using both a flexible defence and entrenchments like those employed by Robert E. Lee in Virginia in 1864–5 during the American Civil War. Had the French had artillery to compare with that of the Prussians then the attacks of the latter, especially at Wörth and Gravelotte, should have been devastating.

The difference was to be seen in 1914 and 1916, although in both offensives the Germans also suffered from their failure to keep an 'open' campaign zone with room for manoeuvre and a tempo permitting the retention of the initiative as the Elder Moltke had done; the strategy of envelopment failed in 1914 and, in 1916, the strength of the French defence compensated for the exposed nature of the Verdun position. More generally, the expanded range of modern weaponry in World War One limited the possibilities of flank movements and attacks. This made envelopment more difficult and thus made it more likely that defeated forces would be able to retreat and set up a new effective defensive line, avoiding both destruction and a speedy enforced peace. Nevertheless, on the Eastern Front in 1914 the Germans showed that their strategic concepts were not without merit, although their decisiveness was shown in a defensive success rather than an offensive triumph.

The campaigns of 1866 and 1870 did not demonstrate that the Prussians were bound to win, although they did show the value of winning the opening battle in a short war. This looked forward towards the danger of assuming that German successes in 1939 and 1940 demonstrated the ineluctable superiority of *Blitzkrieg*. A past parallel was that of Frederick the Great of Prussia in 1740–2, 1744–5 and 1756–63. His successes did not imply that his methods were in some way a paradigm of military perfection or his army the best in the West. Instead, they showed that it was appropriate for the tasks it was expected to undertake; and that these were carefully kept in line with Prussian capability. Even so, Prussian failures in offensive operations, as in 1744 and 1778, suggested that the Prussian military system had deficiencies. These were in addition to the limitations of its restricted 'tasking', namely its inappropriateness for amphibious and colonial operations, neither of which were tasks it was likely to have to fulfil. 'Tasking' was also important in the Wars of German Unification. In neither 1866 nor 1870 did Prussia have to conquer its opponents. To that extent, the wars more closely approximated to Napoleon I's attacks on Austria than to his invasions of Spain and Russia.

Indeed, Prussia and the Prussian army were not really up to the task of conquering their opponents. After successes in the decisive battles fought near the frontier in 1870, the Prussians encountered difficulties as they advanced further into France, not least supply problems and opposition from a hostile population. More generally, the resources for the total conquest of Austria and, later, France, including, for example, possibly resisting a war of *revanche* mounted from France's major overseas territory, Algeria, were simply not present. This was not the option the government or Moltke sought; they wanted a swift and popular conflict with relatively low casualties. The rate at which resources were used up militated against a long war. In 36 hours at Sedan, the Prussians fired 35 000 shells.

Yet, as it turned out, in 1870–1 the Prussians did not win the war against France by destroying much of its army near the frontier. Due to political factors, the replacement of Napoleon III by the Third Republic, proclaimed at Paris on 4 September, the war continued: Sedan was not a Sadowa. Determined not to surrender territory as the price of peace, Léon Gambetta's Government of National Defence raised new forces. After the French surrender at Sedan, the Prussians advanced on Paris which they had surrounded by 19 September. There was no attempt to storm the city, which indeed had a garrison of 300 000 troops, spread out over a sixty kilometre long fortified defensive perimeter. Moltke relied on starvation and Bismarck persuaded Wilhelm I to add bombardment. Relying on new draftees, troops from Algeria, *Gardes Mobiles*, and American arms shipments, the French assembled armies to relieve the city, leading to a series of battles from early October to late January 1871.

The Prussians were in a strong position, with their centre point the forces besieging Paris, and now able to use the French railways, although they suffered from wartime damage to the railways and from their inadequacy in keeping the massive force besieging Paris supplied. The Prussians also benefited from the prestige they had gained in victory, as well as from the surrender at Metz, of the last major professional French force, and from the disorientation of their opponents. Prussian morale was high due to their initial stunning victories.

In response, the new French Republic appealed to the tradition of French revolutionary enthusiasm to repel the invader at all costs, only to be disabled by a different internal revolutionary force – the Paris Commune. Nonetheless, helped by the superiority of the *chassepot* over the Dreyse rifle, the republican armies still won some small actions and showed themselves capable of defensive operations, especially if in fortified positions, although they lacked the ability to mount successful attacks. Instead, they proved vulnerable to Prussian artillery and were repeatedly defeated in the open. However, in 1870–1, unlike in 1864 and 1866, there were no marked technical advantages on either side; the Prussian artillery included a lot of old-fashioned guns, but many shooters preferred the Dreyse rifle to the *chassepot* as it was more soldier-proof.

The French also discovered, as the Americans had done in 1861, that rapidly raising large forces created serious problems of supply, training and command. These were made much worse because France was already experiencing defeat, division and dislocation. Numbers alone could not suffice; it was the way in which men had been integrated into already existing military structures that was crucial, as the Prussians showed, and this could not be done quickly or easily, given the demoralised state of the French army. The forces in Paris failed in their attempts to break out of the city; the confidence of republican enthusiasts in a *sortie en masse* proved misplaced. Defeats elsewhere led to an armistice, signed on 28 January, and to the French National Assembly accepting Prussian terms.[2]

France had also been defeated in both 1814 and 1815, and forced to accept political settlements decreed by its opponents, but German success in 1870–1 was far more rapid than the long-drawn-out process of reducing Napoleon I had been, and was obtained without the help of the large alliance system that had defeated him. The Prussians had been able to grasp success in the process of change that was affecting Western warfare. The idea that tactics and formations should change markedly in response to the last war can be seen in the sequence of Franco–Austrian (1859), Austro–Prussian and Franco–Prussian wars. This encouraged a degree of built-in responsiveness to the possibility of change within the military system. Adapting force structures, armament and tactical doctrine did not take place in a vacuum, but rather with reference to the character of and threat from potential opponents. An understanding of the dynamic nature of military change necessitated armies and navies continually evaluating what others were doing and updating themselves. The professional expertise and flexibility of the

Prussian army enabled Moltke smoothly to introduce innovations such as timed stages in mobilisation. Peacetime war games,
staff rides and manoeuvres ensured that plans were tested and
capability enhanced. This process contributed greatly to the sense
of armies as organisations that could be made to respond to
central direction in an effective and flexible way.[3]

As Western militaries became more institutionalised and professional, so planning came to play a greater role interacting
with international arms races as well as influencing foreign policy.
Military plans, such as the German Schlieffen Plan of 1905, drove
policy.[4] Campaigns were analysed at length in military institutions and publications in order to prepare better for the future.

There was an emphasis on the virtues of an initial all-out
offensive. Throughout Europe planners drafted blueprints for
offensive operations, which were seen as the sole way to secure
success. This both reflected Clausewitzian ideas and arose from
the dissection of the conflict of 1870–1 for lessons by the generation of officers ultimately to hold high command positions
in World War One, for example Franz Conrad von Hötzendorf,
Chief of the Austrian General Staff from 1906 until 1916, and
his French and Russian counterparts.

The Schlieffen Plan called for an offensive envelopment of
the French army, followed by the use of the same strategy against
France's ally, Russia. Schlieffen envisaged an invasion through
neutral Belgium against weak French forces, turning south, en-
veloping Paris and swinging southeast to hammer the main
French forces from the rear against the Franco–German and
Swiss borders. It would then be possible to advance further into
the interior. The strategy's author, Field-Marshal Alfred von
Schlieffen, a veteran of the Austro-Prussian and Franco-Prussian
wars, was Chief of the General Staff in 1891–1906:[5] he had to
plan for a much greater problem than had faced Prussia in
1866 and 1870–1, namely war on two fronts. German tactics and
peacetime manoeuvres accordingly emphasised the offensive.
Schlieffen envisaged an initial massive onslaught in the West to
inflict swift defeat on the French before turning on the Russians;
i.e. two sequential, not simultaneous, offensives.

Sir Ian Hamilton, then British Adjutant General, observed
the manoeuvres in September 1909 of the Saxon army, part of
the German forces. Noting that 'the spirit of the offensive [was]

sedulously fostered', he wrote 'the Germans are ever preaching
fire effect, but here we find fire effect prematurely discarded in
favour of that primitive *arme blanche* [shock action] which is the
negation of modern armaments . . . not a single entrenchment
worthy the name was ever even attempted.' However, Hamilton
was also most impressed with the quality and nature of planning: 'quite astonished by the general dissemination of knowledge
right through regimental officers and staff . . . [all] instruments
in the general military scheme . . . the greater facility and rapidity with which staff work is carried out in the field.' Yet Hamilton
also detected weaknesses. He was most impressed by the cooperation of infantry, cavalry and artillery: 'In the earlier stages
of a manoeuvre; on the march; during the reconnaissances; at
the issue of orders and in the opening phases of an engagement the cooperation thus secured is the feature which, above
all others, renders the German Army so potent an instrument
of war.' However, he observed that this broke down in the final
phases of combat, and also thought the younger Helmuth von
Moltke, Chief of the General Staff in 1906–14, neither brilliant
nor adroit.

Hamilton's observations looked towards World War One. He
told Wilhelm II that the Saxon army 'was carrying the good
idea of the offensive beyond all reason' only to meet with the
rejoinder 'in war time it would correct itself only too quickly.'
Hamilton felt the attacks were on too narrow a front and that
the compact forces would be vulnerable, which was indeed to
be demonstrated in the war; but he also noted 'machine guns
in Germany seem to play a more leading part in manoeuvre
than in England'.[6]

The offensive philosophy also held sway in Germany's likely
opponent, France. Mistaken analysis of the failure of 1870 by
officers such as Colonel François-Jules-Louis Loyzeau de
Grandmaison, Director of Military Operations 1908–11, led to a
doctrine of *offensive à l'outrance*, the offensive at all costs, which
was seen as the best way to express and sustain the nation's martial
fervour, a concept that was important in the culture of the period;
as well as to balance the expected superiority of German numbers.[7]
Furthermore, attacking appeared to be the most appropriate way
to encourage and hold the enthusiasm of the troops and thus
ensure superior morale to that of the defenders. This was an

important element in thought about war in the period. Better morale appeared valuable tactically as a means to overcome the lethal character of defensive firepower, but also operationally providing a crucial capability gap between similarly armed forces. The emphasis on morale is a reminder of the danger of considering military developments largely in terms of improved technology, although it would have been better for both sides had they more fully appreciated the massive advantage of defensive firepower in 1914 which could not be suppressed by superior morale. Tactically, the stress on the offensive was linked not only to the *élan* and morale of the attacker, but also to a belief in the value of the bayonet. The quality of the generalship was also believed to be an important factor, with it being argued, for example, that German commanders could have won for the French in 1870, and their Japanese counterparts had they been in command of the Russians in the Russo–Japanese War.[8]

For the French, the 'spirit of the offensive' was seen as a necessary counter to German numerical superiority. It also seemed the only way to regain Alsace-Lorraine, which had been ceded to Germany in 1871 and the loss of which was keenly felt. Thus political objectives played a major role in framing strategy and tactics. They were to lead to heavy losses and failure in 1914.[9] At the same time, taking the offensive seemed the only way to deny the Germans the initiative. The French Plan XVII, which was in effect when World War One broke out, was a plan for attack.

We should not ignore the wider cultural context that affected both military planning and the willingness of the average male citizen to acquiesce in the burdens of military spending and, in Continental Europe, of peacetime conscription. The Social Darwinism of the late nineteenth century, with its emphasis on natural competitiveness, encouraged interest in aggressive military planning and this was supported, both with resources and psychologically, by the tremendous demographic expansion of the period and by the major increase in industrial capacity.

Academics, scientists, artists, clerics and intellectuals also contributed to formulating rationales and objectives for expansion and conflict. War was seen as a glorious means to renew people and escape decadence. Most intellectuals were convinced nationalists: internationalism was of only limited appeal. A concept of triumphant will linked the prevailing Romanticism to international relations. Millenarian theology and providentialism both also contributed to a sense of the rightness of conflict. Educated elites came to believe in the moral value of war. This was a 'rationality' centred on themes of sacrifice and ideas of vitalism. Contributing to the same end, industrialists pressed the economic and social utility of weapons programmes. However there were powerful Liberal elites in Britain and France who repudiated or at least challenged this thinking, and they were supported by Socialists. Nevertheless, the absence of conflict helped to make military service popular: it was a no-risk rite of passage, at a time when other male rites of passage had been discredited.

With the offensive in vogue, Clausewitz's chapter on defensive warfare (the longest in *On War*) was largely ignored; some translations omitted it altogether. To sustain the offensive and achieve victory in the face of ever more lethal technology on the battlefield, strategists and tacticians called for ever larger armies and emphasised the value of conscription and the substantial reserve forces that universal military training permitted; having fulfilled their allocated period of permanent military service, conscripts moved into the reserves, where their military effectiveness was maintained by annual manoeuvres. This ignored the strategic impact, in the West at least, of squeezing ever larger armies into the same area.

Pressure for larger armies led to a concern about population size and birth rates, especially in France where they were lower than in Germany. An alliance with the vast Russian army, over a million strong, excluding reservists, in 1900 came to appear crucial to French politicians; the two powers were allied from 1894. The Russian army was far larger than that of Germany and, once the Russians started investing in enhanced effectiveness, especially after defeat in 1905, it became a more serious threat. The net effect of conscription was the availability of millions of men trained for war. The British tradition of volunteer service ensured that their military thinkers faced the dilemma of how to fight a future mass-army war without conscription.

At the same time, there was a major increase in the battlefield and general capability of Western militaries. This owed much to the size and flexibility of the industrial base of the major powers, although industrialisation itself accentuated stresses in society, creating a situation in which war appeared as a viable solution to domestic crisis. Thanks to the flexibility of modern industrial culture and the availability of organisational expertise, investment capital and trained labour, it was possible to translate new concepts rapidly into new or improved weapons, and, through mass-production, to have such weapons adopted in large quantities. Germany was able to double the complement of field-guns to 144 per corps between 1866 and 1905. The British War Office report on developments in 1910 noted: 'The general tendency is still to increase the artillery and new guns are being acquired in almost every country.'[10] The most effective was the French 75 mm rapid-firing field gun that was introduced by the firm Schneider-Creusot in 1893. Although light, the gun was stable as a result of compressed air counteracting energy. This ensured accuracy as well as rapid deployment, and the combination helped to make the open battleground dangerous for opposing infantry. The impact of this gun was increased by foreign sales.

More generally, guns became more powerful, and benefited from new propellants. They were necessary to silence opposing artillery and to kill opposing infantry. The logistical strain created by such artillery was immense, especially in offensive operations. Aside from moving the guns themselves, it was also necessary to provide sufficient ammunition; pre-war planners totally underestimated the voracious appetite of the artillery in World War One. As guns and ammunition were heavy and could best be moved on paved roads, logistical problems increased, as did the need to match plans to communications. Advance by paved road became an adjunct to mobilising by railway.

British Intelligence reported in 1901, 'Russia has lost no time in realizing that infantry is unlikely to be employed in the future without its own proportion of guns always with it'.[11] The Russians obtained guns both from foreign suppliers and from domestic production. Already, in 1900 the Russians were ordering 1000 quick-firing field-guns from the Putilov iron works, which was producing artillery as good as that from elsewhere in Europe.[12] Resources for such expenditure came from economic growth which permitted very high rates of peacetime expenditure on military preparations. In 1907–13, Russia spent heavily on both army and navy: defence spending increasing from 608.1

million roubles in 1908 to 959.6 million in 1913, a rise well above inflation. The percentage of Russian government expenditure on defence rose from 23.2 per cent in 1907 to 28.3 per cent in 1913.[13]

Growing Russian strength led to pressure in Germany for a pre-emptive war. Russian spending on the military, combined with the development of her strategic railroad net, was one reason why the young Moltke pressed for war in 1913–14; he feared that Germany might not be able to win a war with Russia later.[14] More generally, budgetary competition between states played a major role in military expenditure,[15] as states scrutinised the spending plans of rivals.

The availability of improved weaponry owed much to continually improving technology and better steel production methods, particularly the Bessemer steel converter and the Gilchrist-Thomas basic steel process, thanks to which steel output rose dramatically from the 1870s. Earlier methods of casting guns became obsolete, as it was not possible to cast uniform guns. Alfred Krupp of Essen had developed a crucial expertise in producing breech-loading steel guns.[16]

There were also continued design improvements in infantry firepower. This included, in the 1880s, the adoption of smokeless powder, which burned more efficiently and permitted an increase in the range and muzzle velocity of bullets, and the development of an efficient system of magazine feed, permitting reliable repeating rifles, such as the French Lebel (1886) and the German Mauser (1889), using spring action to feed cartridges at a rapid rate. Smokeless powder also ensured that the field of vision was not blocked and that it was harder for opponents to discern the source of fire. The development of the spitzer or boat-tail bullet provided a smaller, more aerodynamically stable, and longer-range bullet.

The machine-gun, an automatic repeating weapon, was a metaphor of the application of industry to war. The most famous, the Maxim gun, patented by Hiram Maxim in 1883, used recoil energy and eventually became both reliable and readily transportable. It was water cooled and fully automatic. Early models of the gun readily broke and got fouled by the black powder used as a propellant, so Maxim patented an improved gunpowder.[17] Improvements in the manufacture of cartridges reduced jamming. The Vickers-Maxim machine-gun, adopted by the British army in 1912, fired 250 rounds per minute: the fire of many riflemen. Although it was to be famous in World War One as a defensive weapon, the machine gun was seen before the war as a useful tool for attack, especially by clearing ground of defenders. The rate of fire of this and other weapons, however, ensured that supply needs for ammunition rose and this in turn led to pressure for a rapid victory. The extent to which enhanced weaponry led to uncertainty about how best to employ it and about the likely tactical consequences of its use was captured by General Roberts, then commander in chief of the British Madras army in India. Reporting on experiments with machine guns in 1884, he noted

> The accuracy and power of a weapon which when worked by men unskilled in its use, can fire 777 shots in 2 minutes at a range of 1,200 yards, and obtain about the same number of hits as fifty first class shots, firing for the same time with Martini-Henri rifles, must be acknowledged by all. It seems clear, therefore, that machine guns must play an important part in future warfare . . . Great diversity of opinion exists as to the tactical position which should be assigned to machine guns, and this because there has been no practical experience of any value to decide the question.
>
> Personally I am not in favour of machine guns forming part of the equipment of artillery. They appear to me to be essentially an infantry weapon: there is nothing in their manipulation that requires any knowledge of artillery matters, and their fire is but a multiplicity of infantry fire.
>
> In what way machine guns can best be utilised in war can never be satisfactorily settled until some opportunity offers to try them, but I am inclined to think they are better suited for defence than offence.[18]

Enhanced firepower was an obvious threat to cavalry and, already in 1866 and 1870, attacks by Austrian and French heavy cavalry had been bloodily repelled by Prussian infantry and cannon. Thereafter cavalry came to play a smaller role in armies and military planning, but there was much resistance to this process. This reflected the continued role of traditional notions about military activity, the superior position among officers that cavalrymen had in European society, the part played by cavalry in colonial wars, and the search for strategic mobility in the event of a European conflict.

Improved firepower was also a threat to fortifications. There had been much investment in defensive positions in the middle decades of the nineteenth century. In the 1850s, the British had constructed forts along the Channel coast, especially near Portsmouth, for protection in the event of French invasion. After 1871 the French created an extensive defensive belt to prevent further German advances from the east in the event of another war: the French had less space to manoeuvre in than hitherto. Military bases, such as Belfort and Verdun, were surrounded with fortified positions. Russia also spent heavily on fortresses and fortress artillery.

However, the effectiveness of traditional fortifications was affected by advances in artillery, especially the development of rifled steel breech-loaders, improved pneumatic recoil mechanisms that obviated the need for re-siting, and delayed action fuses.[19] Krupps developed some massive fortification-busting guns used in World War One. As so often in military history, an enhanced capacity for the offensive led to improvements in the defensive, in this case changes in fortification design and construction techniques, including lower profiles for the batteries and the use of steel and reinforced concrete. Much was spent on fortifications in the years before World War One, particularly by Belgium, France, Germany, Austria and Russia. They were designed both to resist offensives and to support them by securing supplies and communications and by freeing troops for operations. In some respects this looked forward to the use of trenches in World War One; they were defensive systems that fused the characteristics of fortifications and field entrenchments.

Initially only a small number of European thinkers anticipated the horrific casualties that developments in military methods and the expansion of army size were likely to produce in any future major war. The Marxist Friedrich Engels argued that the American Civil War (1861–5) indicated the likely massive destructiveness of future intra-European conflict, and he thought that this would undermine existing state and class hegemonies and make revolution possible. In his *War of the Future in its Tech-*

nical, Economic and Political Aspects (1897), part of which was published in English as *Is War Now Impossible?* (1899), the Polish financier Ivan (or Jean de) Bloch suggested that the combination of modern military technology and industrial strength had made great power European warfare too destructive to be feasible, and that if it occurred it would resemble a giant siege and would only be won when one of the combatants succumbed to famine and revolution. Bloch argued that the stalemate on the battlefield that came from defensive firepower would translate eventually into collapse on the home front.

However, fears about the consequent impact on casualty figures and military morale, and emphasis on the dangers of battlefield stalemate and of breakdown on the home front only encouraged an emphasis on preventing the stalemate by winning the initial offensive.

Military commentators could search for clues of the future character of war both in recent and in current conflicts. The American Civil War had provided indications of the potency of defensive firepower, but the broader relevance of trench warfare at Petersburg in Virginia in the winter of 1864–5 became apparent only 50 years later. The impact of the American Civil War on European military thought was negligible on the Continent, where the leaders of professional armies and the officer corps saw no lessons in a war fought by mass militia armies.

Furthermore, despite the experience of the Civil War, the American army continued to emphasise the offensive. Field service against Native Americans provided education neither in the manner in which firearms became more deadly in the last third of the century, nor in the problems of handling large numbers of troops. Instead, there was in American military thought more emphasis on morale and spiritual qualities, than on massive firepower support or the indirect approach, as the means to get across the killing zone provided by opposing firepower.

The major wars of the years 1882–1913 fought between 'Western' armies, at least in the sense of forces armed with modern weaponry, were not waged in Europe itself, with the exception of the peripheral Balkans. As later with the Cold War, there was no clash between the major powers. Furthermore, unlike during the Cold War, the wars that did occur were not closely linked to great power rivalry. Nevertheless, they were followed carefully by observers from those powers keen to establish if the conflicts offered any relevant lessons. The four major wars were all international conflicts; there was no major civil war, either social or secessionist in character in this period. They were the Spanish–American war of 1898, the Second Boer War of 1899–1902, the Russo–Japanese War of 1904–5, and the Balkan wars of 1912–13.

The first was a consequence of the rise of American economic and naval power. In 1898, bellicose political pressures within the USA helped lead to a war with Spain that the government did not want. The Spanish government and army could not face the prospect of abandoning Cuba, although they were aware that the USA was a formidable foe. Neither the Spanish fleet nor the army was in good shape. The army had been intensely politicised for decades, and this affected both the quality and the quantity of command: there were far too many officers. The financial implications, combined with the limited extent of industrial development and the determination to restrict expenditure, ensured that the Spanish army lacked training. It was also inexperienced.

Nevertheless, the Americans also lacked appropriate experience. Their army was small and untrained for such operations. Furthermore, the climate and terrain of Cuba created problems for the Americans. Fortunately for them, the Spaniards fought badly at the operational level. They failed to dispute the American landing in late June 1898, retired into a poor defensive perimeter round Santiago and did not attack American communications. The Spaniards were more successful tactically than operationally, and did not collapse when Santiago was attacked. However, crucial positions were lost to frontal attack on 1 July and Santiago surrendered on 17 July.

The fighting indicated the importance of entrenchments and the firepower provided by magazine rifles firing steel-jacket, high-velocity, smokeless rounds. The German Mauser rifle used by the Spaniards proved particularly effective, and their artillery was also superior as a result of the use of smokeless powder which kept their position secret. The war was a more obvious triumph for the newly developed and powerful American fleet than for the army.[20]

All the Continental armies sent observers to the Boer War in southern Africa between Britain and the Boers (Afrikaners) but, afterwards, there was considerable disagreement over whether to consider it just another colonial war (therefore, in contemporary views, the source of no lessons relevant to Europe), or as a war between two opponents of European stock, and thus somewhat less irrelevant. German and Austrian commentators used the Darwinian language in vogue in reference to the 'racial characteristics' of the Boers, praising them as warriors while at the same time underscoring their uniqueness as opponents. Most Continental military experts saw little in the conflict that was relevant to European warfare. Wilhelm II told Hamilton in 1909, 'It is you who have led us all astray with your South African War experiences, experiences altogether exceptional.'[21]

Many analysts correctly observed that factors such as the long-range marksmanship of the Boers and their tenacious guerrilla warfare of 1900–2 were not likely to be duplicated in clashes on the Continent among the great powers. Nevertheless, the war had important implications for World War One, including the use of indirect artillery fire, smokeless powder, long-range rifle fire and camouflage. Hamilton suggested to the Royal Commission on the War in South Africa the value of equipping soldiers with entrenching tools, and also proposed wheeled shields for the infantry. Due to the still notorious unreliability of early machine-guns, they did not dominate the Boer War battlefield.[22] That, however, gave scant guidance to the extent to which improvements would rapidly enhance capability; although that in turn depended in large part on appropriate circumstances and use. More generally, there was a technological leap forward between the Boer War and World War One, similar to that from the early string-tied aeroplanes of the 1900s to the nippy, useful planes of 1914–18.

A far larger conflict broke out in 1904. Competing Russian and Japanese interests in the Far East interacted with domestic pressures, including the view in some Russian governmental circles that victory would enhance the internal strength of the government, and a foolish unwillingness to accept Japanese strength, interests and determination because they were a non-European power. The government did not seem to have been looking for a war, but it failed to see that serious dialogue with

Japan was necessary if it was to be avoided. The Tsar and his advisers did not think the 'yellow devils' would dare to fight. Russian behaviour and arrogance did much to create ultimate unity in Tokyo in 1904. The 'moderates' agreed that Japan had to fight while she enjoyed a temporary advantage over the potentially stronger Russians, and this was to be repeated in 1941 in the preparations for Pearl Harbor. The Russians paid the price for treating the Japanese as a lesser people. The Japanese, however, had gained great confidence in their military system as a result of their victory over China in 1894–5.

In one respect the war was a triumph for Europeanisation in the form of Western military organisation. The Japanese won by employing European military systems and technology more effectively than the Russians; their army was modelled on the German, their navy and its methods on the British. Yet the Japanese victory was also a shock, in part because of Western racialist assumptions.

The fighting featured many elements that were also to be seen in World War One, including trench warfare with barbed wire and machine-guns, indirect artillery fire, artillery firing from concealed positions, a conflict that did not cease at nightfall, and a war waged with continuous front lines. Advocates of the offensive argued that the Russians stood on the defensive and lost, while the Japanese took the initiative, launched frontal assaults on entrenched forces strengthened by machine-guns and quick-firing artillery, as at Port Arthur and Mukden in 1905, and prevailed, despite horrific casualties. Observers came away noting that frontal assaults were still feasible and the bayonet still relevant, the latest technology notwithstanding.

As was often the case, the situation was more complex. For example, in the battle of Liaoyang (25 August – 3 September 1904) the Russians were attacked by a larger force on three occasions and repulsed them on each, but the commander, Aleksei Kuropatkin, believed himself defeated and retreated. He came closer to success than is sometimes appreciated, not least at Sandepu (26–7 January, 1905). Moreover, if he had been able to fight as he had wanted to, luring the Japanese deep into Manchuria while bringing to bear the overwhelming Russian superiority in numbers, they might have been defeated. Hamilton, who had been an observer in the war, felt when he attended the Russian manoeuvres in 1909 that he could detect an overreaction to the unsuccessful Russian defensive tactics in that conflict: 'a false principle seemed to underlie the tactics of both commanders, the principle namely that any and every problem can be solved by the adoption of a rash and desperate offensive.'[23]

At the Prussian manoeuvres in 1906, Hamilton 'saw the lessons of Manchuria eagerly assimilated and as a result the German Army of 1906 is a very different and much more advanced military machine than the same army when I last had an opportunity of seeing it, in 1902.'[24] However, at the Saxon manoeuvres in 1909, Hamilton felt that Wilhelm II's preference for compact rather than extended formations in attack was a false lesson learned from Manchuria.[25] He was also worried about the ability of the British to learn. Hamilton claimed that the experience gained in the war that artillery should be 'held a long way back' was not sufficiently appreciated.[26] He also felt that the British cavalry training regulations of 1907 had ignored the lessons of the Boer War and led to a misplaced confidence in shock tactics and to charging infantry and artillery,[27] a practice derided by the playwright George Bernard Shaw in his *Arms and the Man* (1894). Hamilton had been criticised by the War Office when his reports from Manchuria disparaged the role of cavalry.

Most commentators overlooked the extent to which land battles had not been decisive militarily, but had instead only caused the Russians to fall back, and ignored the extent to which the conflict so strained Japan that it could not afford to pursue the Russians deeper into Manchuria. Japanese victory owed much to political weakness in St Petersburg. The government had a revolution to confront in 1905, a revolution in part fostered by Japanese military intelligence. The distance of Manchuria from the centres of Russian power also did not help. Japanese success ensured that the tactical superiority of the defence revealed in the American Civil War was not seen as the problem the First World War was to show it to be. Given contemporary racist attitudes, European experts concluded that the infantry of the superior races of Europe would be capable of at least similar deeds, albeit at a heavy cost.[28]

From 1905 army leaders fully expected to suffer one-third casualties in a European war before they won.[29] This expectation dramatically altered thinking on manpower needs and provided the impetus for programmes to expand army size. Pressure for more men across Europe interacted with an increase in armaments[30] to produce a growth in military preparedness. In Russia, defeat at the hands of Japan was followed by a period of reform, including the establishment of a Council for State Defence in 1905, a major increase in military expenditure and the introduction of very modern artillery.

However, large numbers in European armies created problems of effectiveness. This was true of soldiers and also of officers, especially the high command, which had no experience of effectively controlling and directing the millions now under arms. Enhanced preparedness was a matter not only of more men and material, but also of improved organisational means and systems that permitted their integration and increased their effectiveness. These included railways, steamships, telegraphs, telephones and, eventually, radio. They were incorporated into war plans and military manoeuvres. However, the machinisation of the European military should not be exaggerated. When World War One broke out, there was an average of only one machine-gun per thousand troops; although the German army had more. The Serbs in part relied for their communications on 192 homing pigeons.[31] Despite heavy expenditure, there were important equipment deficiencies in the Russian army, in part, it has been argued, because a successful combination of government and industry to foster effective rearmament had not been achieved.[32]

Prior to World War One, European observers had an opportunity to observe a conflict nearer home. The First Balkan War (1912–13) arose from the ethnic and territorial rivalries of a Balkan world where violence was the principal method of pursuing disputes. The long-standing drive to partition Turkish possessions in the Balkans led Bulgaria, Greece, Montenegro and Serbia to attack. The Turks were beaten, being especially heavily defeated by the Bulgarians at Kirkkilese/Lozengrad (22–4 October, 1912) and Lyule Burgas (29 October – 2 November). In these battles the Bulgarians benefited from taking the initiative and from maintaining tactical fluidity. This was seen particularly in successful flanking operations. The Bulgarians also benefited from good leadership, disciplined infantry with good morale who attacked boldly making good use of bayonets, and effective artillery that inflicted heavy losses amongst the Turks. These were the most intense battles of the two Balkan Wars and they showed how heavy fighting could lead to a decisive result.

Victory in battle gave the Bulgarians control of most of Thrace, although they were, in turn, to be hit by logistical problems and cholera. Furthermore, they failed to exploit their successes rapidly enough and, by the time they had advanced towards Constantinople, the Turks had improved a line of fortifications and natural features at Chataldzha. These were assaulted on 17 November 1912, but the Bulgarian artillery had failed to destroy its Turkish counterpart, and the latter blunted the Bulgarian infantry assault. The power of entrenched positions supported by artillery when neither had been suppressed by superior offensive gunfire had been abundantly shown well before it was to be displayed on an even greater scale on the Western Front in 1915, and by the Turks that year at Gallipoli. Defeat at Chataldzha persuaded the Bulgarian General Staff not to launch an assault on Adrianople.

Further west, against far weaker resistance, the Greeks had gained entry to Macedonia by successfully storming Turkish positions in frontal attacks at the Sarantaporos Pass on 22 October, 1912. At Kumanovo on 23–4 October superior artillery helped give victory to the Serb frontal attacks and the latter were also effective at Prilep on 5 November and Bitola on 16–18 November. Under the Treaty of London of 30 May 1913 the Turks lost most of their European empire.

However, the victors fell out and, in the Second War (1913), Bulgaria fought the others, as well as Romania and a revived Turkey. The Bulgarians achieved defensive victories against the Greeks and the Serbs but a Romanian crossing of the Danube on the night of 14–15 July, advance to near Sofia and link-up with the Serbs on 25 July, led Bulgaria to settle. Bulgaria lost important recent gains, including Adrianople/Edirne, which had been regained by the Turks in July.

In some respects, these conflicts were the first blows of World War One, at least in the Balkans. Important signs of what was to come included the unsuccessful Bulgarian attacks on the entrenched Turkish positions at Chataldzha, in which Turkish artillery and infantry inflicted considerable casualties. In addition, aeroplanes were used by all participants, except for Montenegro, mainly for reconnaissance, although cities were also bombed.

Overall, however, the Balkan Wars did not challenge contemporary military assumptions. Due to difficulty in obtaining reliable information, an emphasis on strategy rather than tactics and a focus on success rather than casualties, observers saw the wars as confirming their faith in the offensive, more specifically in massed infantry assaults. This lesson was in particular taken from the Bulgarian victories of 1912, which appeared to show the effectiveness of high morale and of infantry charging in to the attack. There was a general failure to note the degree to which the effectiveness of rapid-firing artillery and machine guns might blunt infantry attacks.[33] It is too easy to close with the observation that observers were rapidly to be proved wrong. Instead, it is necessary to turn to the problems of waging successful war between great powers.

3. The First World War

SPENCER TUCKER

In August 1914 what had been threatened half a dozen times over the previous decade actually occurred: a war began in Europe that involved the great powers and soon became world-wide. The war was hardly a surprise, for Europe was armed to the teeth. In order to maintain the largest armies possible with the latest military equipment, governments had strained their limited national resources, often at the expense of rising popular demands for social services. The continent as a whole was never as ready for war as in 1914.[1]

The conflict might indeed be called a war for all reasons. It resulted from nationalism, rival alliance systems, economic rivalries, national and personal ambition, bluff and simple miscalculation.[2]

The excuse for the war so universally anticipated came on 28 June 1914, with the assassination of Austrian Archduke Franz Ferdinand in Sarajevo by members of a Serbian nationalist society. Austro–Hungarian leaders seized on this to rid themselves of the threat posed to their polyglot empire by Serbia's aggressive pan-slavism. Vienna planned to mask a declaration of war in the cloak of an ultimatum that Serbia would have to reject.

An attack on Serbia, however, ran the risk of bringing in Russia and producing a general European war, and for that reason Austria–Hungary needed German support. As it had done in early crises, Berlin stood firmly behind its only ally, fully realising that Austrian policy might bring war with Russia and France. There were those in Berlin, especially in the German military, who worried about Russia's rearmament and who actively sought a war in 1914 while Germany might still win it. Only belatedly did German and British civilian leaders try to secure an arrangement that might prevent world war.

A European war was inevitable when Russia attempted to bluff Austria–Hungary down by mobilising its own forces. German leaders, driven by their own country's war plan, demanded that

Russia halt its military preparations and, when that country refused, Berlin declared war on Russia.

Germany's war plan also dictated a declaration of war against France when it refused to make known its intentions in the war between Germany and Russia. Britain joined the conflict on the German invasion of neutral Belgium. Thus five of the great powers were at war: Britain, France and Russia (known as the Allied or Entente powers) versus Germany and Austria (the Central Powers). Japan joined the Allied side to secure Germany's possessions in the Pacific Ocean and China; Turkey joined the Central Powers. Italy remained neutral until 1915, when it joined the Allies on promise of territorial reward at the expense of Austria–Hungary. Thus the conflict was world-wide, with fighting in Asia, Africa and the Middle East.

The war of 1914–1918 was not only world-wide, it was total in that it involved entire populations. It dwarfed all previous conflicts in numbers of men mobilised and in resources expended. On paper the Allies were far stronger. One calculation is that in August 1914 they fielded 199 infantry and 50 cavalry divisions to 137 and 22 respectively for the Central Powers. The combined population of the Allies was also much larger: 279 to 120 million.[3] Thus, if the war could be prolonged, and all other factors remained equal, economics and demography might bring an allied victory.

In August 1914 there was a near-universal expectation of a short war. Almost alone, British Secretary for War Lord Kitchener predicted a long conflict. 'We must be prepared,' he said, 'to put armies of millions of men in the field and maintain them for several years'.[4]

Those who posited a short war pointed to books by Ivan Bloch (*War of the Future*, 1847) and Normal Angell (*The Great Illusion*, 1910). Both had declared that there could be no economic winners in modern war. Europeans misinterpreted this to mean that because a long conflict would be an economic calamity for victor and vanquished alike it would not happen.

The war was in fact hideously prolonged and infinitely more destructive than virtually all had dared imagined. Men died at the appalling rate of more than 6000 a day.

War plans on both sides soon went awry. Austria–Hungary, strained by having to fight a two-front war, failed to defeat Serbia.

Russia also divided its resources, between Austria–Hungary and Germany. Only defeat of Germany could win the war, but Russia committed substantial resources against the Dual Monarchy to punish it for its invasion of Serbia and to achieve its war aims in the Balkans. The Russians then divided their forces yet again, this time against Germany, although this was driven largely by topography – the natural barrier of the Masurian Lakes. General Pavel K. Rennenkampf's First Army was to sweep north of the lakes while General Aleksandr V. Samsonov's Second Army went south of them. The two armies were to link up west of the lakes for a drive on Berlin.

Although the Russians were victorious in the southwest against the Austro–Hungarians, they were soundly defeated in the north by numerically inferior German forces. The Germans gambled boldly. Utilising a plan drawn up by Colonel Max Hoffmann, Generals Paul von Hindenburg and Erich Ludendorff shifted resources over the excellent German railway, concentrating and destroying first Samsonov's army, then that of Rennenkampf (the Battles of Tannenberg and the Masurian Lakes respectively). The Russians generally defeated Austro–Hungarian forces, but themselves almost always fell victim to superior German firepower and generalship.

Spectacularly successful in the East, the Germans failed in the West. Developed by former Chief of the German General Staff General Alfred von Schlieffen, the German war plan had in fact triggered the general war. Faced with the certainty of a two-front war, Schlieffen would employ the vast majority of German military resources against France, the more formidable opponent. Once it was defeated in a quick blow, then Germany could turn to deal with a slow-mobilising Russia. This called for violation of neutral Belgium as the fastest way to strike France, even though such a step would undoubtedly bring Britain into the war. The German armies would capture the Channel ports to prevent resupply from Britain and swing wide, encompassing Paris and smashing the French armies against Lorraine. Because of this plan, Germany was unwilling to allow Russia the time to mobilise. Of the divisions committed against France, 59 would comprise the right wing and only 9 the left wing.[5]

Schlieffen's successor, Helmuth von Moltke (the Younger), lacked his predecessor's daring and seems to have been selected by Kaiser Wilhelm II for high command largely as a consequence of his illustrious military lineage. The plan he inherited was flawed. Historian Gerhard Ritter has shown that German forces would be moving largely on foot, whereas French forces would be able to utilise rail lines to mobilise and bring up reserves.[6]

In any case, Moltke finished off any possibility of success by weakening the plan in two respects. Of nine new divisions that came available in the years before the war, only one went to the right wing. Eight went to the German left to defend against an anticipated French thrust against Alsace and Lorraine. Moltke was correct in his anticipation that the French plan (War Plan XVII) called for an invasion of Alsace–Lorraine, but in providing the means to thwart it he also made it easier for French commander General Jacques C. Joffre to shift resources to meet the major German drive to the north. Thus when the German drive in the north unfolded, it was far weaker in proportion than Schlieffen intended.

Moltke also erred when the campaign was in progress. Because the Russians moved faster than the Germans anticipated, he detached five divisions from the right wing and sent them to East Prussia. As it turned out, the troops were not necessary for German victory in the East and might have made the difference in the critical Battle of the Marne.

The French also miscalculated. Joffre's offensive in Lorraine failed to anticipate the German drive from Belgium. He did not believe the Germans would utilise reserves on the front line. Such short-sightedness almost brought disaster for France.

Fortunately for France, Joffre's offensive was not as rigid as that of the Germans and when it failed early it allowed him to shift resources north by rail. The Germans, moving on foot with a long supply line reaching back through Belgium, were thus relatively weaker than the Allied forces in the war's most important battle on the Marne.

That the Battle of the Marne (6–12 September 1914) developed as it did resulted from German Second Army commander General Kluck's own modifications. In executing a shorter hook north of Paris, he failed to coordinate effectively with First Army commander Bülow. A gap in the German line, detected in air reconnaissance, allowed a French reserve army in Paris to strike into the breach, and the French held. The Marne was clearly the decisive battle of the war because it denied Germany the quick victory over France it needed to win the war.[7]

Germany and Austria–Hungary did enjoy an important advantage in interior lines. From their central location they were able to shift resources where needed over the efficient German railway network much easier than could the Entente powers on the periphery. The Central Powers also had near unity of command, as Germany controlled military policy.

The Allies were widely separated geographically. British troops had to be transported to the continent by ship. Russia was cut off from her allies save by sea, and Japan was far removed from the fighting in Europe. The Allies did not have unity of command and too often there was little or no coordination or planning, especially early on. It was not until almost too late, in April 1918, that Allied leaders instituted a unified command structure under General Ferdinand Foch.

Once the German drive had spent itself, both sides attempted flanking movements. The Allies held on to the Channel ports, vital for resupply from Britain, and the war in the West then settled into stalemate. Germany's failure to achieve a quick victory, however, brought Italy into the war on the Allied side in 1915.

Although the Western allies mounted a series of offensives, they were unable to expel the Germans from France and Belgium. In 1915, Britain did try to break the stalemate in the West by utilising its sea power to open a new front: the Dardanelles Campaign. The promise of this was great, but it was poorly planned and implemented. What was to have been originally an action by ships alone to drive Turkey from the war, ended up as a land assault of the Gallipoli peninsula. Had these troops been sent at the outset, the campaign probably would have been successful. Certainly the course of the war would have been different and perhaps Russian history profoundly altered. With the Gallipoli campaign a failure, the Allies finally withdrew from the peninsula at the beginning of 1916.[8]

In February 1916 General Erich von Falkenhayn, who had replaced Moltke as commander of the German Army, launched a great offensive at Verdun, designed to shatter French morale and bleed the French Army to death. As with Stalingrad in the Second World War, Verdun became a matter of honour for the Germans as well. During the first ten months of 1916 the French sustained 378 777 casualties at Verdun; German losses were about 337 000. Taking into account fighting there before and after the 1916 battle, the total number on both sides at Verdun reaches 420 000 dead and another 800 000 gassed and wounded. Each side fired about 10 million shells during the battle.[9]

The Battle of Verdun forced a premature British offensive on the Somme, another costly bloodletting and the greatest battle of the war. It claimed 419 654 British casualties, 194 451 French, and perhaps 650 000 Germans. Verdun also brought the great Russian Brusilov offensive in the East.[10]

Allied offensives continued through 1917, when General Robert Nivelle's Spring (Champagne) Offensive, which gained little ground at great human cost, produced widespread mutinies in the French Army. General Henri Philippe Pétain, hero of the French stand at Verdun, then replaced Nivelle as commander of the French Army and went over to defensive warfare.

In April 1917 the United States joined the war on the Allied side. This tipped the scales substantially in the Allied favour. Time was the key in making American manpower resources count, but the mere entry of the United States into the war was a tremendous boost to Allied morale.

US belligerency was the first big event of 1917. The second was that Russia left the war. In the East, the war had proceeded more or less according to German expectations. The Russians had suffered appalling casualties, and it is a testimony to the extraordinary endurance of a long-suffering people that Russia was able to remain in the war as long as it did.

The fighting in the East seesawed back and forth, but over the next years the Russians were steadily driven back. Noting the Allied failure in the Dardanelles, in 1915 Bulgaria joined the Central Powers and Serbia was at last crushed. In 1916 Romania joined the Allies. At first victorious in its invasion of Hungary, Romania was soon defeated by German reinforcements.

Russia, meanwhile, was reeling. Although all sectors of the Russian economy registered gains during the war and Russia was producing ever greater quantities of war supplies, its primitive economic and transportation systems broke down under the strain of the conflict and this brought shortages in the cities, riots and revolution.

In March 1917 Tsar Nicholas II was forced to abdicate. The

new regime then made the critical mistake of continuing the war. Military reverses followed, and in November the Bolsheviks, supported by an infusion of German money, seized power in a coup d'état and soon thereafter took Russia out of the war.[11]

In the punitive March 1918 Treaty of Brest Litovsk, Germany stripped away much of European Russia, taking the bulk of its industry and foot-producing areas. This was a true *Diktat*. Germany had now secured its chief war aims, but its leaders wanted total victory.

Russia's defeat enabled Germany to shift resources to the West and, in the spring 1918 Ludendorff Offensives, Germany attempted to win a complete victory over France, Britain and the United States. This offensive came close to succeeding – Germans troops again reached the Marne – but US forces, which had grown to 1.3 million men in France – were critical in stopping the Germans in July. General Foch seized the initiative and the Allies steadily forced the German armies back until the conclusion of the armistice on 11 November 1918.

The war on the seas had also developed differently than expected. In the years preceding the war, Germany had built the world's second largest navy. Unfortunately for Germany, this was not large enough to challenge Britain for naval mastery. The British had a quantitative lead in ship classes, although they did always have the qualitative edge.[12]

On the war's outbreak, a series of sea fights around the world drove German shipping and warships from the high seas. But the great naval battle for world mastery, anticipated by both sides, failed to occur. There was only one great fleet encounter – the 31 May–1 June 1916 Battle of Jutland. Seeking to cut off and destroy a portion of the British Grand Fleet with their entire High Seas Fleet, the Germans then fled when the entire British Grand Fleet appeared. Germany claimed victory and indeed had an edge in ships sunk, 14 to 11, and nearly twice the tonnage sunk, but the British still controlled the seas and their fleet was ready to continue operations, whereas the High Seas Fleet was not.[13]

From the beginning of the war the British used their naval strength to impose a blockade on Germany. Although there were serious leaks in this until US entry into the war in 1917 (largely because US goods sent to neutral states were then transshipped to Germany), the blockade was critical in denying Germany strategic resources and food and in driving it from the war. Most histories of the war pay too little attention to this and its influence.

Each side made major military blunders in the war, both in strategic and tactical terms, some of which have already been noted. Certainly Germany's decision to build a powerful battle fleet before the war was a major mistake. Justified as a 'risk fleet' and a means of frightening Britain into becoming a German ally, it instead drove Britain to the side of France. It proved impossible for Germany to maintain both the world's most powerful army and most powerful navy. Had the resources expended on the navy gone into the army, Britain might not have been alienated. Regardless, Germany would have won the war on land.

Stymied in surface warfare and stung by the British blockade, Germany retaliated with the submarine. This was no less contrary to international law than the blockade, yet when Germany gambled on a renewal of unrestricted submarine warfare on 1 February 1917, it brought the United States into the war. Berlin embarked on this because it believed Germany could drive Britain, which was dependent on food and raw materials imports, from the war before American military resources could be sufficiently mobilised to count. U-boats did exact a frightful toll. In February 1917 the Germans sank about 540 000 tons of Allied shipping, and in the three months from April to June 1917 they sent to the bottom another 2 million tons. In April alone the tally was 350 ships of 849 000 tons, a monthly figure never attained by the more powerful German U-boats of the Second World War and well beyond what German planners calculated would be necessary to win the war. Belatedly, the Allies shifted resources into a convoy system and adopted new techniques to defeat the U-boats. The number of German submarines was also inadequate for the task at hand; as would be the case in World War II, Germany had the wrong type of navy.

Had Germany not embarked on unrestricted submarine warfare, Russia would still have left the war and America would not have come in when it did. Again, Germany would have won.

Another major German blunder lay in Ludendorff's failure to move more men from the Eastern Front after the end of fighting with Russia. Although a million men were ultimately transferred, only half of these were present for his March 1918 offensive. A bit more manpower earlier and the German drive would have succeeded, despite American troops.

Other military mistakes included Russia's misdirection of resources before the war, especially in concentrating on fortresses rather than meeting the needs of its field armies. Russian soldiers fought bravely but they were appallingly led and even worse provided for in weaponry, clothing and other supplies. And, as previously noted, Russia's division of resources between its two adversaries at the beginning of the conflict was a major mistake. Defeat of Germany would have forced the far weaker Austro–Hungarian Empire into terms.

The French squandered great resources up to 1917 on costly and futile attacks on the Western front. Joffre called them 'nibbling attacks' but they were actually a form of attrition warfare that were terribly costly in manpower to the attackers and without great gains. There was also First Lord of the Admiralty Winston Churchill's obstinacy in the Dardanelles campaign. There were more than a sufficient number of blunders in that campaign: the signaling of intent, the failure to anticipate the problems of mine sweepers' operations while under fire from mobile howitzers ashore, but above all the failure to see until too late the need for ground troops, thus allowing the Turks and Germans to build up defensive positions. Indeed, the only positives to the Gallipoli Campaign were the splendidly executed evacuation and its lessons for World War II amphibious warfare.

There were of course many tactical failures as well. In 1914 few commanders anticipated the effects of long-range rifle fire, machine guns and modern artillery on the battlefield. By 1914 small numbers of machine weapons – particularly the machine gun – could destroy the concentration of men necessary to overwhelm a given number of their enemy faster than the latter could be moved across the battlefield. In order for attacking infantry to advance, artillery had to reduce the defender's fieldworks, barbed wire, machine gun-nests and artillery defences.

Tactical doctrine called for a protective prolonged bombardment at a depth of 3000 yards or so, yet small numbers of reserves with machine weapons and the ever-present barbed wire could stop offensive movement. In any case attacking infantry were exhausted after advancing over fire-swept ground.

Even if an enemy front were to be seriously cracked by these heavy blows, attackers could not take proper advantage of the situation because cavalry, the traditional exploiting arm, was vulnerable to machine guns and barbed wire.

Increasingly long preliminary bombardments were not the answer. The week-long preliminary bombardment at the Somme in 1916 did not eliminate all the defences and indeed merely rearranged the barbed wire, forcing attacking troops to bunch up in order to pass through. The tearing up of the earth in the bombardment also prevented the rapid movement forward of essential stores.

While the major powers understood the importance of the machine gun in warfare in Africa and Asia (a half dozen machine guns were the chief weapons in the slaying of 11 000 Dervishes at Omdurman in 1898 – but see p. 157, and both the Russians and Japanese sustained appalling losses in fighting in Manchuria in 1905) no one seems to have understood its implications for European warfare. At 450 to 600 rounds per minute, one machine gun could equal the fire of 40 to 80 riflemen. It also had greater range than the rifle, enabling indirect fire in support of an attack as was practised later in the war.

Germany was at least better prepared than its counterparts in this regard. In the German Army machine guns were deployed in companies, as opposed to dispersing them among infantry formations. This facilitated their concentration in needed sectors.

Light machine guns, such as the excellent British Lewis Gun, appeared later. Still, all armies in 1914 tended to regard machine guns as minor artillery weapons.[14]

It was artillery fire, however, rather than the rifle or machine gun, that was the chief killer of the war. An estimated 70 per cent of all wounds were inflicted by shell fire.[15]

In the half century preceding the war, artillery changed from a direct fire weapon to largely an indirect fire weapon. In 1882 the Russian Carl Guk published a system for firing on an unseen target using a compass, aiming point and a forward observer. The Japanese refined this method and, in their defeat of Russia in 1905, used indirect fire with great success. By the 1890s most European armies had standardised the techniques of artillery fire, allowing for the massing of fire on remote targets.[16]

The howitzer also increased in importance. This mid-trajectory weapon could fire at longer ranges than mortars. It came to be the preferred artillery piece in World War I because its high arc of fire allowed highly accurate plunging fire against enemy entrenchments. The Germans augmented their corps artillery with batteries of howitzers rather than field guns.[17]

Artillery changed from light guns useful in open mobile warfare to trench mortars, howitzers and heavy siege guns capable of long-range fire against the reinforced obstacles that now appeared along the stabilised front. Shrapnel, useful only against troops and horses in the open, was largely ineffective against entrenchments and every effort was made to produce more and heavier high-explosive rounds.

French artillery shows this transition. In 1914 French Army artillery was preponderantly mobile field guns. Of 5108 artillery pieces on hand that September, 4098 were field guns (3840 were the famous light-weight 'French 75', perhaps the finest of its type in the world) and 192 were mountain guns; only 389 were heavies. But 75mm shells were too light to smash entrenchments and most of those on hand were in any case shrapnel. The French mistakenly believed that what the 75mm gun lacked in hitting power it could make up for in its high rate of fire. Yet France started the war with only 1300 rounds per gun, about a three-week supply at best, and most of these were shrapnel. Heavier guns became increasingly important. At war's end the French had 5600 heavy guns as opposed to 6000 field pieces.[18]

Thanks largely to artillery, the machine gun and barbed wire, from the end of 1914 until early 1918 there was no change of more than ten miles in the front lines on the Western Front. The sole exception was the 1917 voluntary German withdrawal in the Noyon salient. Until 1918 defenders were always able to plug breaks in the line by rushing reinforcements to the threatened point.

There were four principal ways for an attacker to resolve the dilemma of the superiority of the defence. One was to exhaust an enemy through one's own superior defence and firepower. A second approach, offensive attrition warfare, advocated continued conventional attacks to wear down an opponent. A third option would utilise new technology, such as the tank, poison gas or airplane, to achieve a breakthrough. The fourth was an indirect strategy that avoided attacking the enemy's major defensive lines and striking elsewhere, as in the 1915 Dardanelles Campaign. For the most part, World War I generals chose the second method, with disastrous results for the men they commanded.[19]

Mass armies and rapid-fire weapons created tremendous logistical problems. During the 1870–1 Franco–Prussian War, the Prussian Army provided 200 rounds of rifle ammunition per man, which was carried by the individual soldier and in the supply train. The average expenditure in six months of war was only 56 rounds per man. In 1914 the number of rounds per man had increased to 280, but all were gone in the first weeks of the war. In 1870–1 Prussian artillery pieces had fired an average of 199 shells apiece. The 1000 rounds per gun available in 1914 were all gone within six weeks of the start of the war. Ammunition demands soon vastly exceeded pre-war estimates, and both sides experienced shell shortages, which had political ramifications, especially in Britain.[20]

Throughout the war both sides continued to maintain large numbers of largely useless cavalry in order to exploit possible breakthroughs. British General Sir Douglas Haig planned to use cavalry for this purpose at the Somme in 1916. Horses eat about ten times as much by weight as men; simply feeding the large number of them in all armies imposed heavy demands on already strained logistics systems.

During the war there were important changes in weaponry, including the tank, submarine, warplane and poison gas. At sea the traditional race between armour and ordnance had produced steel-armoured ships and new, more powerful, breech-loading guns. The battleship was still the queen of the seas, but it underwent tremendous change in the years before the war, reaching the apogee of its development in HMS *Dreadnought* of 1906, the first all-big gun, geared-turbine battleship. Its guns could all be fired from one central fire-control location and, at 21 knots, it was the fastest ship of her type afloat.[21] All major naval powers then constructed their own dreadnoughts.

First Sea Lord Admiral Sir John Fisher introduced the battle cruiser. Conceived on the same principles as the dreadnought, but of higher speed and greater armament, the battle cruiser was battleship armament on a high-speed cruiser hull. The first three British battle cruisers, completed by mid-1908, had a main battery of eight 12-inch guns and a speed of more than 26 knots. But battle cruisers sacrificed armour for speed and British battle cruisers also suffered from a serious design flaw, the lack of sufficient armour on the top of the gun turrets and inadequate flash protection for the magazines, which became apparent in the 1916 Battle of Jutland.[22]

The war speeded up the transition from coal to oil as fuel for ships. Oil had great advantages in that much more of it could be carried and refueling was much faster and easier; it was even possible while underway. This in turn led to intense British interest in the Persian Gulf.

The modern submarine had already appeared. Originally thought of for observation purposes, submarines came into their own during the First World War. It was an ideal weapons platform for the automotive torpedo, the effectiveness of which was demonstrated early in the conflict when one German submarine sank three old British cruisers in an afternoon. Ironically, in 1914 Britain had more than twice the number of submarines of the Germans (73 to 31). In any case, none of the major naval powers, focusing on a decisive fleet action, initially gave much attention to the submarine as a commerce destroyer.[23]

Ground transportation underwent great change, although most soldiers still moved on foot. Railways proved extraordinarily important in rapid, mass troop movements. Their vital importance was demonstrated in the first month of the war. Armies also experimented with motorised transport. The British Army went from 827 cars and 15 motorcycles in 1914 to 56 000 trucks and 34 000 motorcycles in 1918.[24]

Tanks also made their appearance in World War I. In 1915–16 the French and British had independently developed armoured fighting machines. Neither coordinated with the other, leading to a profusion of machine types and no clear doctrine of tactical employment. Winston Churchill in the autumn of 1914 allocated Admiralty funds for construction of 'trench spanning cars'. In February 1915 Churchill formed a Landships Committee at the Admiralty. Before he resigned following the Gallipoli fiasco he convinced his successor, Arthur Balfour, not to drop the experiment.[25]

The French called their new weapon a *char* (chariot). The British knew theirs as a 'tank', the term used to disguise the contents of the large crates containing the vehicles when they were shipped to France.

The key figure in British tank development, Colonel E. B. Swinton, thought of tanks in ambitious terms. He believed they could have a decisive impact on the battlefield. Rather than reveal the tanks prematurely, Swinton wanted to build a large number and then employ them *en masse* without the warning of a preliminary bombardment. Infantry would follow the tanks to exploit the breakthrough, with artillery performing counter-battery work against enemy guns. This concept seems reasonable today but was thought ridiculous at the time.

By the summer of 1915 both the British and French were producing large numbers of these weapons. The British planned to build 150, the French 400. In the summer of 1916 Haig thought that even a few of them might be sufficient to tip the balance in the stalemated Battle of the Somme. Swinton, who strongly opposed this, was replaced.

The Mark I tanks used in the Somme Offensive weighed 28 tons each fully loaded; they had a top speed close to 4 mph – over rough ground only 2 mph – a crew of eight men and .5-inch armour. The 'male' version had two 6-pounder naval guns in its sponsons and four Lewis machine guns. The 'females' had six Lewis guns.[26]

Of the original 150 tanks, only 59 were in France when Haig made his decision to employ them; of these only 49 reached the battlefield. Plagued by mechanical problems, only 35 got to their point of departure; 31 of these crossed the German trenches; only nine tanks surmounted all problems and pushed on ahead of the infantry.[27]

The tanks were far from impressive in their debut, in large part because they were too widely dispersed and not used according to a plan. Their crews were also not well trained. Still, the few that did get into action had such a psychological impact that Haig immediately ordered 1000 more.[28]

The French tank programme began later than the British. In December 1915 Colonel Jean Estienne, an artillery commander, wrote Joffre suggesting that the French build caterpillar-type vehicles similar to Holt tractors he observed in use by the British to service their artillery. Joffre ordered 400 of these from the Schneider works. In 1916 Estienne organised and commanded the 'Artillerie d'Assault'. He called for tank assaults to be mounted in early morning and, if possible, in fog. Attacks would be continuous with the tanks followed by carriers with fuel and supplies. Estienne also stressed the need for thorough coordination beforehand with infantry, artillery and air forces. Estienne and his superiors regarded the new weapon as 'portable artillery' supporting infantry.[29]

Armour doctrine evolved dramatically in the course of the war. The British initially deployed their tanks in small packets, but for their offensive at Cambrai (November–December 1917) they had more than 400 under their own commander, General Hugh Elles. These included 376 of the latest Mark IV model, a slightly more powerful version of the 1916 Mark I. To the crews its chief difference from the Mark I was that it would usually keep out the new German armour-piercing bullet. For the first time, tanks were the key element of the British plan and this time they were used *en masse.*

Instead of a long and counterproductive preliminary bombardment, the offensive opened with 1003 British guns laying down a short but intense barrage on the German front line, then shifting fire rearward to disrupt the movement of reserves and blind direct-fire artillery with smoke. The tanks led, each transporting at its front a large fascine (a bundle of brushwood) to allow passage over trenches. They were closely followed by the infantry, advancing in small groups in open order rather than in the usual extended line assault formation.

Although initially successful, the attack at Cambrai broke down on the failure of tank–infantry–artillery coordination and the lack of tank reserves. Too many of the machines had been in the first two waves and were knocked out by German field guns or, more often, suffered mechanical breakdowns. In the first day 65 tanks were lost to enemy action, 71 broke down and 43 got stuck. The great tank armada no longer existed. The next day when the British resumed their attack, cooperative action between tanks and infantry was largely over and the battle reverted to the typical World War I pattern. Still, it showed what was possible with the correct doctrine and sufficient training.[30]

The Battle of Cambrai restored surprise as an attack element on the Western Front. It also showed that the tank and infiltration tactics could restore battlefield fluidity, hallmarks of 1918 Western Front fighting.

The Germans were not much interested in tanks, dismissing them on the basis of the 1916 British performance as unreliable and a waste of effort. In the course of the war they manufactured only 20, although they did use some captured British tanks. The development of German tank warfare was left to the next generation.[31]

On 24 April 1918, during their great Spring offensive, the Germans employed 13 A7V tanks, advancing them in three groups in thick mist. The centre group of six German tanks exchanged fire at 200 yards range with three British Mark IV tanks and drove off the two 'females'. But the German tanks were themselves damaged by cannon fire from the 'male' Mark IV and driven back. Later one of the German tanks in the southernmost group knocked out a British light Whippet tank, one of a group of seven brought up to counterattack German infantry. This first tank-to-tank battle in history underscored the need for tanks to have an anti-tank capability.

The Allies used increasing numbers of tanks. In his 18 July counterattack at Reims, Foch employed 350. In the British Amiens Offensive that August, Haig employed 430 tanks (including a number of new 8 mph Mark A Whippet tanks acting as cavalry).

During the war the French built many more tanks than the British (4800 to 2818). They used them for the first time in the April 1917 Nivelle Offensive.

Perhaps the biggest change in warfare came in the air. Modern aviation may be said to have begun in the United States in 1903, when Wilbur and Orville Wright achieved the first manned powered flight. Soon they had designed a military aircraft for the Army Signal Corps, and in 1910 Eugene Ely flew a plane off the U.S.S. *Birmingham* and the next year he landed another on the U.S.S. *Pennsylvania*.[32]

Aircraft first went to war in the 1911–12 war between Italy and Turkey over Libya. Most were unarmed and used solely for observation purposes. Although aviation made rapid strides, in 1914 generals and admirals still thought of it primarily as useful for observation and scouting. General Foch remarked that 'aviation is a good sport, but for the army it is useless'.[33] Nonetheless, all powers built aircraft. In August 1914 Britain had

270, including seaplanes, but not airships, Germany, 267; Russia, 190; France, 141; Austria–Hungary, 97; and Belgium, 24. The importance of aircraft during the war is revealed in production figures; during the conflict more than 161 000 were built.[34]

The most important World War I aircraft were two-seaters used for reconnaissance, aerial photography and artillery observation. Tethered balloons were also used for these purposes, but aircraft were far less vulnerable. Control of the air over the battlefield soon became vital, with most aerial combat occurring over or near the trench lines where the bulk of reconnaissance and spotting took place.

Both sides developed anti-aircraft guns to shoot down planes from the ground. The Germans knew anti-aircraft fire as 'flak', an acronym for *flieger* (plane) *abwehr* (defence) *kanone* (cannon). To the British, it was 'ack-ack'. Anti-aircraft artillery steadily increased in effectiveness during the war thanks to advances in munitions, sound location, searchlights and crew training.

But the best way to shoot down enemy aircraft was to arm one's own planes. As aircraft became useful for observation purposes, it became necessary for the other side to shoot them down. Pilots and observers on both sides began carrying small arms and taking occasional shots at enemy aircraft. Not long afterwards they also carried machine guns aloft. These were mounted either for an observer to fire or fixed in order that the pilot could aim the plane at a target. The machine gun became the key weapon of the air war. A biplane could mount a gun with a drum magazine on its upper wing in order to avoid the propeller arc. But aiming and reloading were difficult and when the gun jammed, clearing it by hand was both arduous and dangerous.

In 1915 Dutch aircraft designer Anthony Fokker, working for the Germans, developed an effective cam-operated synchroniser that allowed bullets to pass through the arc of a propeller and miss the propeller altogether. He combined this with the Spandau or Parabellum machine gun mounted on an Eindecker (monoplane). August 1915 began an eight-month period known as the 'Fokker Scourge', when the Germans dominated the skies over the Western Front before the Allies developed their own effective synchroniser gear.[35]

Specialised aircraft appeared. Two-seaters were the mainstay for observation purposes. There were also single-seater 'scouts', 'fighting scouts', or 'fighters' as they came to be known. They were used not only to shoot down enemy aircraft in 'dogfights' but also in ground attacks.

The planes themselves underwent considerable change. No fewer than five generations of fighter aircraft appeared during the war. The last, just before the end, were single-wing all-metal craft. By the summer of 1917 a series of outstanding Allied fighters, including the SE5 and Sopwith Camel, began to reach the front, giving the Allies a qualitative superiority that they held for the rest of the war.

During the war, aircraft were consumed at a high rate. Pilots were an exclusive club but those who flew fighter aircraft were the prima donnas of the war. Contrary to popular myth, overall pilot fatalities were not out of line with the infantry on the ground, although loss rates for aces were higher.

Fortunately for the Allies they were able to build more aircraft than Germany. At the end of the war the French had a front-line strength of 3700 aircraft, the British 2600, and the Germans 2500.[36]

By 1917 the Allies developed an integrated doctrine of air power, using fighters in connection with artillery fire to attack observation balloons and ground troops. This culminated in the 1918 St. Mihiel offensive in which no fewer than 1481 Allied airplanes took part. Under the command of American Colonel Billy Mitchell, Allied air forces flew trench-strafing, close air support, interdiction and air superiority missions pioneered by the British. In the process Mitchell demonstrated the potential of air power for the future. He even tried to convince his superiors of the feasibility of parachuting an entire division behind enemy lines.

Bombers developed later than fighters. Early bombing was, more often than not, random. The British Royal Naval Air Service may have conducted the first effective 'strategic' bombing raids of the war in September and October 1914, when planes carrying 20-pound bombs flew from Antwerp to strike Zeppelin sheds at Düsseldorf and destroyed one airship.[37]

The Germans used lighter-than-air Zeppelins for both aerial reconnaissance and bombing missions. The Zeppelin was in fact the first strategic bomber. Although more vulnerable than airplanes they had much greater bomb-carrying capacity. In 1914 Germany had some 20 of them supporting both its army and navy. On 6 August 1914, *L6* initiated a twentieth-century practice when it flew from Cologne to attack Liège, Belgium. Its bombs killed nine civilians before, holed by Belgian ground fire, it crashed near Bonn.

In January 1915 Germany carried out its first aerial bombing raid on Britain, using Zeppelins. The largest raid was on London on 13 October. The material damage inflicted by Zeppelins was relatively modest. A total of 51 Zeppelin attacks (208 sorties) during the war on the British Isles dropped 196 tons of bombs, killing 557 people and wounding 1358. British sources estimated that the raids inflicted £1 500 000 in property damage.

Countermeasures against the Zeppelins included searchlight batteries, anti-aircraft guns and aircraft machine guns firing incendiary bullets, to which the hydrogen-filled Zeppelins were particularly vulnerable. The raids declined steadily thereafter.

Aircraft were not as vulnerable to anti-aircraft fire as Zeppelins. By early 1915 the first bombing directives had appeared, making these aircraft an extension of the artillery, able to strike well beyond the range of conventional guns. During the March 1915 Battle of Neuve Chapelle the British were the first to use bombers as an extension of the land campaign. Hoping to disrupt the flow of men and supplies to the fight in progress, they sent them against railway installations.

The planes used for these missions were former observation aircraft adapted for the purpose. The French were the first to form units of aircraft specifically dedicated to bombing missions. Most early bombing was, however, extraordinarily inaccurate and problems grew with increases in anti-aircraft guns and fighter aircraft.[38]

The Germans developed the twin-engine G plane or *Grossflugzeug* (known as the Gotha, after one of its builders) and multi-engine *Riesenflugzeug* or 'R' series bombers, some of which could carry up to a 2200-pound bomb. The first Gotha/R raids began in May 1917. Most of these were at night with London the target. In all the Germans mounted 435 bomber sorties over Great Britain. Their attacks killed 1300 people, injured another 3000 and inflicted a fair amount of material damage. Virtually all the belligerents engaged in strategic bombing during the war and every capital, save Rome, was struck.[39]

The British had their twin-engine Handley-Page bomber. Similar to the Gotha in appearance, it had an endurance of eight hours and a bomb load of nearly 1800 pounds. Despite this the British largely ignored it as a strategic bomber. By September 1918, the British air force commander, General Hugh Trenchard had 120 aircraft, mainly Handley-Pages, for long-ranging bombing. In October 1918 Marshal Foch agreed to the creation of an Inter-Allied Air Force with Trenchard in command.

In May 1918 the British had flown a prototype of their Handley-Page V/1500. This four-engine bomber could carry 7500 pounds of bombs and stay aloft for more than 12 hours. Three were fuelled and loaded for a raid on Berlin when the Armistice intervened. Had the war continued into 1919, the Allies would have launched massive bombing raids against Germany.[40]

Aircraft were also employed at sea, where they were especially useful for hunting submarines, locating enemy battle fleets and adjusting naval gunfire.[41] The British experimented with using them to launch torpedoes against ships. In 1915 they sent seaplanes armed with torpedoes against Turkish supply ships in the Dardanelles. Few naval officers, however, thought in terms of attacking warships in this fashion.

Aircraft carriers appeared, although none had full-length flight decks. Planes taking off from them were expected to land on shore or, in exceptional cases, in the water alongside, where they would float on air bags until they could be hoisted aboard. Only the Royal Navy used aircraft carriers in combat. Its *Ark Royal*, although not with a full flight deck, was the first ship commissioned in any navy that might be called an aircraft carrier. The first clear-deck carrier was the British *Argus*. Converted from a cruiser, it did not undergo sea trials until October 1918.[42] Aircraft carriers did not come into their full potential until the Second World War.

April 1918 saw the creation of the world's first independent air force. The Royal Air Force, formed of the Royal Navy Air Service and Royal Flying Corps, had 22 000 aircraft and 291 175 personnel.[43]

Poison gas was another new, and deadly, weapon. At the end of October 1914 the Germans had fired shells with an irritant gas in the Neuve Chapelle sector of the Western Front, but without apparent effect. They first used tear gas, xylyl bromide (codenamed 'T-Stoff'), on the Eastern Front in January 1915, when they fired some 18 000 gas shells against the Russians at Bolimov. The weather was so cold that the gas failed to vaporise; it froze and sank into the snow.[44]

The Germans then decided to try chlorine gas on the Western Front. Chemist Fritz Haber, who had charge, was certain it would be successful and urged his army superiors to exploit it. Sceptical about the project and strapped by the shift of significant German manpower to the Eastern Front, they saw it as an experiment and refused to allocate reserves to exploit any breach it might effect in the enemy line. Haber was also forced to release the gas from commercial metal cylinders and depend on the wind for dispersal, delaying the attack.[45]

There had been clear warnings of an impending gas attack. In March the French took prisoners who described preparations for such an attack and on 13 April a German deserter described to his French interrogators 'tubes of asphyxiating gas . . . placed in batteries of twenty . . . along the front'. This information was ignored as was the deserter's crude respirator gas mask. Accurate reports reached Second Army commander General Sir Horace Smith-Dorrien, but he neither issued a general warning nor ordered precautionary measures.[46]

On 22 April French troops holding a section of line in the salient around Ypres spotted an advancing greenish yellow cloud. The Germans had opened 5000 cylinders to release 168 tons of chlorine gas. The resultant cloud wiped out two French divisions manning a four-mile section of front, killing and incapacitating the defenders or causing them to flee their positions. German troops, cautiously advancing behind the cloud, captured 2000 prisoners and 51 guns. By the end of the day 15 000 Allied soldiers were casualties, 5000 of them dead. Still, the Germans lacked sufficient manpower to exploit the situation and Allied reserves soon sealed the breach. A second gas attack on 14 April was less successful. Canadian troops used handkerchiefs soaked in water or urine as crude respirators. Thereafter the Allies developed their own poison gases; the British employed gas for the first time at Loos on 25 September 1915.[47]

First World War gases were of three main categories: chlorine;

phosgene, which attacked the lungs and caused them to fill with fluid, literally drowning the victim; and mustard gas. The latter, introduced in 1917, burned and blistered the body, resulting in great pain and, in some cases, temporary blindness. Both sides also introduced gas masks, which by 1916 had become standard issue, and the result was a stalemate of sorts.[48]

World War I poison gas incapacitated or wounded far more men than it killed. From the standpoint of the attacker, this was an advantage because each wounded enemy soldier neutralised additional other soldiers and increased the burden on enemy logistical and medical systems.

Both sides provided their troops with protective masks that were designed to filter the harmful agents, thereby preventing the most serious types of gas injuries. The combatants also developed improved delivery means, primarily through the use of artillery or mortar shells. The British also developed the Livens projector, a metal tube 4 feet long buried in the ground and angled towards the enemy.

One study of chemical use in the Great War states that all sides used a total of 125 000 tons of toxic chemicals. Estimates of total gas casualties vary, but they numbered more than one million and nearly 100 000 of these died.[49]

During the war all armies experimented with new tactics on land to break the stalemate, but only after the conflict's sheer carnage forced innovation. Although others gave considerable thought to this, General Aleksei Brusilov, the best senior Russian general of the war, first implemented them on a large scale in his 1916 offensive against the Austro–Hungarians.

Brusilov's four Southwestern armies (40 infantry and 15 cavalry divisions) faced an Austro–Hungarian army group of 49.5 divisions (38.5 infantry – two of them German – and eleven cavalry) strongly entrenched in three fortified belts. Brusilov insisted on a simultaneous dispersed attack along the entire 300-mile front to make it impossible for his enemy to shift resources.

Short of material resources such as artillery and shells, Brusilov came up with new tactics. He had his men sap their front-line trenches forward to within 75 to 100 yards of the Austrian lines. The men dug tunnels under the Austrian wire, stockpiled reserves of shells and constructed huge dugouts to hold infantry reserves. They also made accurate models of the Austrian defences and trained in them.

Brusilov held a manpower advantage of about 100 000 men (600 000 to 500 000) and 1938 guns as opposed to 1846. Only 168 of these were heavy guns, however; his opponents had 545.[50]

Brusilov used aerial photography to locate enemy guns and his artillery and infantry worked closely together. Another tactical innovation was positioning the bulk of his guns no further than two kilometers (a little over a mile) from the front.

The Russians achieved surprise. On 4 June they began a massive and accurate barrage that silenced many enemy guns. The next day Brusilov's infantry advanced. The Austrians had already been hard hit in their front-line positions by accurate Russian fire, and three of Brusilov's four armies broke through. Within the first day the two Russian flank armies advanced ten miles. By 6 June Brusilov had taken 41 000 prisoners and 77 guns; by 9 June it was more than 72 000 prisoners and 94 guns. The Austrian Fourth and Seventh Armies were routed.[51]

The Germans also utilised new tactics. Those of Brusilov were by necessity; the German tactics were by design. They were first employed on the Eastern Front in September 1917 at Riga.

Western military analysts came to call these 'Hutier' tactics, after German General Oscar von Hutier.[52] The Germans refined these in the Battles of Caporetto (October–November 1917) and Cambrai (November–December 1917). They culminated in the final German offensive in the West, in March 1918.

The new tactics relied heavily on decentralisation of authority and two different types of divisions: the standard *Stellungsdivisionen* (trench) and new *Angriffsdivisionen*. The latter were the elite *Stosstrüppen* ('shock troops'). Their *Sturmbattallione* (assault battalions) contained the healthiest and most motivated men. They were preferably young bachelors because of expected high casualty rates. Highly trained, they received the finest equipment and better rations.

The tactics included massing the fully briefed assault forces at the last moment. Secrecy was attained by covert night movements and concealment by day. The attack, launched in early morning darkness hopefully with ground fog, would begin with a short, massive artillery bombardment. This was immediately followed by infiltration-style assaults employing combined-arms platoons of about 50 men each armed with light machine guns and the 9mm submachine gun to sweep enemy trenches. Pioneers cut paths through enemy wire; the assault troops also had light, direct-fire artillery. Attackers bypassed enemy strong points, flowing into enemy weak points and leaving the strongly held areas for follow-on elements. No limits were set on divisional advances; these were determined by forward attack elements. Assault formations were followed by support elements with light trench mortars, flamethrowers and heavier direct-fire artillery that could reduce all but the heaviest strong points. Reserve elements came next. They consisted of conventional troops who freed advance elements to continue the attack. Such tactics isolated enemy front-line units, disrupted communications and allowed attackers to reach the enemy rear areas before significant reserves could arrive.[53]

Artillery played a key role. Lieutenant Colonel Georg Bruchmüller had developed a system of responsive and flexible artillery support that he coordinated throughout the 1918 offensives. Artillery was massed secretly before the offensive, even the night before, in order to catch the enemy by surprise. There was no registration firing prior to the attack and the initial short, intense bombardment consisted mainly of smoke and gas shells to create maximum confusion and blind enemy gunners. Forward observers with the leading infantry elements controlled subsequent artillery fire, using Very pistols or flares to signal commands.

The Germans made virtually no use of tanks, but they did integrate aircraft into their assault. These were to secure command of the air over the battlefield and locate enemy guns and troop reinforcements. Heavier aircraft carried out bombing missions to disrupt enemy communications, while lighter planes assisted advancing elements with strafing runs against ground targets. Pilots communicated with the troops by ground panels or by radio.[54]

These new tactics nearly brought the Germans victory in their spring 1918 offensive, but they lacked sufficient numbers to succeed. Nonetheless, the tactics were the foundation upon which the Germans would build for the next war. Unfortunately for the Allies, they were too little studied in their staff colleges after World War I.

World War I differed from previous conflicts in that victory was almost indistinguishable from defeat. No power won the war. Human costs were staggering. More than 68 million men had been mobilised; of these at least 10 million had died (8 million from combat and the remainder from disease and malnutrition). Another 21 million men were wounded and nearly 8 million had been taken prisoner or declared missing, and at least 6.6 million civilians perished.

The war was much more than a vast military holocaust. It toppled all of continental Europe's dynastic empires: the German, Austro–Hungarian, Turkish and Russian. The First World War occupies central place in the rise to power in Germany of Adolf Hitler, and it is hard to imagine the Bolsheviks coming to power in Russia without it.[55]

The war reshuffled the balance of power and made the United States the leading creditor nation and world financial capital. It greatly stimulated unrest in the colonial areas of the world, paradoxically advancing both Zionism and Arab nationalism. US President Woodrow Wilson's statements calling for 'self-determination of peoples' and 'fighting to make the world safe for democracy' found ready acceptance overseas. The First World War was quite simply the most important single event of the twentieth century.

4. The European Civil War: Reds versus Whites in Russia and Spain 1917–39

FRANCISCO J. ROMERO SALVADÓ

When hostilities broke out in Europe in 1914, the rulers of the belligerent countries expected that a fast and effective victory on the battlefield would silence the domestic opposition and rally the support of their citizens. In fact, this proved to be a huge miscalculation. The war drove European society to the edge of an abyss, ushering in a new era of political instability, ideological polarisation and popular strife that exploded into even greater brutality in 1939.

As the war dragged on, the initial displays of patriotism gradually gave way to increasing resentment at a conflict that was neither understood by most people nor bore any relation to their more immediate concerns. In this context of increasing bitterness and alienation, the Great War constituted a watershed: the awakening of the masses. The killing of millions at the front and scarcity of basic commodities at home prompted soldier mutinies, peasant riots and industrial unrest. The armistice of November 1918 failed to produce a new era of social stability. Instead, four years of appalling losses intensified the protest movements that had existed before 1914. Added to the existing economic dislocation and social distress was the plea of displaced national minorities and the revisionist feelings of the losers of the Great War. Thus the inter-war years became an unprecedented era of popular upheaval and political radicalism that can be regarded as a European Civil War, a period of revolution and reaction during which liberal political orders were swept away and replaced with new authoritarian formulas of social control.

The Russian and the Spanish civil wars represented the most

violent manifestations of this confrontation between left and right, Reds versus Whites.[1] Bridging the two World Wars, they shared not only the horrors of a fratricidal conflict but also an unprecedented impact upon the international balance of power.

No other belligerent state was as affected by the Great War so much as Imperial Russia. While the mobilisation of fifteen million peasants destroyed its traditional fabric of society, the country's industrial capabilities proved unable to match the military needs of modern warfare. As the precarious transport system virtually collapsed, the army constantly suffered from shortages of clothing, rifles and munitions. Simultaneously, mounting inflation and food and fuel rationing shattered the home front. War-weariness and popular discontent were exacerbated by scandals of corruption in the court, large-scale profiteering and hoarding. As soldiers began to desert in large numbers, industrial militancy rocked the cities. Eventually, on 23 February 1917, a spontaneous women's protest in Petrograd against the rising price of bread became a revolution when first the workers and then the local garrison turned against the authorities. After days of bloody clashes, the regime collapsed and Tsar Nicholas II himself was advised by his officers to abdicate on 1 March.[2]

The February Revolution produced an exceptional political formula, the co-existence of a Provisional Government formed by members of the last monarchist parliament and Soviets of soldiers, workers and peasants which sprang up with the demise of the old order. Dominated by Mensheviks and Socialist Revolutionaries (SRs), the Soviets allowed the existence of the Provisional Government and then in June their main leaders joined it. Political liberties were introduced but any major decision was postponed until the election of a Constituent Assembly by universal suffrage.

To a large extent, the fate of the new regime lay in the military question. In June a new offensive was launched with the objective of restoring the morale of the troops and enhancing the prestige of the government. It was a gamble that failed to pay off.[3] After the German counter-attack, crippled by massive losses, desertions and defeatism the Russian army ceased to be an effective standing force. The reputations of the Socialist ministers, in particular that of the SR Alexander Kerensky, War Minister and Prime Minister since July, were tarnished. The main beneficiaries were the Bolsheviks, the only Socialist party that had opposed the Provisional Government and was attracting increasing popular support by demanding an end to the war, power to the Soviets and redistribution of the land.

In September the Bolsheviks obtained majorities in some of the main cities. Trotsky was appointed Chairman of the Petrograd Soviet and rapidly set up a Military Revolutionary Committee to which, by 23 October, every regiment in the capital had sworn its loyalty or guaranteed its neutrality. At 2 a.m. on the 26th a combination of armed workers or Red Guards, detachments of sailors and soldiers toppled the Provisional Government with hardly any resistance.[4]

Until early 1918, the Bolsheviks, now renamed the Communist Party, did not meet much opposition as their control spread from the capital to the provinces. The distribution of land and the initiation of peace negotiations with the Central Powers gained them mass support. Dubbed by Lenin as 'the triumphal march of Soviet Power', this first stage of the civil war was characterised by the absence of proper armies or even battles. There was hardly any support for the discredited Provisional Government, let alone for a monarchist restoration. A battalion of Cossacks raised by Kerensky to wrest back power ended with the fraternisation of the troops and with the former Prime Minister escaping capture by disguising himself as a sailor. His own soldiers lynched the new Commander-in-Chief, General Dukhonin, in the army's headquarters, Stavka.[5]

In a war that was largely decided by the fast transport of troops and armament to the front, possession of the railway network was paramount. The Bolsheviks shipped Party agitators, Red Guards, and above all the 35 000 strong three regiments of Latvian Rifles, the only disciplined military force they had at their disposal, via the railway to neighbouring regions. Taking advantage of the reigning chaos, they soon established Soviet hegemony and then moved on to the next destination.[6] However, two key decisions were soon to turn the chaotic and relatively bloodless clashes of this period into full-scale war.

In January 1918, the dissolution of the democratically elected Constituent Assembly after just one session persuaded other political groups to take up arms against the new regime. In particular, the SRs, the largest party after the elections, set up a counter-government, the Committee for the Salvation of the Revolution and the Motherland, and urged their followers to organise uprisings throughout the country.[7] More worrying for the survival of the Communist regime was the arrival of foreign armies on Russian soil.

After three months of stalling in the peace negotiations, the Bolsheviks were unprepared for a new military onslaught. Thus, when the Germans resumed hostilities in February, their swift advances stormed through the badly disciplined Red Guards and forced the Soviet government to accept onerous conditions. By the Treaty of Brest–Litovsk of 3 March 1918, Russia recognised the independence of Finland, the Ukraine and Georgia, and renounced sovereignty over Poland, the Baltic States and the Moon Sound Islands. Batum, Kars and Ardahan were conceded to Turkey.[8]

Disengaging Russia from a catastrophic war echoed the demands of a war-weary population. Yet it raised the stakes for the survival of the new government. The peace treaty stripped the former Russian Empire of a third of its population, 40 per cent of its agricultural harvest, 26 per cent of its railway tracks, 80 per cent of its iron and 90 per cent of its coal production. Furthermore, under German protection rabidly anti-Communist states were created in the Ukraine, the Baltic States and Finland.[9]

The unilateral agreement with the Central Powers provided the Allies with the excuse to send military expeditions. Supposedly to safeguard military depots, they were soon providing military support for the different White armies led by former Tsarist officers then being formed on the periphery of the country.

From the spring of 1918, the war entered a new stage marked by the emergence of proper armies engaged in major military confrontations. Nevertheless, to understand the final outcome of the Russian Civil War, it is vital to emphasise that it was far more complex than simply a confrontation between Reds and Whites. It was a gigantic struggle of Russians against non-Russians, Socialists against Monarchists, Soviets against Tsarist officers, and countryside against town.

From the very beginning, the Bolsheviks had an important advantage. Having seized power in the main cities and central regions of Russia, they retained control of a large and compact area which was densely populated and contained most of the industrial resources as well as fertile land. Operating from the centre, they could shift from one front to another and, when forced to retreat, they gained the benefit of shortened lines of communication as the web of railways converged on Moscow.[10]

By contrast, the huge areas that fell under the control of the anti-Bolshevik forces were sparsely populated and lacked significant industrial infrastructure. The Whites were not only unable to present a common front with the SRs but also had to build up their bases in distant areas from the centre largely inhabited by non-Russians who, though sharing their anti-Bolshevik feelings, had independence as their basic priority.[11] Due to their geographical position, Russian chauvinism proved militarily suicidal.

In Central and Eastern Russia constant in-fighting plagued the anti-Bolshevik forces. The former Tsarist officers abhorred democracy and loathed the SRs who also fought under a red flag. After a Soviet offensive, the SRs retreating from the Volga reached an agreement in September 1918 with the White officers based in Siberia to establish a single anti-Bolshevik administration or Directory. On 18 November Admiral A. V. Kolchak, initially appointed Minister of War by the Directory, accepted dictatorial powers after a military coup overthrew his own government. Although, for a short time, the other White Chieftains recognised him as Supreme Leader, Kolchak's fifteen-month reign was above all an ill-fated adventure. Initial military success, like the seizure of Perm in December 1918, only consolidated the Whites' unwavering optimism that an all-out military offensive would be enough to defeat the ill-trained Reds. This fatal underestimation of the enemy led them to believe that co-ordination with the Whites operating then in the South was not necessary to guarantee victory. A concerted plan with Finland under the White General, Mannerheim, would have divided the Red Army into two fronts but Kolchak refused to accept the independence of that nation. Thus the three-pronged attack initiated by Kolchak's troops in March 1919 soon ran out of steam. After advancing hundreds of miles into the Urals, their supply lines were overextended and the rear was in constant turmoil. Beginning a retreat in June, the White Army disintegrated as entire areas fell under partisan attacks, SRs' uprisings, and the activities of independent warlords. By November their capital, Omsk, fell without a fight. Kolchak himself was captured and executed in February 1920.[12]

The Whites in Southern Russia achieved a more successful military record than their Siberian counterparts but ultimately shared a similar fate. Under General Anton Denikin, former Commander-in-Chief of the south-western front in 1917, the so-called Volunteer Army, raised in the Don and Kuban Cossack territories, became one of the finest military units of the civil war. From a tiny force of 3000 officers in February 1918, it had grown, in less than a year, to 100 000 strong after merging with local Cossack troops. In the first months of 1919, the now re-named Allied Forces of South Russia began their advance into the Ukraine and the Caucasus. In July of 1919, at the zenith of his fortune, Denikin launched an offensive to seize Moscow. By October the Whites were only two hundred miles from that objective and near Tula, a crucial arsenal town. Yet, as in eastern Russia, the White thrust turned into appalling defeat as it could not withstand a combination of Red counter-attack in the front, harassment of the supply-lines by peasant bands, and combat on the western flank against Ukrainian nationalists. Having succeeded Denikin in 1920, Baron Wrangel launched his last offensive in June coinciding with the outbreak of full-scale hostilities between Poland and Bolshevik Russia. Yet this exceptional cooperation with a non-Russian force came too late. When the Reds sealed an armistice with the Poles in October, they could concentrate on the last White front. By November 1920 the Whites had been driven back to the Crimea from where 150 000 troops and civilians were evacuated by the French fleet.[13]

General N. N. Iudenich led the third important White Army in the north-west. His offensive against Petrograd in the autumn of 1919 was doomed as it was not co-ordinated with Finland and Estonia. Once again military priorities were undermined by Russian chauvinism.[14] In fact, the more shrewd Bolsheviks at this crucial moment had offered these nations full recognition provided that they stay out of the war. This promise was fulfilled as Finland and the Baltic States became new states in 1920.

Their geographical position left the Whites with an extremely poor communication network. Physically separated by huge distances, it took four months for an envoy to travel between the areas controlled by Denikin and Kolchak. Telegraphic exchanges were possible though only via Paris, taking over a month.[15] Thus the main military offensives turned out to be strikingly uncoordinated adventures. Denikin's operation against Moscow was launched after Kolchak's offensive had failed. Iudenich's drive on Petrograd followed Denikin's retreat. Additionally, their military campaigns were impaired by deficient transport facilities. For instance, the Trans-Siberian Railroad, the arterial network for Kolchak's army, proved unable to maintain vital supplies from the port of Vladivostok in the Far East to the front line in the Urals 4000 miles away.[16] By contrast, under a unified command and in control of the main railway lines, the Reds presented a homogeneous effort co-ordinating military operations and checking White attacks by transferring the bulk of their troops from one front to another as the military situation required.[17]

Foreign intervention was crucial to keep the White war effort alive. Unlike the Reds, who had inherited the entire Tsarist arsenal and possessed the main industrial centres, the Whites were completely dependent on external aid. However, though fundamental in prolonging the civil war, foreign intervention lacked the consistency and quantity to alter its outcome.

In May 1918 the Bolsheviks suffered one of their greatest military setbacks when the so-called Czechoslovak Legion, a well disciplined force of 40 000 former war prisoners of the Austro–Hungarian Empire en-route via Vladivostok to France, revolted. Mutual distrust between Soviets and Czechs led to an accidental clash and to the latter's rebellion. In a few weeks, the Legion had proved the fragility of Soviet authority. City after city fell into the hands of the Czechs who effectively took charge of the Trans-Siberian Railroad and cleared a huge area, from central Russia to the Pacific, of Bolsheviks. In the process, they helped the SRs to seize the vital Volga region where they established the capital of their government, the Komuch, dominated by delegates of the disbanded Constituent Assembly. The Legion also aided the SRs' own military force, the People's Army.[18] However, the Czechs' priority was always to fight for their own independence. Their initial enthusiasm for the anti-Bolshevik cause soon turned into despair as SRs and White officers fought one another in a conflict in which they remained neutral. Throughout 1919, although still playing the vital role of guarding the Trans-Siberian, the Legion did not take any leading part in the war.

Red fears that the Czech rebellion was the spearhead of a major foreign invasion never materialised. The main concern for the Allies remained their conflict with the Central Powers. Afterwards, they simply could not commit the manpower and resources necessary to ensure a White victory since it might have sparked off a massive revolt among their own war-weary populations and troops. As a result, despite the feelings of politicians like the British Minister of War, Winston Churchill, the French Premier, George Clemenceau, and the Allied Commander-in-Chief, Marshall Foch, the Russian affair could not be turned into a full-scale anti-Bolshevik crusade.[19]

In the summer of 1918, British and French expeditionary forces landed in the Black and the Baltic seas, and several nations sent troops, military advisers and diplomatic delegations to Vladivostok. However, their military contingents were small in numbers and lacked common purpose and clear objectives. After some skirmishes in the Ukraine in March 1919, in which Greek and French troops suffered about 400 casualties, French sailors in Odessa mutinied. France abandoned the Russian adventure and began to push for containment of Bolshevism through a *cordon sanitaire* of new states on the western border of the Soviet Union. With one thousand casualties and one hundred million pounds spent, Britain was the main supporter of the White cause. Generals Knox and Poole played an important role in the headquarters of Kolchak and Denikin respectively. Yet there was never uninterrupted aid, effective naval action or significant numbers of modern weaponry such as aeroplanes or tanks.[20] Furthermore, vital military help was hampered by the long distances to the Russian ports and then by the dragging journey to the front lines. By 1920, the collapse of Kolchak's offensive and Denikin's retreat persuaded Britain that the best solution was that of peace negotiations and mediation in the conflict.[21] Only Japan sent a massive force, 72 000 strong, but it remained in the Soviet Far East, away from the front line and instead fostered all types of mischief-makers and miscreants in order to prevent the emergence of a single and united Russian administration.[22]

The limited presence of modern equipment meant that the

main battles were based on the unchanged military strategy of the Great War of mass infantry and cavalry charges. Mechanisation was minimal and the only widespread use of new technology was that of the machine-gun. In a struggle of all against all, there were no fixed fronts and the lines were thinly held with troops moving along the railway leaving large areas unoccupied. Armies were often formed not in the rear but in the vicinity of the battlefield and thrown with little or no training into combat.[23]

The Czech Rebellion and the emergence of large White forces convinced the Reds to replace early revolutionary concepts with pragmatic tactics. Leon Trotsky as Commissar for War was largely responsible for the rejection of the early improvised militias and the creation of a proper army based on universal conscription and compulsory military training. Officers were no longer elected by the troops; instead their authority was restored. Political Commissars were attached to every unit so that the armed forces were subject to political control and propaganda.[24]

As the war increased in intensity, the victory of the Red Army was ultimately clinched by its ability to mobilise the rural economy behind the Soviet state and its superior success, compared with their rivals, in enlisting millions of peasants for military service.[25] With over 80 per cent of the population, the countryside became the main source of manpower for all sides. In general, the peasantry was appalled by the idea of the Civil War and wished to remain aloof from a conflict they regarded as an alien political struggle. Often peasants resorted to acts of violence and sabotage and even formed their own Green or partisan units fighting both Whites and Reds, a clear expression of fierce hatred for everything connected with the city.[26]

All the warring camps were plagued by staggeringly high numbers of desertion but the Bolsheviks retained a much larger degree of loyalty in rural areas. The peasants' dislike of the Reds was not as powerful, and certainly not as ingrained, as their fear of the old order and the return of the former landowners. As a result, the Red Army had both overwhelming numerical superiority and found it much easier to replenish their losses. In August 1918 it consisted of some 331 000 men that had grown to 700 000 by the end of the year. It was much larger than all the armies it would meet in 1919 (at the peak of their fortunes the SRs' Army numbered 30 000 soldiers, Kolchak

120 000, Iudenich 17 000, Denikin 111 000, and Wrangel 37 000). In 1920, the Red Army stood at five and a half million men, although naturally only a part of them was serving at the front.[27]

With the White Armies defeated in the battlefields in 1920, the Reds only had to mop up small pockets of resistance in the Far East and liquidate the various peasant groups active in rural areas.[28] The introduction of the so-called New Economic Policy, a market system with liberalisation of trade, was a major concession to the countryside that eventually diminished the support for armed struggle against the regime.

By 1921, the Soviets had won the civil war but, despite all their predictions, the Communist gospel had failed to succeed abroad. In fact, the Bolsheviks had always believed that the example of the consolidation of a workers' state in Russia would act as the spark for Socialist revolution throughout Europe. Indeed, developments on the continent in the post-war years appeared to confirm the imminence of revolutionary upheaval.

The October Revolution initiated the richest period of revolutionary activity in Europe since 1848. Economic dislocation, food shortages and the scale of casualties borne by the working classes intensified the class struggle and ensured a ready audience for Bolshevism. The years 1919–21 represented the peak of the offensive. In March 1919, a Communist International (Comintern) was created with the objective of coordinating all subversive initiatives. The disintegration of the former Austrian and German empires created a vacuum of power in Central and Eastern Europe which facilitated the advance of Communism. For a short spell, there were Soviet states in Bavaria, Slovakia and Hungary in 1919. Most of Europe was shaken to its roots by urban strikes, rural uprisings and revolutionary euphoria. By 1920, with the victorious Red Army advancing toward Warsaw, there was the widespread belief that the capitalist world was in its death throes.[29]

Paradoxically, one of the more bizarre consequences of the Soviet success in Russia was that the initial momentum of revolutionary elan was followed by an era of virtually uninterrupted working-class defeat. The Comintern's sectarian methods led to painful divisions within the Socialist movements. The newly-born Communist Parties failed to attract the bulk of organised labour, placed their highest priority on combating the other left-wing forces and gradually became little more than appendices of Soviet foreign policy.

By 1921 the tide began to turn. The Red Army had been defeated in Poland and the European labour movement was hopelessly divided. The revolutionary challenge had either been brutally crushed, as in Hungary and Germany, or channelled towards reformist goals in most of Western Europe. Even the Comintern switched tactics calling those who had hitherto been vilified for a United Front strategy to defend the workers' daily interests. However, it was too late to stop the wave of political reaction. Significant sectors of the ruling social and economic classes rejected parliamentarian methods as a valid system of defending their interests. Authoritarian solutions were advocated, not so much to suppress revolutionary Socialism, which had already run out of steam, but to wipe out the gains in social legislation that the labour movement had achieved since 1914. The establishment of a dictatorship in Hungary in March 1920 heralded the advance of the forces of nationalism, militarism and anti-liberalism. Fascism seized power in Italy in 1922; military dictatorships were established across Southern and Eastern Europe in the 1920s and 1930s; in 1933 Hitler annihilated democracy in Germany and within one year Austria had met a similar fate. Thus the outbreak of the Spanish Civil War in July 1936 constituted the latest battle in a European class conflict that had been under way since the Bolshevik triumph of 1917.[30]

As in the rest of Europe, Spain was caught in this spiral of social violence and ideological militancy. Its ruling regime, an elitist Liberal Monarchy, faced its first real test of survival when a Socialist-led general strike in August 1917 sought to emulate Russia's February events and install a democratic republic. However, unlike Petrograd, the army remained loyal to the monarchy and repressed the revolt with sheer brutality. The post-war economic recession and news of the Bolshevik triumph increased social turmoil. A small Communist Party was created after a split in the Socialist movement. Yet, the Anarcho-Syndicalist *Confederación Nacional del Trabajo* (CNT) was in charge of the offensive. Between 1918 and 1923, short-lived governments in Madrid were unable to control the growing upheaval which reigned in the country. Starving peasants rose throughout Southern Spain demanding 'land and bread'. Syndicalists paralysed the industrial centres, in particular Barcelona, with massive strike action. The final blow to the ailing system came in the summer of 1921 with a major military rout at Annual (Morocco) where over 12 000 Spanish troops were massacred. It was in this climate of political vacuum, social warfare and colonial disaster that the Captain General of Barcelona, Miguel Primo de Rivera, staged a coup d'état on 13 September 1923 and was immediately offered dictatorial powers by King Alfonso XIII.

Two exceptional historical developments distinguished Spanish events. Firstly, Spain was the only place where an authoritarian regime collapsed and gave way to a modern democratic order in inter-war Europe. Praetorian intervention in 1923 not only destroyed the old oligarchic system but also produced a profound split within the army[31] that eventually led to the fall of the Monarchy and the proclamation of the Second Republic in April 1931, the country's first genuine exercise in mass democracy. Secondly, unlike many other European countries whose constitutional regimes were overthrown in this period with hardly a struggle, the Republic only collapsed after a vicious conflict that lasted almost three years.

Indeed, a military coup had been planned immediately after the electoral victory of the Popular Front in February 1936 to prevent the introduction of wide-ranging social and economic reforms. The conspirators had not anticipated massive popular resistance, let alone a civil war. They were confident that their uprising, in a country with a long tradition of military intervention, would lead to a relatively swift takeover. However, the insurrection, which began on the night of 17 July, failed in its main objectives. After the first three days, the Spanish Whites or Nationalists had only succeeded in their strongholds, that third of Spain which voted for the Right in February 1936: the Catholic heartland (Galicia, Old Castille and Navarre) and Morocco. Exceptions were Oviedo, Zaragoza and a strip of land around Seville. Yet here the triumph was far from secure; surrounded by hostile territory, they were captured only through the audacity of officers who, after initially proclaiming their loyalty to the government, switched sides striking by surprise against the confident authorities. In the main industrial cities and the rural south, the uprising was defeated by the swift action of trade unions and political parties. Furthermore, a majority of senior officers, and large sections of the peninsular troops and police forces remained loyal to the Republic. The fleet, the tiny air force and the gold reserves were also in the hands of the government. The African army, the pro-Nationalist professional force in Spanish Morocco that could decide the outcome of the war, was paralysed by the problem of transport across the Straits of Gibraltar.[32]

Like their Russian counterparts, their geographical position seemed to be a significant factor against the Nationalists. Anchored in agrarian areas, they were cut off from each other: General Mola was in charge of a rump state in North and Central Spain; General Queipo de Llano controlled the area around Seville; and General Franco was in Spanish Morocco. Furthermore, they had lost their overall leader, General Sanjurjo, in a plane crash in Portugal on 20 July.

However, unlike the Russian Whites, huge areas did not separate them. By early August, the African troops had crossed the Straits of Gibraltar and initiated their march towards Madrid soon uniting their southern and northern regions. More importantly, vital issues such as unity and state re-construction were better solved by the insurgents than by the government.

Wherever the rebellion succeeded, political activity automatically ceased to exist and authority passed into the hands of the army. Military imperatives indicated the need to establish a unified leadership under a Commander-in-Chief to replace Sanjurjo. In September, a gathering of Generals appointed Franco Head of the State and Generalissimo of all the armed forces.[33] Despite the tactical differences of the various civilian forces that supported the uprising, there was more that united than actually divided them. They all had not only collaborated between 1931 and 1936 in the common goal of destroying the Republic but also during this period had undergone a process of 'fascistization', sharing a similar anti-democratic, ultra-catholic and authoritarian programme. Accepting that in order to wage a successful war they had to subordinate their activities to military command, they hardly presented any resistance when amalgamated into a single political force in April 1937.[34] The Catholic Church became the ideological cheerleader of the movement. History was rewritten. The insurgents were not rebels, but blessed as the heroes of a crusade to liberate Spain from the godless hordes of Moscow. Franco himself was referred to as *Caudillo*, the name of the medieval warrior chieftains.[35]

By contrast, despite the widespread recognition that collaboration was imperative to victory, unity eluded Red Spain until the end. In the areas where the coup was defeated, the authority of the central administration was not formally challenged but real power lay in the streets and not in the ministerial offices in Madrid. The state machinery was swept away by a wave of revolutionary fervour and for practical purposes bypassed by a myriad of popular committees, constituted depending on the local balance of power. A coherent standing armed force collapsed. Out of the 100 000 troops in mainland Spain in July 1936, less than half of them joined the revolt. Yet soldiers who might have opposed the rebellion deserted their units as workers' militias took control of re-establishing order in the streets and organising military operations. Most professional officers, if not shot or imprisoned, were not employed because of doubts about their political background.[36]

Although initially smaller in numbers, the Nationalist troops were a coherent fighting force led by regular officers, most of them *africanistas* whose careers had been made in the Moroccan wars. It included the 40 000 strong Army of Africa composed of the Foreign Legion and Moorish mercenaries. They conducted war as if it was a colonial struggle with the hostile population playing the part of natives and terror used consciously as a military and political instrument.

Ill-disciplined and poorly armed Republican militias fared badly in open battle. Despite their overwhelming superiority in numbers, they failed to advance against thin lines defended by organised troops under the command of seasoned officers. Their performance was even worse against the African army marching towards Madrid. Military operations were hampered by constant disputes between rival political forces with the militias holding votes before an attack and refusing to obey orders from professional officers. There was no single strategy as the Republicans were chaotically fragmented and focused their resistance in merely local terms.[37]

With the war approaching the capital, a new government presided over by the veteran Socialist leader Francisco Largo Caballero was established in September 1936. The objective was to reconstruct the authority of the central state, to harness all the Republic's resources in a concerted war effort and to mould the unruly militias into a cohesive force, the Popular Army. It was a daunting task which was never fully accomplished as it ran against the autonomist plans of the Catalan and Basque administrations as well as the deeply-rooted rivalries between rival forces. Indeed, to the traditional antagonism between the two largest working-class movements, the Socialists and the Anarcho-Syndicalists, was added the growth of a powerful Communist Party. These rivalries often exploded into random violence and killings. In May 1937, Barcelona underwent a mini civil war when Anarcho-Syndicalists and Marxist dissidents fought at the barricades against the Catalan government backed by Communists and Socialists.[38] The May Days were the worst but neither the only nor the last display of internal fighting within the Republic.

The Communist Fifth Regiment with its stress on discipline, its political commissars and its use of professional officers, became the role model for the Popular Army. Eventually, throughout 1937, the chaotic rag-tag militias of the first months gave way to a much better disciplined regular army. Under the leadership of some regular officers, like General Rojo, who rose to be Chief of the General Staff, the Reds organised in 1937 and 1938 a series of well-planned offensives seizing the initiative and surprising the enemy. However, small advances were often followed by painful losses of human and *matériel* which could not be replaced. Moreover, unlike the Whites, the Popular Army suffered from a shortage of suitable senior and middle-rank officers with infantry combat experience, while the separate political colour of different units persisted.[39]

Ultimately, defeat was not produced by the constant domestic squabbles within the Red camp but because of the internationalisation of the conflict. Unlike Russia, the role played by the Great Powers in Spain not only prolonged the conflict but also determined its course and outcome. It seems reasonable to speculate that, but for foreign intervention, the insurrection might have petered out from lack of military supplies and the African troops might have been left stranded in Morocco. Thus the diplomatic context of 1936 proved crucial.

Under the authoritarian regime of Antonio Salazar, Portugal sided with the insurgents. The head of the rebellion, General

Sanjurjo, established the headquarters of the conspiracy there. Portugal became the perfect spot from which foreign aid was delivered, and served as the liaison for the divided Nationalist zones. Also ten thousand Portuguese 'volunteers' joined the rebels.[40]

Much more significant in military terms was the assistance provided by Germany and Italy. Their activities brought modern warfare techniques to the Spanish arena, foreshadowing the horrors of the Second World War. Both dictators heeded the Spanish Whites' requests for aid spurred by a combination of ideological zeal and strategic opportunism. On 25 July Hitler set in motion 'Operation Magic Fire'. In a few days, a German vessel, the *Usaramo*, left Germany loaded with ten transport planes Junkers 52, six escort fighters Heinkel 51, anti-aircraft guns, bombs, ammunition and a full crew of pilots, mechanics and instructors. Ten more Junkers 52 were also on their way.[41] On 29 July, the Italians began to dispatch a dozen Savoia-Marchetti transport and bomber planes, followed by twelve Fiat C.R.32 fighters to Spanish Morocco.[42] By early August, the first success-ful airlift of troops from Morocco was under way. Thousands of soldiers of the elite African Army began their inexorable ad-vance towards Madrid leaving behind a staggering trail of blood, desolation and carnage. A secret meeting on 4 August between the heads of the German and Italian intelligence services, Admiral Canaris and Colonel Roatta, sealed the military collaboration of both countries in Spain. They agreed that their activities should continue beyond the airlift, increasing the number of military advisers and *matériel* aid, and allowing their air-forces to engage in fighting and bombing missions.[43]

Fascist aggression contrasted with the stance of the Western Democracies. Initially, the French government, a Popular Front coalition similar to that of Spain under the Socialist Léon Blum, responded in positive terms to the pleas for military aid. How-ever, once the decision was leaked to the press, a mounting campaign by right-wing circles and the possibility of domestic strife at home led to a split in the cabinet. The tacit opposition of Britain, France's vital ally, tilted the balance. On 25 July, the initial French commitment to help the beleaguered Republic was reversed.[44]

While the French government remained sympathetic to the

Republic, the British presented a very different attitude. Ruled by a National Government, Britain adopted a policy of tacit neutrality that in fact concealed veiled support for the White cause. For reasons of class and upbringing, they detested what a left-wing Republic stood for, and approved of the anti-revolutionary objectives of the Spanish insurgents. Additionally, Britain controlled about 40 per cent of all foreign investment in Spain. Thus while the Republic was viewed as a Soviet under mob rule, General Franco was considered a good military man, who was prudent and conservative. The heart of the problem for British diplomacy was that formal Republican legitimacy was in the same camp as the dreaded social revolution, while the counter-revolution remained formally illegitimate. Consequently, although maintaining for the home audience an image of scrupulous neutrality, the real position of the British administration was perfectly encapsulated by the instructions of the Prime Minister, Stanley Baldwin, to his Foreign Minister, Anthony Eden, on 26 July: 'On no account, French or other, must you bring us into the fight on the side of the Russians!' Britain's attitude proved crucial in the first days of the conflict. On 22 July the British administration accepted Franco's requests to close the ports of Gibraltar and Tangier to the Republican navy which was blockading the Straits. Then they restrained their French ally from helping the Republic. Simultaneously, they turned a blind eye to those prepared to intervene in favour of the rebels.[45]

The accidental landing of three Italian Savoia Bombers in French Morocco in early August ended the supposed secrecy of foreign support for the Spanish officers. Once again British pressure and French divisions led to Blum proposing an intermediate solution: a Non-Intervention Pact or the introduction of an arms embargo on both sides. Before France unilaterally adhered to non-intervention on 8 August, Blum arranged with the Air Minister Cot the dispatch of twelve Dewoitine fighter planes and 8 Potez 54 bombers, most without armament or supply parts to Spain. Also the pursuit of a policy of 'relaxed non-intervention' or connivance in the smuggling of armaments over the Pyrenean frontier was expected to help crush the rebellion.[46] What Blum had not envisaged was that his ill-fated retreat from intervention was to spell doom for the Republic.

Indeed, although signed by twenty-seven nations, including

all the Great Powers, the Non-Intervention Pact never went beyond a diplomatic charade. It was the ideal instrument to achieve the objectives pursued by the British Foreign Office. It prescribed an arms embargo towards the combatants, granting the same status to the legal government as to the rebels; it served to confine the war within Spain; it restrained French participation; it maintained for the domestic audience neutrality in a respectable fashion; and avoided confrontation with Germany and Italy. Given that Germany and Italy continued their vital support for the rebels, despite their signing of the Pact, the upholding of the embargo, followed under duress by France and others, clearly damaged the Republic.[47]

By early October 1936 everybody assumed that Madrid was about to fall and that the war would soon be over. However, the Nationalists were held at the gates of the capital. The African Army, invincible in open field, proved less suited than the militias at barricade and street-fighting. Furthermore, the arrival of the first significant amount of foreign aid represented a crucial *matériel* and moral boost for the defenders. So far, Mexico had been the only state siding with the Republic, sending food, some 20 000 7MM Mauser rifles, twenty million cartridges and clothing.[48] The Soviet Union finally decided to back the Spanish Popular Front. The Comintern organised the transport of volunteers to Spain, the so-called International Brigades, thousands of men and women from all continents who travelled to Spain to fight in what they regarded as the last ditch-battle against the march of Fascism. At the same time, the first important deliveries of Soviet weapons began to arrive in October 1936 including Chato and Mosca fighter planes, Katiuska bombers and T-26 tanks.[49] Madrid was now the stage for an epic battle, the scene of air combats and massive duels of artillery and tanks. By 23 November, with all frontal attacks repelled and his armies decimated Franco had to halt the offensive.

Despite the Non-Intervention Pact, the dramatic escalation of foreign aid transformed Spain into a miniature world war in all but name.[50] The Republic ultimately failed to achieve victory because of the strength of international forces arrayed against it. From May 1937, the last Republican government led by the Socialist Juan Negrín struggled not only to combat the Axis-equipped Nationalist armies but also a crippling embargo which not only prevented the Republic from ever engaging on an equal military footing, but also undercut attempts to sustain the physical fabric and morale of the home front, crucial to a war of resistance.[51]

Merchant ships laden with military equipment left Russia for Spanish ports delivering, in 58 voyages, 623 aircraft, 331 tanks, 60 armoured cars, 302 field-guns, 64 anti-aircraft guns, 427 anti-tank guns, 15 008 machine-guns, 379 645 rifles, and 2000 personnel.[52] As the Mediterranean route became increasingly dangerous, Russian weapons were sent from Murmansk to French Atlantic ports and were then smuggled into Spain. International volunteers continued to arrive until reaching a maximum of about 40 000. They were present in all the main battles of 1937 and 1938, losing approximately a third of their total number.[53]

In turn, the Spanish Whites relied on oil deliveries from the main Anglo–American companies: Texaco, Shell, Standard Oil and the Atlantic Refining Companies. Without them, their campaigns would have come to a halt in days.[54] Also the Fascist Dictatorships committed enough manpower and military equipment to decide the outcome of the conflict. Italy was all but in name at war with the Republic. Her involvement included about 80 000 troops organised in mechanised divisions, the so-called *Corpo di Truppe Volontarie*, 759 aircraft, 6600 cannons, mortars, and machine-guns, 7400 motor vehicles, hundreds of thousands of rifles, 7.7 million shells and 319 million small-arms cartridges.[55] Hitler dispatched the Condor Legion, the finest airforce of the period. It consisted of a permanent squadron of approximately 5000 troops (some 20 000 would serve at different times), anti-aircraft guns, 200 Panzer tanks and 140 of the most modern bombers and fighter planes in the German arsenal including the Junker 87B 'Stukas' and Messerschmitts 109 (in total around 700 aircraft were sent).[56]

Fascist aid gave Franco a vital air and artillery superiority with which to follow his strategy of attrition, bleeding the enemy and leaving no pockets of resistance in his rear. Yet *blitzkrieg* tactics combining tanks, aircrafts and artillery were pursued in some instances as in the decisive offensive through Aragón in the spring of 1938 reaching the Mediterranean and cutting Red Spain in two. Other new military techniques included the indiscriminate bombing of cities to terrorise the civilian population into submission. The ancient Basque city of Guernika was destroyed by the Condor Legion in the campaign to conquer Northern Spain in 1937. Barcelona and Madrid became the first two large European cities to be constantly under air attacks by Italian and German bombers. Italian submarines and aviation played a vital role in sinking merchant fleets transporting military and food supplies through the Mediterranean.

It was evident that unless Non-Intervention was either abandoned altogether or genuinely enforced the Republic was at a clear disadvantage. There was a staggering difference in terms of the quality, quantity and regularity of aid received by both sides. Italy and Germany camouflaged their troops as volunteers fighting Bolshevism. In fact, they were professional soldiers constantly re-supplied and equipped with the best available *matériel*. By contrast, the International Brigadiers were civilians who had to be armed, trained and fed by a besieged Republic. The long distance between the Soviet Union and Spain, and the Italian blockade also meant a more irregular source of supplies. Furthermore, unlike the Nationalists who always could obtain their supplies promptly and on request, the diplomatic embargo forced the Republic to operate in the open arms market. In consequence, purchases from so many sources meant irregular deliveries, different types of armament with the subsequent shortages of accurate supplies and accessories, and over-priced and obsolete equipment from private arms dealers. Indeed, despite an abundance of gold, purchasing agents were faced with a wall of intrigue and deception, and forced to pay inflated prices for useless equipment wherever they turned. Poland, the second provider of weapons to the Republic, sold 100 000 rifles, 180 million cartridges, 11 123 light machine-guns and 294 artillery pieces that were little better than junk. Even the Soviet Union participated in this fraudulent practice. Apart from the excellent quality of planes and tanks, and 150 Degtyarev light machine-guns, most weapons were old, dating from nineteenth-century wars. Additionally, by fiddling with the exchange rate, the Russians charged almost twice the normal price for their arms.[57]

Nevertheless, the escalation of German expansionism gave the Republic a glimmer of hope in 1938. In March Germany annexed Austria and laid plans for her next prize, the Sudetenland in Czechoslovakia. Blum's attempts to intervene more actively in the Spanish conflict ran against the hostility of the French senior officers and of the British government. Fearing the isolation of France in a European war, Blum had to settle for a half-hearted formula: the total opening of her border to the delivery of Russian weapons.[58] The Blum administration lasted only one month and was replaced by a more right-wing government led by Daladier on 8 April. The British exerted all sorts of pressure on the new French government to reverse Blum's decision and close the border. According to them it was the French attitude, not the blatant Axis display of force in Spain, which flouted the principles of Non-Intervention and was leading Europe to the verge of war. Spain was thus worth sacrificing on the altar of appeasement. After relentless coercion, Daladier finally gave way and the border was closed on 13 June cutting off the only safe channel of arms to the beleaguered Republic.[59]

The worsening of the Sudetenland question in the summer of 1938 seemed to favour the Republican strategy of resistance until war started in Europe. The international crisis coincided with the launching of the last all-out offensive by the Popular Army, the battle of the Ebro. However, as the slaughter raged on, the eyes of the combatants were focused on events on the continent. As soon as hostilities broke out, the Republic would declare war on Germany and link its fortune to that of the Allies. Thus the Munich Pact was the last pyrrhic victory of appeasement and in effect the last nail in the coffin of Republican Spain. All hopes of being rescued by the Western Democracies were shattered. Furthermore, the Ebro campaign became the war of annihilation always pursued by Franco. On 16 November, the battle ended. It had taken the Nationalists almost four months to push the Republicans out of the territory captured in July. The toll was the heaviest of the entire war: each side suffering over 50 000 casualties.[60] Both armies were exhausted. However, whereas the Republic lost some of its best troops and equipment which could never be replaced, Franco could afford the appalling cost. On 18 November Hitler agreed to requests for massive deliveries of armament in return for mining concessions. In fact, by the end of the year, eager to see off the Spanish problem, Germany surpassed Italy, for the first time, in her scale of involvement.[61]

On 23 December 1938 Franco initiated his final push against

Catalonia. Starved of supplies and heavily outgunned, the Republican defences collapsed. On 26 January 1939 Barcelona fell. On 1 April and after a struggle of thirty-two months, Franco announced his final and total victory.

In conclusion, both Russian and Spanish Civil Wars constituted much more than mere fratricidal conflicts. They marked the beginning and the end of a European Civil War which shook Europe in the inter-war years. They also encapsulated the evolution of European events. Whereas, in 1919, the Bolshevik leaders talked of the dawn of a new era, twenty years later both revolution and democracy were in retreat before the triumphal march of reaction. Foreign involvement in Russia served to prolong the war but ultimately there was never the commitment in troops and arms to prevent a Red Victory. By contrast, in 1936, the internationalisation of the conflict in Spain determined its final outcome. Even before the *Anschluss* of Austria and the break-up of Czechoslovakia, Spain became a test case for Western appeasement and Fascist aggression. The sacrifice of a Red but democratic Spain seemed to British and French policymakers a reasonable price to avoid conflict with Italy and Germany. Instead, it only served to embolden the Fascist Dictatorships, sealing the Axis Pact and using Spanish battlefields as testing grounds, while increasing their territorial ambitions. Also, the evolution of the Spanish conflict persuaded the Soviet Union to switch its international strategy of Popular Front to one of *rapprochement* with Germany. The conclusion of the Nazi–Soviet Non-Aggression Pact in August 1939 astonished the world. The memories of the Spanish Civil War were still fresh as Europe was about to face the horrors of the Second World War.

5. The Second World War, 1939–45

S. P. MACKENZIE

The 'twenty years peace' that separated the two world wars allowed soldiers and statesmen time to draw lessons from the Great War experience as well as to forecast ways in which technological and other changes would alter the nature of any future conflict fought on a similar scale. The opening campaigns of the Second World War would demonstrate the degree to which the great powers had correctly or incorrectly anticipated the shape of things to come, as later campaigns would show their capacity to learn from mistakes and adapt in the face of new realities. The earlier struggle had already demonstrated the extent to which European warfare had become 'total' in terms of the harnessing of all the human and material resources of the modern industrial state to the war effort. If anything, the course of this new round of continental conflict would involve even more comprehensively integrated national exertions. For the purposes of study, however, warfare in the Second World War in Europe can be divided – albeit somewhat artificially – into eight forms or types.

There were, to begin with, regular ground operations, conducted with or without air support and in some instances dependent on the success of amphibious or airborne operations. Land operations can be divided both chronologically and structurally between the years of German-led Axis dominance and the years of the eventually crushing Allied and Soviet response. There were also irregular low-to-medium intensity campaigns fought behind the front. In several cases there were strategic air campaigns designed to alter the course of the war. All the warring states undertook psychological operations designed to buttress or undermine the will to win, and engaged in intelligence-gathering and deception campaigns. Then there were the efforts to combine available resources, both human and material, into an all-out war effort. Last but not least there was warfare as grand strategy, how nations and alliances structured and ran the strategic decision-making process at the highest levels.

GROUND OPERATIONS, 1939–42

Different nations drew different lessons from the battles of the First World War, and from subsequent advances in aviation and vehicle technology. Those that had been on the winning side tended, by and large, to be more complacent than those that had been among the defeated.

In France, Britain, Italy and the United States horses were increasingly supplanted by motor vehicles, experiments undertaken with concentrated tank forces, and some recognition afforded the growing importance of air support in the latter 1920s and 1930s. Structural innovation was ultimately limited, however, both by institutional complacency and conservatism, and in many cases also by budget restrictions. In Germany and the Soviet Union (USSR), meanwhile, similar experiments, with fewer institutional or budgetary constraints, were followed through with the development of operational doctrines and force-structures – large armoured formations and operation-centred air forces – in which fast-moving and concentrated mechanised operations with air support played a leading role. Innovations of this kind in the USSR were curtailed and even reversed as a result of the Red Army purges in the latter 1930s; but the Wehrmacht, though its infantry and artillery divisions were still heavily dependent on horse-drawn transport, had by the outbreak of the Second World War developed a way of war emphasising initiative, speed of manoeuvre, and concentration of vehicular force for which the more traditionally equipped and trained forces of its opponents were ill-prepared to deal.[1]

It was this, rather than a clear superiority in numbers or equipment, that largely determined the outcome of the major land campaigns of the first half of the war in Europe. The Wehrmacht not only rapidly overcame comparatively weak opponents (Poland in 1939, Denmark and Norway along with Holland and Belgium in 1940, Yugoslavia and Greece in 1941) but also defeated major powers with unexpected ease. France fell in the space of six weeks (1940), and British land and air forces were forced to evacuate on the three occasions they attempted to help stem the German tide (Norway, France, Greece). When Hitler then turned his forces against the Soviet Union (summer 1941), the Red Army suffered a series of horrendous defeats that made it appear likely that the USSR would collapse.

Though efforts were made to speed up development of large-scale armoured formations and air support to match the panzer divisions and Luftwaffe, neither Allied nor Soviet forces were organised to fight the kind of fast, combined arms deep-penetration battles of manoeuvre and encirclement that the *Wehrmacht* unleashed in 1940–1. (It should be noted, though, that the German armed forces were ill-prepared to undertake large-scale amphibious operations, as the ad hoc and abortive nature of the plans to invade Britain and the very costly invasions of Norway and Crete indicate.)

The French army had neither the time nor the space to recover and adapt when the enemy invaded in 1940. The British army, protected by the English Channel after being driven off the Continent, did its best to learn from defeat while conducting a campaign against the Axis from Egypt. Yet while able to best the poorly trained and organised Italian army, British forces in the Western Desert as often as not found themselves thwarted or driven to retreat by the smaller but better integrated Afrika Korps in 1941–2. The vast expanses of Russia, coupled with huge reserves of manpower and material, allowed the Soviet Union to reorganise and fight on even with the Wehrmacht at the gates of Moscow; but the limited success of the Red Army winter counterattacks of 1941–2, and the utter failure of the big offensive the following spring, suggested that Soviet forces were not yet as well led, trained or organised for bold action as those of the enemy.[2]

Only time would tell if Germany's opponents – to whom Hitler added by declaring war on the United States after the Japanese attack on Pearl Harbor in December 1941 – would develop the capacity to decisively defeat the Wehrmacht in battle. Meanwhile, as the war continued, other components of the war effort began to take on importance.

IRREGULAR WARFARE

The sheer speed and scale of Nazi advances in the first half of the war contained at least one potential hazard in the form of segments of conquered populations that might seek to continue the fight and do serious damage. This certainly was the hope of those in London and Moscow suddenly tasked with aiding the growth of sabotage and related activities behind the lines (no planning for such a contingency having taken place).

In the West, indigenous resistance activity was at first quite limited. But as Nazi rule became more onerous and logistical and organisational support began to be offered by the British through the Special Operation Executive (SOE), later added to by the American Office of Strategic Services (OSS), the size and scale of underground activity grew. The ultimate aim was to build up forces strong enough to mount a general campaign of sabotage and guerrilla activity that would seriously disrupt enemy activity behind the lines when the Allied armies returned to the Continent. Linked in kind to such activity were the raids on the enemy coast and behind enemy lines carried out by special units such as the commandos and special air service.

To the East, organised resistance activity developed more quickly and on a larger-unit scale, partly in response to harsher Nazi occupation policies and partly because – at least in places – a wilder landscape offered more opportunities to rally forces secretly. SOE played a supporting role from Poland to Greece, but faced difficulties to a greater extent than in the West in trying to coordinate the activities of Communist resistance organisations, especially in Yugoslavia, that were ultimately beholden to the Kremlin. In the occupied portions of the Soviet Union, meanwhile, groups of Soviet soldiers cut off behind the lines as the Germans advanced – many of them members of the Communist Party – went to ground and fought on as guerrillas. By the end of 1942 the surviving bands were under the central direction of the Political Administration of the Red Army, and from 1943 onward were used extensively to disrupt enemy communications in concert with Red Army offensives.

The effectiveness of such irregular warfare varied. In regions where the local population was hostile to the former regime, as in parts of the occupied Soviet Union, partisans could find it virtually impossible to operate for long. In response to guerrilla activity the enemy carried out severe reprisals against the civilian population – often ten or more hostages shot for every German killed. Political and other rivalries could make coordination of underground activity difficult, and arms and ammunition were necessarily limited in size and quantity to what could be captured or dropped by parachute from Allied aircraft. In consequence, if forced to fight heavily armed German troops, resistance units could and did suffer very heavy losses. On the other hand hit-and-run attacks forced the enemy to divert troops / albeit often not men of the highest calibre and supplanted in some cases by pro-Axis local militias / to guard vital points and engage in anti-partisan sweeps. Furthermore, coordinated sabotage campaigns against road, rail and telegraph links could and did seriously impede the arrival of reinforcements at the front at critical points in time.

Taken all in all, such activities were a useful adjunct to, rather than a substitute for, regular military operations. Though at times units of several thousand fighters could be formed and underground command structures could become quite sophisticated, the fact remained that, in occupied territory, resistance forces of whatever size did not possess the capacity to train for, or the logistical support necessary to sustain, full-scale conventional warfare. Without the timely arrival of Allied or Soviet ground troops, or at least an escape route to hand, resistance and special service forces were almost invariably crushed in open battle.[3]

STRATEGIC BOMBING

As every field commander knew or discovered in the course of the war, adequate air support for ground operations – particularly big offensives – had become a vital component of modern warfare. Tactical air sorties, however, or even theatre air operations, were not what many senior Allied air officers saw as the main function of a modern air force. It was strategic air power, specifically the ability of long-range bombing of enemy cities and industry to bring about victory, which occupied centre stage in the minds of the so-called 'Bomber Barons' of the Royal Air Force (RAF) and United States Army Air Forces (USAAF).

Though some attention had been paid to strategic bombing in Germany in the pre-war years, technical difficulties combined with the need to build rapidly and maintain a force capable of supporting the Wehrmacht meant that the Luftwaffe was primarily trained and equipped to fight operational rather than strategic air campaigns. Technical, logistical and organisational problems meant the same was largely true of the Italian and French air forces, while the purges and an emphasis on unit output had oriented the Soviet air force (VVS) toward aircraft and doctrine suitable mainly for battlefront operations. In Britain and the United States, however, true believers in the war-winning potential of strategic air power, such as Air Marshal Arthur Harris and General Carl A. Spaatz, held sway. They were thus able to oversee the development by the middle years of the war of huge fleets of multi-engine bombers deployed in England and used primarily to cripple key war industries (the B-17s and other aircraft of the USAAF) or undermine worker morale (the Lancasters and other long-range aircraft of the RAF) to the point where the German war effort would collapse. In neither case did strategic bombing prove to be quite so decisive.

Daylight operations by American bomber formations aimed at specific factories produced heavy losses for minimal gains due to the absence of fighter cover, while night raids on German cities by RAF bombers, though less susceptible to interception and capable of laying waste many acres of urban landscape, did not cause civilian morale to crack. (The same was true of smaller-scale German attempts to strike at London and other centres with bombs at night in 1940–1 and then with rockets in 1944.) The efficiency of civil defence and related organisations, combined with the fact that truly devastating attacks occurred only sporadically, limited the numbers killed and the psychological effect.

Yet while never a war-winning formula unto itself, the advent of long-range escort fighters and improvements in navigation and related aids meant that the strategic bombing did achieve some real successes in 1944–5 (e.g., the RAF reducing steel production in the Ruhr and the USAAF causing serious fuel shortages as a result of attacks on oil industry targets). The sheer scale of the air assault on Germany, furthermore, forced the Luftwaffe to concentrate on the defence of the homeland at the expense of other commitments and eventually took a severe attritional toll on experienced pilots. The ethics of strategic bombing and whether the Allies themselves would have been better off diverting some of the resources devoted to it to other aspects of the struggle remain hotly contested subjects.[4]

HEARTS AND MINDS

In a struggle in which all working people were potential con-tributors to the war effort – whether serving in the fighting and related services, working in the factories and fields or keeping the home fires burning – it is not surprising that the belligerents took the issue of morale seriously. Efforts were made not only to maximise the normative will to win of one's own people but also to undermine that of the opposing side.

As far as influencing the outlook of the home population was concerned, the totalitarian powers had the advantage of already possessing state propaganda organisations. In Nazi Germany the ministry of propaganda under Josef Goebbels, in Fascist Italy the ministry of popular culture and its ilk, and in the Soviet Union state-run organs such as the TASS news agency and the Moscow artists' and writers' union simply directed their work into new channels. Civilians were exposed to a steady stream of posters, radio broadcasts, newspaper articles and films promot-ing the cause and manipulating war news to advantage. Domestic propaganda in Italy was not terribly effective, partly due to a lack of bureaucratic coherence and above all because defeats in North Africa undermined the credibility of official news releases. Attempts to maintain the will to win in Germany were much more successful. The conquest of much of Europe in the first half of the war reinforced the message of Nazi superiority over the decadent, plutocratic democracies in the West and the Jewish–Bolshevik terror-state to the East. When the victories then ceased and it was enemy forces that were closing in on the Reich, Goebbels was able to capitalise on fears concerning the conse-quences of defeat – given the stated refusal of the Allies to continence anything other than unconditional surrender – to add the strength of desperation to people's commitment to the war effort.

Meanwhile the sheer barbarity of Nazi occupation policies in the western portions of the Soviet Union made it easier for citizens to accept Moscow's stress on the need to exert every sinew in working to eject the foreign invader. It helped that such propaganda was usually couched in nationalist terms (freeing Mother Russia) rather than in terms of furthering Communism, the latter a goal that did little to stir the hearts and minds of those not already in the party. In addition a pervasive secret police apparatus and informants, especially in Germany and the Soviet Union, made it relatively easy to identify and clamp down on any subversive opinions running counter to the official line.[5]

The democratic powers had a more difficult task, as they had to build from the ground up wartime propaganda apparatuses that balanced freedom of the press and other liberties with the need to influence public opinion. The initial, sometimes counterproductive efforts in Paris were overshadowed by the military débâcle of 1940, but in London the Ministry of Information and then in Washington the Office of War Information eventually struck the right note. The general policy was to always tell the truth – sometimes rather selectively – so as to foster public trust. At the same time, efforts were made to nudge the media into explaining to both men and women how the nature and goals of the Axis, above all Nazi Germany, made the war both necessary and just. Though some campaigns on specific issues were less than successful, and war propaganda did not prevent a number of strikes or criticism of the conduct of the war to be voiced when things were going badly, on the whole Allied efforts to promote the cause at home were relatively successful.

Efforts were also made to more closely involve Allied troops in the ideological side of the struggle through such means as the 'Why We Fight' films developed for the US forces and the discussion sessions organised by the Army Bureau of Current Affairs in British units. Just how effective such activity was remains open to debate, but it certainly did no harm. Commissars served as disseminators of state propaganda within the Red Army, while National Socialist Leadership Officers sought to buttress the commitment to Nazi ideals within the Wehrmacht in the

later stages of the war. Backing up these normative efforts, especially in the Russo–German struggle, were brutally coercive
measures of a type unknown in Allied armies, not least frequent recourse to the firing squad for real or suspected deserters
and shirkers *pour encourager les autres.*[6]

The belligerents also sought to undermine enemy willpower
by psychological means, chiefly through leaflets and radio broadcasts designed to sow doubt in the minds of soldiers and civilians
about the rosy picture of events being painted by their own
authorities. Even when the source of such propaganda was dis-
guised it won few converts in the West. On the Eastern Front,
to be sure, there were cases where soldiers felt so strongly that
they had been let down by their own side that they proved susceptible to enemy blandishments and either deserted or switched
sides after surrendering, the Wehrmacht in particular thereby
acquiring a useful source of auxiliary labour.[7] Nevertheless, in
no case did a campaign or operation of war succeed to any
significant extent through efforts to undermine enemy morale.[8]

Taken all in all, successful propaganda tended to reinforce
existing views rather than make converts. But in the war for
hearts and minds all the powers were successful in the sense
that they avoided the kind of general psychological collapse
that had overtaken Germany in the last stage of the First World
War.

INTELLIGENCE AND DECEPTION

It always helps to know the intentions of the foe, and all sides
in the conflict in Europe attempted to gather the secrets of the
enemy while protecting their own. This form of warfare was pursued by traditional means (reconnaissance and spies) and through
more recent innovations (electronic eavesdropping and code-
breaking).

The effectiveness of reconnaissance operations, including aerial
observation and photography, depended on how well integrated
intelligence activities were in the command structure and on
the ebb and flow of conventional operations – an advancing
army usually having the edge over a retreating enemy. Therefore it is not surprising to find that the Third Reich did best in

the first half of the war while the Soviets and especially the Western Allies dominated in the second. Spies were another matter. In this sphere Germany was at a disadvantage even at the height of Nazi conquest. Code-breaking successes allowed MI5 to pick up (and turn) practically every German spy who landed in Britain. Conversely, and in spite of some successful counterintelligence work in Holland and elsewhere by the *Abwehr* and Gestapo, the occupation forces were not able to prevent local inhabitants or agents from various Allied departments (SOE, the Secret Intelligence Service, OSS) from organising spy rings in much of occupied Europe. Meanwhile the Soviet Union could draw on information provided by a large number of moles and other spies, including the extensive 'Red Orchestra' network.

However, it was from signals intelligence rather than human sources that the most up-to-date and comprehensive picture of the enemy could be drawn. The various and often rather unco-ordinated German intelligence organisations concerned with deciphering enemy radio traffic scored some important successes on occasion, but it was the Allies who mostly held the upper hand in the code-breaking war. This was largely due to the success of the British government code and cipher school (Bletchley Park) in deciphering the signals of the German and Italian armed forces, in turn dependent on the possession of examples of the Enigma enciphering machine used by the enemy. The information thus gleaned, known as Ultra, was of immense importance, allowing access to messages which gave vital clues on enemy strength, location and intentions of enemy units at sea as well as the Mediterranean theatre and later in North-West Europe. Information was often incomplete and sometimes not taken with enough seriousness by field commanders, but there is no doubt that Ultra provided the Allies with a window of observation denied to the Axis. By late 1942, furthermore, the Red Army had caught up in the art of using radio intercepts to pinpoint the size and location of enemy units on the Eastern Front. The Reich's foes also became very good at mounting deception operations involving among other things fake signals designed to mislead the Germans as to the location and poten-tial size of Allied landings in France in 1944 (Fortitude) and the direction of the main Soviet summer offensive of the same year.[9]

Long the 'missing dimension' in examinations of the Second
World War and then subject to sensational exaggeration, enough
substantiated details of intelligence activities have emerged for
a balanced assessment to be made. When all is said and done,
there can be little doubt that, through a combination of
organisational skill and luck (for example, the fortuitous acquisition of an Enigma machine from Poland), the Allies gained
more from their intelligence activities than the Axis at the strategic level. At the front, as in other areas, they gradually matched
and then outstripped the Germans in the sophistication and
effectiveness of tactical intelligence-gathering and deception
techniques. Taken all in all, intelligence activity was a highly
significant contributing factor to Allied victory in the field.

MOBILISATION FOR TOTAL WAR

Of even greater significance were the latent human and material resources of the various belligerents and above all the
ability of the states concerned to develop and harness them
effectively for total war. Here again it was the anti-Axis coalition
that ultimately triumphed.

Shortages of raw material, poor economic management and
organisational deficiencies meant that both the quantity and quality
of Italian tanks, aircraft and much other equipment was inferior. More important, however, was how production and manpower
matters were handled within Germany itself and the conquered
territories. In the opening years of the struggle Hitler sought
to minimise the disruptive effect of war on the home population by operating what was essentially a modified peacetime
economy. In the early, speedily victorious phase of the struggle
it proved unnecessary to massively expand the output of key
raw materials and finished war products, or the size of the armed
forces, or indeed to replace (rather than upgrade) the weapons
being produced.

By 1942, however, with the war dragging on and the Reich
now facing a coalition of three great powers with no immediate
end to the struggle in sight, a rapid shift began towards operating a true war economy. Production of war goods was streamlined
and rationalised, progressively more stringent rationing of food

and clothing along with wage and price controls was introduced, and much of the civilian population of Germany and the conquered territories drafted into armaments factories and other war work. The result was a spectacular rise in war production. There were, however, comparative limits to what was achieved. A reluctance fully to integrate the female population into the industrial workforce and turf wars between government bodies whose spheres of authority overlapped (for example, the armaments and labour ministries) did nothing to aid the war effort. Though artificial substitutes and the plundering of occupied Europe somewhat ameliorated the problem, Germany remained short of key natural resources such as rubber and petroleum. Furthermore, while some important new weapons were developed such as the Panther tank, the emphasis on producing more from existing production lines meant that in some areas – for example, conventional fighter aircraft and bombers – the Reich qualitatively fell seriously behind its opponents, particularly in the West.

A long struggle having been the basis of pre-war planning, in some respects Britain was well prepared for total war in terms of rationally manipulating the economy (wage and price controls, rationing of food and goods, the progressively wider compulsory allocation of labour, including women) to maximise war production while minimising civilian consumption. Long-range planning also meant that in some areas – such as aircraft production – quality as well as quantity increased over the course of the war, and while much raw material had to be imported, overall Allied control of the Atlantic meant that Britain had access to resources denied to the enemy, as well as help from the Empire and Commonwealth. There were, however, inherent limits to what Britain could achieve. It took time for dominions such as Canada to develop the war industries necessary to support their growing armed forces, while structural weaknesses in British industry meant that even the best weapons were comparatively slow and costly to produce. Some weapons, furthermore, including tanks, were so poor in design as to continuously lag dangerously behind their German counterparts in quality. More immediately significant was the fact that by 1940–1 wartime expenditure, particularly purchases from the USA, exceeded national income to the point where the country faced virtual bankruptcy.

Luckily Britain could look to the United States for indirect
help even before the formal American entry into the war; through
the Lend–Lease agreement and other deals the necessary imports were provided virtually free of charge. The latent economic
strength of the country in terms of human and material resources and knowledge of the latest mass-production techniques,
coupled with the willingness of the Roosevelt administration to
engage in deficit financing, meant that US industry truly did
become the arsenal of democracy. Under the supervision of the
War Production Board and related bodies the expansion of output
was truly phenomenal. Enough tanks, guns, aircraft and other
tools of war were produced both to assist America's allies and
also to lavishly equip the rapidly expanding and ultimately huge
US armed forces fighting both in Europe and against Japan.
Furthermore, what was produced, however quickly and cheaply
in overall costs, was always reliable and usually of high quality:
for example, bomber aircraft. All this was achieved with comparatively limited state intervention in the form of rationing
and direction of labour.

Even more impressive, in the light of difficulties that had to
be overcome regarding the horrendous territorial, material and
manpower losses of the first year or so of the war in the East,
was Soviet industrial output. The state apparatus was able to
oversee the relocation of industrial plant and, with continued
access to key natural resources such as iron ore and coal as well
as workers (male and female), demand increases in output to
compensate for reverses and equip new units of the Red Army.
With maximum state direction and control, and at enormous
cost to the civilian economy, war production expanded. Through
concentration on producing and further developing the most
ruggedly simple yet effective weapons available (such as the T-
34 tank) the Soviet Union was able not only to replace what had
been lost but also to equip new division after new division. Lend–
Lease supplies aided the Soviet war effort, but there can be no
doubt that the vast bulk of war material was produced by the
Soviet Union itself. By the last months of the war, manpower
and other resources were stretched to the limit, but the Red
Army had been given what it needed to roll back the invader.[10]

Table 5.1   *Annual aircraft production*

State	1939	1940	1941	1942	1943	1944	1945
Italy	1800	1800	2400	2400	1600	–	–
Germany	8295	10 247	11 776	15 409	24 807	39 807	7540
*United Kingdom**	8190	16 149	22 694	28 247	30 963	31 036	14 145
United States	5856	12 804	26 277	47 836	85 898	96 318	49 761
Soviet Union	10 382	10 565	15 735	25 436	34 900	40 300	20 900

*Includes Commonwealth.
Source: Derived from Paul Kennedy, *The Rise and Fall of the Great Powers* (New York, 1987), p. 354.

Table 5.2   *Annual tank production*

State	1940	1941	1942	1943	1944
*United Kingdom**	1400	4800	8600	7400	5000
Germany	2200	4800	9300	19 800	27 300
Soviet Union	2700	6500	24 400	24 000	28 900
United States	400	4200	23 800	29 400	17 500

Source: Derived from I. C. B. Dear and M. R. D. Foot (eds), *The Oxford Companion to the Second World War* (Oxford, 1995), pp. 459, 1183, 1213, 1231.

Superior numbers do not always bring victory, but there can be little doubt that one of the principal reasons for Axis defeat in the Second World War was that the output of the opposition was so much greater (see tables 5.1 and 5.2). In part this was simply a matter of available material and human resources, but it also had to do with how production was organised. Nazi Germany made great strides in the second half of the war, but these were more than matched by the combined efforts of the anti-Axis coalition members.

WAR AT THE TOP

A further area in which the Allies had the edge on the Axis concerned the formulation of grand strategy; that is, deciding on why, when, where and how the armed forces should be employed to bring about victory. In this aspect of warfare the differences in the personalities of war leaders and bureaucratic structures of command – both within states and between allies – were of decisive importance.

As far as the Axis alliance in Europe was concerned there was little in the way of real partnership. Hitler and Mussolini both went to war and started campaigns without informing the other of their plans beforehand. Joint operations did evolve in North Africa and elsewhere, but given the disparity in the size and effectiveness of the respective armed forces these tended to evolve into a form in which strategic and operational direction rested rather arrogantly in German hands. The increasingly dictatorial nature of Nazi demands, combined with the deterioration of the war situation, was why Italy attempted to switch sides in the spring of 1943 (thereby ending up in a situation in which the country was split between warring regions dominated by the Germans and the Allies). The smaller allies were even more subordinate to the Reich and mostly suffered greatly when attempts were made to negotiate an independent peace.

Lack of trust and effective joint command structures might not have mattered if the senior and overwhelmingly dominant Axis partner had possessed the bureaucratic mechanisms and expertise to develop a successful strategic vision. At first the concentration of military decision-making power in the hands of the Führer caused no problems, as he proved willing to listen to professional advice that helped bring about the collapse of France. From late 1941 onward, however, as victory began to give way to defeat, he was increasingly at odds with anyone at *Oberkommando der Wehrmacht* (OKW) or in the field who argued with his refusal to countenance retreat and constant attempts to mount offensives. Surrounding himself with yes-men at OKW and appointing and relieving field commanders on an increasingly arbitrary basis, Hitler took more and more to micro-managing operations himself. Such interventions played havoc with the normal command structure and more often than not led to disaster (Stalingrad being one outstanding example). His insistence on diverting resources to the militarily pointless war against the Jews also did nothing to improve Germany's strategic situation.[11]

The Allies, by way of contrast, not only managed to develop the bureaucratic mechanisms necessary for a true partnership but also formulated strategic priorities and ran operations in an orderly and logical manner. This was achieved through a combination of

summit diplomacy and the setting up of bureaucratic mechanisms such as the Combined Chiefs of Staff (CCS). There were
still plenty of disagreements and tensions, but also a willingness
to thrash out frictions and pursue a joint strategy. Hence, despite
much disagreement, the development of Anglo–American operations in the Mediterranean theatre (the British preference) and
later in North-West Europe (the American preference). The smaller
allies such as Canada, to be sure, had little say in strategy, and as
the relative strength of US arms grew in the last year of the war
in comparison to those of Britain it was the Americans who tended
to determine the thrust of future Allied operations. A real degree
of cooperation and trust, however, did evolve. Furthermore, the
strategic decisions reached, while sometimes complicated by political considerations, were grounded on the expertise of military
professionals – who were, by and large, left to get on with the job
once the green light had been given. Even Churchill, who sometimes sought to intervene at the operational as well as strategic
level, could usually be persuaded to heed professional objec-
tions. The result was that while mistakes were made, campaigns
were not characterised by the kind of confusion and illogicality
present at Hitler's headquarters.[12]

Achieving a similar level of cooperation and coordination
between the Allies and the Soviet Union proved a more elusive
goal, in spite of summit diplomacy and an ongoing exchange of
signals. Stalin's main concern was to see a second front opened
in Western Europe as soon as possible so as to draw off pressure
on the Red Army. The postponement of Allied cross-Channel
operations until 1944 did nothing to allay suspicions that the
western powers were unwilling to assume a proportionate share
in fighting the Wehrmacht. However, since the war in the East
was geographically distinct from the war in the West, it mattered little that joint strategy was in effect confined to rough
coordination of the timing of Allied and Red Army land offensives.
As far as strategic decision-making in Moscow went, as supreme
commander Stalin was at first loath to allow Soviet generals to
conduct operations without interference, and intervened – with
disastrous consequences – to prevent necessary withdrawals and
push overly ambitious offensives in the first year of the war. Unlike
Hitler, however, Stalin learned from his mistakes, promoting
commanders of proven ability such as Zhukov, allowing the

reorganisation of field command structures and paying attention to what an increasingly efficient general staff (*Stavka*) had
to say. It was this, in combination with the resource gap and
above all Hitler's interventions, which allowed the Red Army to
push the Wehrmacht back from the Volga to Berlin between
1943 and 1945.[13]

CONVENTIONAL OPERATIONS, 1942–5

In the spring and summer of 1942 the superior operational
skill of the Wehrmacht meant that it was still capable of achieving great victories, as at Gazala in Libya and Kharkov and the
opening phases of the advance to the Volga in Russia. By the
autumn and winter of 1942, however, the balance was starting to
shift in favour of the enemy. From then on it was Axis forces
that were on the defensive or retreating.

One problem, which would only get worse as time passed,
involved resource overstretch. Even as Germany geared up for
total war, there were simply not enough men or pieces of key
equipment to go round in comparison to what the enemy was
proving capable of deploying. On the Eastern Front it was only
possible to resume offensive operations in the south, and even
then reliance had to be placed on the weak armies of Axis
satellites to guard the line of advance. Meanwhile, in the Western Desert, the Afrika Korps received only a small proportion
of what was needed in the way of supplies and reinforcements
in order to carry on the offensive. At the same time, both the
Red Army and the Allied forces were growing in size and strength
and would soon have the numerical superiority necessary to
mount major offensives of their own.

Just as important was the restructuring and reorganisation that
was taking place in the Soviet, British and American forces –
changes designed to make them more effective in the field. In a
nutshell this meant acknowledging the centrality of the tank, supported by mobile artillery, infantry and air assets (including on
occasion paratroops) in either exploiting or foiling deep-thrust
breakthroughs. Armoured forces were expanded, efforts made to
integrate ground and air forces, and doctrine and command structures reorganised. The result was that, despite various setbacks

and false dawns, the armies that the Wehrmacht faced in the second half of the war were both better equipped and more capable than those of the first half and (given sufficient numerical superiority) able to prevail.[14]

Hence the battles of the last months of 1942 and early 1943 in which Axis forces were beaten and either surrounded or driven back, culminating in the surrender of what remained of the German forces in Stalingrad and the Allied capture of Tunis, the last Axis stronghold in North Africa. Though Hitler would insist on two more really big offensives, at Kursk in 1943 and in the Ardennes in 1944, the Wehrmacht would for the most part be confined to defensive and counteroffensive operations for the rest of the war. The difficulties encountered by the Red Army in its thrusts westward and by Allied armies moving forward in Sicily, Italy and then Normandy in the 1943–4 period indicated German formations could force their foes to pay a high price for ground gained, and proved adept at counterattacks and delaying actions. Their opponents, however, not only had more of everything – not least air cover – but could use it effectively (if not always very subtly).

Some of the operational lessons of the first years of war, to be sure, were not properly understood or misinterpreted. The Allies, for example, invested heavily in airborne forces after German glider and parachute troops seized key Belgian fortresses (1940) and the airfields on Crete (1941). The latter operation, however, due to the necessarily 'light' nature of the troops employed, unexpectedly strong enemy resistance and poorly conceived relief efforts, almost ended in failure – something that Hitler took to heart but which was ignored by Allied commanders in planning and carrying out the huge and ultimately unsuccessful Anglo–American drop in Holland in the autumn of 1944. Nevertheless, the Allies by necessity became adept at amphibious operations, a form of warfare that the Germans had never had the occasion to develop properly. There were setbacks, most notoriously the Dieppe Raid (1942), but through trial and error the Allies developed the specialised craft and coordinated handling of ground, sea and air forces necessary to land and establish a bridgehead on hostile soil: most impressively of all in the Normandy landings (1944).

France and much of the rest of Continental Europe had succumbed too quickly for her forces to begin to adapt to the

pace and style of German operations. However, fortuitous geographic circumstances – the sea barrier in the case of Britain
and the USA, sheer landmass in the case of Russia – allowed
time for Hitler's determined foes to digest the nature of German methods, learn from mistakes, mobilise resources and begin
to fight in more or less the same manner. Mistakes made in the
early encounters with the Wehrmacht also led, through a process of natural selection, to the rise of generals capable of
comprehending and adapting to the new style of war such as
Montgomery (UK), Patton (USA) and Zhukov (USSR).[16]

CONCLUSION

Having discussed the various forms of warfare that developed
between 1939 and 1945, it is important to recognise that they
were highly interdependent parts of an integrated whole, of a
total war effort (whether national or international in scope).[16]
The course and outcome of the war, however, confirmed the
importance of some approaches while calling into question others.

As far as land campaigns were concerned, German successes
in the first half of the war highlighted the central importance
of the integrated use of concentrated tank units accompanied
by mobile infantry and artillery, supported at the tactical and
operational level by bombing aircraft and, where appropriate,
parachute forces. In practice, limited space and difficult terrain,
along with in-depth defensive positions, meant that campaigns
could and did involve major battles of attrition in the latter
half of the war. The sought-after ideal, however, still achievable
once a front had been broken through, remained fast-paced
manoeuvring by mechanised forces aiming to exploit weaknesses,
turn flanks and where possible cut off avenues of retreat. (The
new consensus concerning the centrality of armour in modern
warfare was reflected in the effort not only to produce tanks in
large numbers but also to improve their ability to survive hits
and their effectiveness in knocking out their enemy counterparts.)

As much through necessity as design, amphibious landings,
hitherto ad hoc affairs, evolved under Allied control into highly
sophisticated operations involving a variety of specialised craft
able to land and maintain fighting forces equipped to establish

a secure bridgehead. Motorised vehicles of all kinds came to be seen as the vital organs of a modern army, though rail transport continued to be important logistically, and horses had continued to play a role on the Eastern Front where both adequate roads and motor transport were scarce.

The activities of underground forces, though arising through circumstance as much as design, had played a useful ancillary role in a number of campaigns. Partisan and guerrilla forces, along with SOE and a number of similar bodies, were wound up once the immediate need for them was past. The armed forces of the European powers and America, however, retained or soon resurrected at least some of the semi-clandestine commando-type groups that had arisen during the war, while the secret services remained very conscious of possible foreign-sponsored sabotage operations in any future conflict.

The strategic bombing of Germany during much of the war had been less successful and rather more costly than its advocates had promised, though there were some successes in the last stages. Questions concerning the efficacy of conventional long-range bombing were in any event rendered moot by the awesome destructive power of the atomic bomb, as demonstrated over Hiroshima and Nagasaki at the end of the war. The advent of nuclear weapons was to provide a powerful argument for the continued development of strategic air forces irrespective of what had, or had not, been achieved prior to this point.

In the liberal democracies – though not of course the USSR – the apparatus of mass psychological manipulation was dismantled after the war, its wartime efficacy open to debate. Governments nevertheless made contingency plans, while the armed forces continued to devote resources to exploring the mechanics of psychological operations. The services also took to propagandising on behalf of the peacetime services to a greater extent than before the war.

The war years had seen intelligence activities, especially those concerned with signals, come into their own. Signs of their ongoing importance were the efforts made to keep certain wartime operations as secret as possible after the war because of their possible utility in a future struggle as well as the development of new, or expansion of old, intelligence agencies.

In terms of the mobilisation and allocation of human and

Table 5.3   *Pre-war population and fatal war casualties (approximate)*

State	Population (millions)	Casualties (military)	Casualties (civilian)
Italy	43	0.4	0.1
France	41	0.25	0.35
United Kingdom	47	0.30	0.05
Germany	68	4.5	2.0
Soviet Union	167	10.0	10.0
United States	129	0.274	N/A

Source: Derived from I. C. B. Dear and M. R. D. Foot (eds), *The Oxford Companion to the Second World War* (Oxford, 1995), p. 290.

material resources in order to maximise war output while maintaining large and effective armed forces, the Second World War witnessed the development of a number of truly efficient and effective war economies on both sides. It was, in many ways, a triumph of logistics. On the one hand, the development of nuclear weapons and all they entailed in terms of a 'come as you are' future war suggested that wartime mobilisation on this scale would not occur again. On the other hand, conscription was maintained in countries that had relied on volunteers for their armed forces before the war, as was, albeit on a lesser scale, research and development in conventional weapons.

Lastly, the war had also provided valuable experience and insights for Allied statesmen and generals into the problems of integrating national war efforts and devising joint strategies. This would prove useful in the early years of NATO. The experience gained, however, had come at an extraordinarily heavy price. In all, somewhere in the order of thirty-six million Europeans had been killed in the conflict (see table 5.3), and economies had been stretched to or past the breaking point. The Second World War in Europe, decided to a considerable extent through the intervention of the great power across the Atlantic, marked the beginning of the end of European primacy in global affairs and the dawn of the new, bi-polar world.

6. Colonial Wars, 1815–1960

BRUCE VANDERVORT

INTRODUCTION

The purpose of this chapter is to provide an account of the wars fought by European armies outside Europe from the age of rapid imperial expansion (1815–1914) to the era of equally rapid imperial decline (1914–1960). In the halcyon days of empire building in the nineteenth century, these conflicts were often called 'small wars' by European military writers to distinguish them from wars waged by Europeans against each other. This label referred not only to the smaller numbers of soldiers engaged in colonial warfare, which was accurate enough, at least for the 1800s, but to a presumed gap in warmaking capacity between European armies and their less advanced foes whose perception owed as much to racialist ideology and a Eurocentric worldview as to rational assessment. In the course of the twentieth century the label lost much of its descriptive power, as colonial wars became increasingly broad in scope and, with the absorption by non-European peoples of nationalist ideology and modern military technology, began increasingly to resemble the 'total wars' waged among Europeans.

The geographical net cast by this chapter will be somewhat more inclusive than has been the case in other accounts of European colonial wars. It will cover not only the colonial campaigns of the two leading imperial powers, Britain and France, but also those of their lesser European rivals, Belgium, Germany, the Netherlands, Portugal, Russia and Spain. The term 'European' has also been inflated here to embrace the European–American armies of the New World, principally those of Argentina, Canada, Chile, Mexico and the USA.

The colonial wars shaped the military establishments of the European and European–American expansionist states far more than is generally conceded. Indeed, their colonial 'missions' obliged most of them to diversify their force structures and command and control processes, even their strategic and tactical thinking, to such an extent that it becomes difficult in retrospect to associate them with anything like an identifiable military model, including the supposed paradigm of the age: the German military machine that emerged from the wars of national unification in the 1860s and 1870s.

The narrative which follows falls into two parts. The first, covering the long nineteenth century, treats European campaigns to expand and defend imperial holdings in Africa, Asia and the Pacific islands, as well as the wars waged by European–American armies to round out their national domains in the latter half of the 1800s and by the USA to create an Asian and Latin American empire in the first decade of the twentieth century. The second part covers the wars fought by these same powers to stem the tide of national liberation which swept the non-European world and ultimately brought about the collapse of European empires in the twentieth century.

I: COLONIAL WARS, 1815–1914

Overview

The long nineteenth century was characterised by the growing superiority of European and European–American armies in colonial warfare and the rapid conquest by those armies of vast territories which were then incorporated into the European and US empires and into the national domains of Argentina, Canada, Chile, Mexico and the USA. The pace of European and European–American advance is generally described as being somewhat slower from 1815 to around 1870 than it would be later, although the evidence for this seems to be considerably stronger for some areas of the globe than it is for others. Africa offers perhaps the most dramatic example of 'retarded expansion'. As late as 1876, less than ten per cent of the continent was in European hands, most of which was accounted for by France's Algerian colony. Just three decades later, in the wake of the European 'scramble' to divide up Africa, only Ethiopia and Liberia remained free of imperial rule. The New World also offers clear demonstrations of late-blooming hegemony. Whereas conquest of the eastern

USA by European–American troops had taken over 200 years of bitter struggle, reaching a conclusion only in the 1840s, it took the 'blue soldiers' of the republic only some 25 years to subdue the Indian peoples of the West, from about 1865 to 1890. In South America, the Argentine and Chilean armies made little headway against Indian opponents in the first half of the century, but then vanquished them in the space of a few years; the Argentines, for example, crushing Indian resistance in a furious two-year campaign in 1878–9.

Historians have for some time tended to explain the quickening pace of imperial conquest after the mid-1800s by highlighting key Western scientific breakthroughs and the widening gap in military technology between the Europeans and European–Americans and their 'native' opponents. While more will be said later about the theme of 'technological determinism', it should be pointed out here that the record of European expansion in Asia during the long nineteenth century tends to call this rationale into question. Some of the most formidable indigenous armies in Asia were defeated before many of the vaunted triumphs in science and military technology came on stream. Britain rounded out its holdings in India, bringing the whole of the subcontinent under its sway – the Maratha dominions in the western part of the subcontinent (1818); Mysore (1831); Sind (1843); Kashmir (1848); the Punjab, in the wake of fierce fighting against the westernised armies of the Sikhs (1849); Burma (1852) – well before the 'breechloader revolution' or the advent of machine guns. This technologically barren era, of course, also saw Britain weather a fundamental challenge to its hegemony in India, in the Sepoy Mutiny of 1857, and impose a protectorate, albeit an uneasy and contested one, upon Afghanistan. It is also worth pointing out that the first ever defeat of Chinese armies by European forces occurred before much of the new military technology was available. This was the British triumph in the Opium Wars (1839–42), which led to the cession of Hong Kong in 1842.

The Russians, meanwhile, were adding to their empire and securing their southern frontier with Turkey by subduing the Muslim peoples of the Caucasus Mountains, principally the Chechens and Cherkesses (or Circassians), in three decades of fighting which culminated in the surrender of the great Chechen leader, Shamil, in 1859 and the defeat of the Cherkesses in 1864. In the same year, the Russians turned their attention toward the Muslim khanates of Central Asia, ostensibly to spread the gospel of Christianity and Western civilisation, but in reality to carry off the fabled treasures of Samarkand and Tashkent and to preempt presumed British designs on the region. A whirlwind campaign brought Russian control over the area by 1868.

Not all European conquests in Asia proceeded so expeditiously. It took the Dutch the better part of a century to secure at least nominal control over the whole of the great Indonesian archipelago, beginning with the hard-fought conquest of Java in 1825–30 and culminating with the conclusion of long, drawnout wars to 'pacify' the Sultanate of Aceh, the key to control of Sumatra, in 1912. France, meanwhile, had only managed to acquire a foothold in Cochin China by the 1860s; conquest of the rest of Indo-China – Annam, Tonkin, Cambodia and Laos – would come only in the 1880s and 1890s.

Further, in response to Kipling's invitation to take up 'the white man's burden', the USA made its entrance on the imperial stage at the very close of the nineteenth century by seizing Puerto Rico in the Caribbean, the Philippine Islands in East Asia and the Pacific island of Guam from Spain. Finally, in an absorption every bit as complete as that in Africa, almost all of the islands of the Pacific Ocean were swept into the imperial net by 1914. Most of them went to the traditional European imperial powers, namely Britain, France and Germany, but some fell under the rule of states that were themselves imperial dominions: Australia (Eastern New Guinea) and New Zealand (Cook Islands).

Conquest also proceeded apace north and south of the US border over the long nineteenth century. Transfer of sovereignty over the vast Canadian West from the Hudson's Bay Company to Ottawa was unsuccessfully resisted by Indian and mixed-blood peoples (*métis*) in 1885. As we have seen, Argentina and Chile brought their Indian wars to a conclusion in the 1870s and 1880s, the Argentines in the 'War of the Desert' of 1878–9 and the Chileans in an equally rapid campaign in 1882 below the Bio-Bio River in the southern third of the country. In Mexico victory over rebellious indigenous peoples proved to be much more elusive. Although the Mexican army managed to occupy the lands of the stubborn Yaqui peoples of the north-western state of Sonora over the course of the nineteenth century, victory was never complete and Yaqui resistance would surface once again, in muted form, in the 1930s. Mexican victory in the 'Caste Wars' of the mid-nineteenth century against the Mayan peoples of the Yucatan peninsula and the neighbouring state of Chiapas was even less decisive, as the Zapatista uprisings in Chiapas during the Mexican Revolution of 1910 and in the 1990s bear out.

Thin red line of heroes

The massive territorial acquisitions outlined above were made in spite of severe manpower problems in all of the European and European–American colonial armies. It should be recalled that imperial expansion took place against a backdrop of increasing tensions among the continental European powers, which precluded the deployment outside Europe of significant numbers of French, German, Italian or Russian troops. Even before assumption of continental European obligations in 1904, the British military was suffering from imperial overstretch. Fears of a Russian descent on India obliged Britain to station at least a third of her regular army in the subcontinent. The unprecedented manpower demands of the Second Boer War (1899–1902), added to those of India, left the British Isles virtually undefended at the turn of the twentieth century.

Similar problems arose in the New World. Domestic upheavals coupled with wars against neighbouring states made it impossible for Argentina, Chile and Mexico to resolve their 'Indian problems' until the second half of the nineteenth century. Significantly, it was only after a certain internal political stability and something like regional equilibrium had been effected after 1870 that the Indian wars in those areas could be brought to a close. In the USA, meanwhile, the war weariness which succeeded the War Between the States (1861–65) led to public demands for a sharply reduced military establishment, with the result that the US Army never had more than 25 000 soldiers to carry out its far-flung operations in the American West.

The 'white man's grave'

The chronic manpower shortages faced by European and European–American colonial armies were made worse by the vulnerability of their soldiers to the diseases and extremes of climate encountered in the areas where conquest took place. Early in the nineteenth century the susceptibility of European troops to tropical diseases such as malaria and yellow fever produced 'a death rate at least twice that of soldiers who stayed home, and possibly much higher'. In the years 1819–36, for example, British military deaths at the Sierra Leone station in West Africa, due almost exclusively to disease, averaged an astounding 483 per 1000.[1]

Beginning in the mid-1800s, medical advances such as the regular use of quinine to treat malaria, discovery of the causes of cholera, and stricter enforcement of hygiene regulations among troops began to reduce the health risks to European soldiers in the tropics. That progress in tropical medicine came slowly and had more impact on soldiers in barracks than in the field, however, was clearly shown by the fate which befell a French expeditionary force in Madagascar in the last years of the nineteenth century. In a ten-month campaign in 1895 to conquer the island, French troops lost some 6000 dead to disease, primarily malaria, and only 20 dead to enemy fire. 'The number of French deaths in those ten months', writes one authority, 'was probably greater than their losses in the conquest of all the territory that was to become French West and Equatorial Africa.'[2]

With European troops still vulnerable to hecatombs such as this, it should come as no surprise that the general public in Europe continued to view the tropics as 'the white man's grave', or that politicians in countries with conscription, such as France and Germany, were reluctant to relax bans against deploying conscripts to tropical regions. Advances in tropical medicine also failed to convince European colonial officers that they could now safely increase the number of European troops under their command. The French commander in West Africa in the 1880s, Colonel Joseph-Simon Galliéni, put the matter in characteristically blunt fashion: 'It would be a good idea', he wrote, 'to get rid of most of the European troops in the [Western] Sudan, who encumber our ambulances and die like flies, and replace them with indigenous troops.'[3]

Also worrisome were the difficulties posed for European troops by the hot and humid climate of tropical areas. Even though by the close of the nineteenth century most European troops in the tropics had been issued with solar helmets and lighter, looser fitting uniforms, they still functioned poorly. In 1901, Captain J. S. Herron of the US Second Cavalry reported to his superiors on the lengths British colonial officers were obliged to go to keep European troops in the field in the tropics. The British employed a system, he wrote, that kept

> the [British] soldier a fighting man and, for all labor which is fatiguing, unhealthy or repugnant, employing natives paid by the state. In the field the British troops are accompanied by numerous drivers, packers, laborers, etc . . . it often happens that noncombatants are more numerous than combatants.[4]

Debilitating medical problems were not confined, however, to colonial armies operating in the tropics. Even on the relatively temperate High Plains of the American West in the 1870s, disease and climate were more formidable foes than enemy fire. 'Wounds were not a major threat to soldiers serving in the West', writes one source, 'but long grueling marches in extreme temperatures as well as severe food and water shortages could have devastating effects on their health. Disease, especially typhoid, malaria, and scurvy, was a great and often victorious enemy.'[5] Argentinian troops paid a heavy price for their victories over the pampas Indians. During long forced marches in pursuit of the foe, 'soldiers were reduced in some cases to drinking horse urine or to placing pieces of metal in their mouths in hopes of inducing salivation. The men ate roots and horsemeat – the latter relished by Indians but abhorrent to *cristianos*.'[6]

Specialised armies

Some continental European armies tried to overcome their manpower problems by creating specialised volunteer units for service in colonial campaigns. It was understood that, for the most part, these units would be based in colonial areas and would be structured, trained and armed for the unconventional warfare they would be obliged to wage in such places. It was believed that forces of this kind could compensate through their fire-power, but also and perhaps especially, through their élan and special skills, for what they lacked in numbers. Britain remained the only European imperial power that relied exclusively upon its regular army for colonial service. The British expeditionary forces that fought in the Ashanti, Mahdist and Boer Wars in Africa and who provided the European contingent of the Indian Army were drawn from Britain's volunteer regular army.

The Indian-fighting armies in the New World often found that budgetary and other restraints forced them to use a mix of militia and regulars on campaign. The Mexican National Guard campaigned alongside regular army conscripts in the wars against the Yaquis and Maya. The Argentine and Chilean armies that defeated the Araucanian and other Indian tribes in the late nineteenth century fielded a mix of regulars and militia, as did the Canadian force which defeated the Indians and métis on the Saskatchewan prairies in 1885. The US Army fought in tandem with National Guard and militia units in the Indian wars, the Spanish–American War, and the Philippine Insurrection, but always with some misgivings, since it viewed the non-regulars as undisciplined and poor fighters.

The European and European–American colonial armies were usually volunteer formations. Italy, Mexico and Russia (after 1871), however, did employ conscripts in their colonial wars, not always with good results. Although France and Germany fielded huge conscript armies in the closing decades of the nineteenth century, very few of these conscripts saw service in the colonies. French law, for example, forbade deployment of conscripts outside Europe except in carefully defined national emergencies. Only conscripts who volunteered to do so could be stationed in the colonies and these were few and far between. An exception was the all-European *Schutztruppe* contingent in German South West Africa, mounted infantry composed entirely of volunteers from the Imperial Army.

France and Italy created special military formations for colonial service. The French formed a Foreign Legion composed of foreign other ranks and officered by Frenchmen, for use as colonial light infantry. Founded in 1831 and based at Sidi-Bel-

Abbès in Algeria, the Legion received its baptism of fire in North Africa but also fought in sub-Saharan Africa (Dahomey) and in Indo-China. France also created special volunteer armies for service in North Africa (*l'Armée d'Afrique*) and in the tropics (*l'Armée Coloniale*). Italy's *Corpo Speciale* was the only European colonial army composed entirely of conscripts. It was structured differently from the French colonial armies, however, maintaining only a small cadre of officers and noncoms at its Naples base and drafting in units from the Italian regular army for colonial service when needed.

Triumphant technology?

European and European–American colonial armies also sought to compensate for their manpower shortages by taking advantage of their technological superiority, particularly with respect to firepower.

Until the middle of the nineteenth century, the technological gap between European and European–American armies and their colonial adversaries was not very large. Military weaponry had advanced little since the Napoleonic era: smoothbore muzzleloaders continued to serve as a standard shoulder arm in all armies using gunpowder weapons; field artillery, still largely smoothbore and muzzleloading as well, was, despite some improvements, still too cumbersome for efficient use in the rain forests and mountains of the colonial world. Nor had naval technology progressed much beyond the days of Nelson. Though the steamship had been a known quantity for some time, navies were slow to abandon the sailing ship in its favour; smoothbore muzzleloading cannon remained standard armament on warships.

Until the telegraph came into general use in the mid-1850s, communications between commanders and troops on campaign largely depended on the rapidity of couriers or, where practicable, the semaphore developed by Napoleon's armies. Capitals relied on fair winds and calm seas to speed their instructions to armies abroad, much to the satisfaction of commanders in the field.

Logistics would remain the Achilles heel of European and European–American armies engaged in colonial warfare down to the liquidation of the European empires in the twentieth

century. The reluctance of the Indian Army to garrison
Afghanistan was due as much to daunting logistical difficulties
as to the fierceness of the hill tribes or Russian pretensions in
the region. Reliance on long, slow-moving supply trains severely
hampered the operations of cavalry and mounted infantry against
more mobile Indian foes on the US Great Plains and the
Argentine pampas. European operations in Africa in the
nineteenth century (and after) were tied to long columns of
porters, whose deaths in large numbers from overwork and
malnourishment were one of the great scandals of the epoch of
imperial conquest.

Where possible, European commanders tried to curb reliance
on supply trains by adopting the venerable Napoleonic expedi-
ent of living off the land. This was the method employed by the
French commander in Algeria in the 1840s, General Thomas-
Robert Bugeaud, to restore mobility to his armies, with the added
benefit that it laid waste to the Algerian countryside and forced
a now destitute Arab and Berber peasantry to seek terms. 'Père'
Bugeaud's stratagem was not widely applicable, however. Low
agricultural productivity in most parts of the colonial world meant
that pickings were often slim for European troops in search of
sustenance. Moreover, raiding for rations also threatened to
further alienate already hostile rural populations.

The rough technological parity between European and
European–American armies and their adversaries that
characterised colonial warfare in the early nineteenth century
began to undergo a profound change in the 1850s and 1860s.
A 'military revolution' can be said to have occurred at this point,
featuring, among other things, the submarine telegraph; steam-
powered iron vessels; breechloading, rapid-firing shoulder arms
and artillery; and, ultimately, the machine gun. Employment of
this technology, it is claimed, made possible the rapid conquest
of those areas of Africa, the Americas, Asia and the Pacific region
gobbled up by the expansionist states by 1914.

Weapons technology was transformed by the 'breechloader
revolution' of the 1860s. This change, together with the rifling
of gun barrels, significantly improved the performance of both
shoulder arms and land and naval artillery. By allowing soldiers
to inject rounds one after the other into the chambers of their
rifles rather than laboriously reload powder and ball at the muzzle

end after each shot, breechloading greatly increased the infantry's rate of fire. The next step in the 'revolution' occurred in the 1880s, with the introduction of rifles with magazines, which automatically fed multiple rounds into the breech. At the same time, breechloading artillery, firing explosive shells rather than shot through rifled barrels, greatly enhanced the destructiveness of the big guns on both land and sea.

What needs to be borne in mind, however, is that these and other technological changes, important though they might have been, did not bestow anything like instant superiority upon European and European–American armies. To begin with, there was a considerable lag between the availability of the new technologies and their actual appearance on colonial battlefields. Also, even when the new technologies were present on the battlefield, success was never guaranteed, as the British disasters at Isandlwana and Hlobane during the Anglo–Zulu War and the Italian débacle at Adowa in 1896 clearly demonstrate.

The weapons that would go on to dominate the battlefield in the First World War seldom had a decisive impact during the colonial wars. To take but one example, the machine gun won very few victories for European and European–American troops against indigenous peoples. French conquest of the Western Sudan and Indochina was accomplished with almost no use of automatic weapons. And, even though the British were quick to employ machine guns in their colonial wars, they rarely proved to be decisive in British victories. Let us take for instance the battle of Omdurman in the Sudan in 1898. While machine guns certainly played a role in the first phase of the battle, the one immortalised in the film 'Four Feathers', in the decisive second phase of the battle, passed over in the film, no machine guns were present. Victory here was assured instead by a determined stand by General Horatio Herbert Kitchener's Sudanese and Egyptian troops, equipped to a man with black powder, single-shot Martini-Henry rifles, first issued to British soldiers in 1871.

The instrument of Kitchener's deliverance provides a clue to a more reliable explanation of European success in the colonial wars than the thesis of triumphant technology: the ability to compensate for serious shortages of European troops for colonial service by recruiting large armies of indigenous soldiers.

Martial races

The conquest of vast territories around the globe by European and European–American nations depended to a very great extent on the ability of the invaders to 'divide and conquer' the indigenous peoples they encountered. Their success in doing so enabled them to recruit large colonial armies to conquer and then to guard their imperial domains. David Killingray exaggerates only slightly when he contends that

> European empires in Africa were gained principally by African mercenary armies, occasionally supported by white or other colonial troops. In what Kipling described as 'savage wars of peace' the bulk of the fighting was done by black soldiers whose disciplined firepower and organisation invariably defeated numerically superior African armies.[7]

What Killingray says about Africa applies to Asia and, to a somewhat lesser extent, the New World as well. Britain's reliance upon indigenous soldiers in the conquest and safeguarding of its Indian possessions is too well known to require comment here. The Dutch conquest of Indonesia could not have been completed without the support of large numbers of Moluccan and Ambonese auxiliaries. Although the French tended to dismiss the Indo–Chinese peoples as too passive to be good fighters, they nonetheless enrolled large numbers of them in their assault columns in the fighting for Tonkin in the 1880s and 1890s. The Russians, finally, made extensive use of irregulars in their Caucasus and Central Asian campaigns. Although they employed Christian and dissident Muslim auxiliaries to good effect in the Caucasus, their most helpful allies were the fierce Cossack cavalry who accompanied Russian armies and often provided a permanent garrison for conquered areas by displacing the enemy population as settlers.

Whereas the European powers raised whole units of indigenous infantry and cavalry in Africa and Asia, European–American states tended to restrict Indian recruits to scouting duties. The US Army liked to recruit its scouts among the hereditary enemies of tribes it was fighting; in the campaigns against the Sioux and Cheyenne, for instance, cavalry officers signed on scouts from the Crow and Pawnee tribes, which had been battling the former for decades over hunting grounds. The Mexican army followed the same practice, for example recruiting Tarahumara scouts for service against their longtime Apache foes. Only in Argentina does the army seem to have recruited sizeable numbers of Indians as irregular cavalry.

While all of the expansionist powers had large populations from which to draw indigenous soldiers, in almost no cases did they simply recruit as they would have done at home, from the populace at large. Instead they fastened their attention on certain selected elements of the population, the so-called 'martial races', from which they proceeded to draw the bulk of their indigenous troops. Thus, Britain's Indian Army recruited heavily among the 'warlike' Punjabis, but tried to avoid taking in 'effeminate' Bengalis or 'lazy' Madrassis. Thus, Britain's Royal West African Frontier Force in Nigeria eagerly sought recruits among the 'feudal' Hausas of the North but shunned the 'bourgeois' Ibos of the South.

The French, too, exhibited a hankering after 'martial races'. In West Africa, they found the bulk of their *Tirailleurs Sénégalais* (Senegalese Light Infantry) among the Bambara people of present-day Mali: 'stocky, powerfully-muscled' and a warrior breed, but also possessed of a 'limitless confidence in his European superiors', and, equally important, much less expensive than their European counterparts. In 1900, Colonel Albert Ditte estimated, it cost Fr. 2127–2540 a year to maintain a French marine infantryman in West Africa, but only Fr. 980.35 to keep a Bambara *tirailleur*.[8]

The recruitment of large indigenous armies was crucial to the creation and maintenance of the vast European empires forged in the long nineteenth century (somewhat less so to the rounding out of the national domains of the expansionist states of the New World). Taking Africa as an example, some of the European powers engaged in the 'scramble' for African territory would have been hard pressed to stay the course without 'native' soldiers. Germany, whose troop requirements at home grew sharply from the 1890s on, employed a larger percentage of African soldiers in its colonial forces than any other European power. In 1912, just 226 European military personnel were serving in Germany's African colonies outside South West Africa, alongside 2664 African troops. Portugal, the poorest of the colonial powers, had no choice but to field largely African armies in its *fin-de-siècle* campaigns in Angola, Guinea-Bissau and Mozambique. Finally, King Leopold II of Belgium was almost entirely reliant upon African levies to control his vast Congo domain. In 1900, his 6000-man *Force Publique* numbered only some 200 European officers and an undisclosed number of European NCOs.

An imperial balance sheet

By 1914, European and European–American expansionist powers had added vast new territories to their domains at a relatively minimal cost in blood and treasure. They had triumphed over a bewildering array of unconventional opponents in dozens of 'small wars' across the globe, not so much because of superior technology or greater martial prowess, but rather because of better command and control and superior discipline and, especially, because of their ability to turn indigenous peoples against each other and, in the process, recruit the large indigenous armies that did most of the fighting in the colonial wars. They had also been helped, it should not be forgotten, by their opponents' misguided tendency to engage them in set-piece battles, a mistake that would not often be repeated in the new century.

These wars exercised a profound influence upon the military establishments of all the expansionist states. Sometimes the impact was direct and physical, dividing the armed forces into distinct metropolitan and colonial elements, with different missions, force structures, weaponry, even doctrine. This dichotomy became most pronounced in the French army, with its huge metropolitan conscript force arrayed against the Germans and its two heavily indigenous colonial contingents permanently based in North Africa and the tropics. But other armies were similarly divided: the British between the home army stationed in the British Isles and the Indian Army with its numerous sepoy regiments; the Russian between the Army of the Caucasus with its Cossacks and Turkmen and the line regiments which garrisoned Russian Poland and the borderlands with the Turks; the US, with its small-unit-oriented, Indian-fighting army in the West and an 'Eastern establishment' lusting after a European-style conventional army.

But the impact of the colonial wars was as much psychological as physical. Just as the Indian Army was two-thirds sepoy in make-up and long on lancers and short on artillery, so it possessed an ethos of battle that distinguished it sharply from the regiments of the home army. The Zouaves and Turcos of France's *Armée d'Afrique* had their own exotic vocabulary and shared with the marines and black *tirailleurs* of the *Armée coloniale* a healthy contempt for the parade-ground soldiers of the French metropolitan army.

In the USA, the spotty performance of the Army in the Spanish–American War (1898–9) opened the way for creation of the European-type professional army sought by the officers of the East Coast establishment. Still, the vicious counterinsurgency warfare waged by Army units in the suppression of the Philippine Insurrection (1899–1902) and the conversion of the US Marine Corps into a light infantry expeditionary force for use in the Caribbean and Central America kept alive the ethos of colonial warfare long after the US Army had donned its Prussian colours.

Colonial combat left its mark on all European and European–American armies, including those of the metropole. Long years of isolation and enforced self-reliance bred a spirit of independence, even insubordination, in the colonial officer corps of many nations that percolated through the military establishment as a whole and in time would pose a serious challenge to civilian control of the military. Other ranks long abroad often felt alienated from their homelands or 'went native', as in Kipling's expressive poem, 'Mandalay'. In more strictly operational terms, the wars on the world's frontiers gave the mounted arm a new lease on life and made the light infantry a privileged mobile striking force. The cult of the offensive and the belief in cold steel as the deciding factor in battle were heavily reinforced as a result of the colonial experience. So was the belief that Western hegemony in global terms depended on the ability to smash the enemy in decisive battle to, in Kitchener's terms, give him 'a good dusting'. These attitudes would inform the *mentalités* of most of the armies that marched off to war in 1914.

The view ahead

Despite their rapid and widespread conquests, however, there were omens of a more troubled future for the imperial powers in some of the colonial wars of the 1815–1914 period. Most disturbing at the time were the defeats sustained by elite formations of the European and European–American colonial armies. In 1876, units of the proud US Seventh Cavalry, led by the Civil War hero General George Armstrong Custer, were annihilated at the battle of the Little Big Horn in Montana by a combined Sioux, Cheyenne and Arapaho Indian force. A troubling aspect of the 'Custer massacre' was that the cavalrymen were not only outnumbered but outgunned by their Indian foes. It was the British army, however, which suffered the most dramatic setbacks. Just three years after the Little Big Horn disaster, a Zulu *impi* decimated elements of the veteran 24th Regiment of Foot at Isandlwana in South Africa. A year later came the massacre of the Queen's 66th Regiment at Maiwand in Afghanistan, followed in February 1881 by a Boer rout at Majuba Hill in the Transvaal of a British force which included the superb Gordon Highlanders. Perhaps more than anything else, these setbacks underlined the consequences of underestimating one's enemy. That this lesson was not properly absorbed was made abundantly clear during the 'Black Week' that opened the Second Boer War (1899–1902), when a British army touted as the finest ever to leave England sustained a series of shocking defeats in pitched battle. Most unsettling in the long term, however, was emerging evidence that European armies faced serious difficulties in coping with guerrilla warfare. This clearly was the case in the second phase of the Second Boer War, when British commanders were obliged to have recourse to a scorched earth strategy and concentration camps to defeat Boer guerrillas. French colonial troops experienced difficulties with guerrillas in some of their West African campaigns, but most notably in Tonkin in the 1890s and in Morocco on the eve of the First World War. Moreover, the mighty German army had so much trouble overcoming Herero and Nama guerrillas in South West Africa in 1904–07 that Berlin briefly considered creating a specialised army for colonial warfare.[9] The Italians, who had formed such a force, still required three decades to subdue guerrillas in the Libyan desert.

II: COLONIAL WARS, 1914–1960

Overview

The colonial wars of the twentieth century were characterised by the initially gradual but then increasingly rapid decline of European and European–American military superiority over 'Third World' opponents, resulting in the eventual collapse of European empires throughout the world and (although it lies outside the scope of this chapter) the defeat of the exemplar of 'the Western way of war', the USA, by the peasant armies of Vietnam. The ebbing fortunes of the Western powers stemmed largely from two factors: the rising tide of nationalist fervour among the colonised peoples, often combined with some form of socialist ideology which enabled the insurgents to mobilise the peasant masses; and the acquisition by nationalist rebels of modern military technology.

Contrary to their general experience during the nineteenth century, European and European–American armies found themselves increasingly confronted by colonial insurgents who eschewed pitched battle in favour of guerrilla warfare. Western armies found this type of insurgency difficult to cope with and were only rarely successful in containing it. Largely ad hoc at first, the practice of guerrilla warfare in the Third World was codified in the 1940s by Mao Zedong in China and applied with local variations by such practitioners as Cuba's Ché Guevara and General Vo Nguyen Giap of Vietnam. The only colonial power that tried to formulate a counter-revolutionary doctrine specifically designed to cope with Maoist guerrilla war was France, in the wake of its defeat in Indochina in 1954. That this counter strategy came too late was demonstrated by France's loss of Algeria in 1962.

The shape of colonial warfare in the twentieth century was accurately forecast in the Rif War in northern Morocco in 1921–5. The conflict pitted a coalition of Moroccan tribes, heretofore rivals but now bound together by a newfound nationalism, against the armed forces of both France and Spain. The war began with one of the most crushing defeats ever administered to a European army by a colonial people: the July 1921 massacre of Annual, in the Spanish Moroccan enclave, which took the lives of 12 000

of 20 000 Spanish soldiers and brought down the government
in Madrid. The Rif insurgents, who came away from the battle
with nearly 400 automatic weapons and some 200 artillery pieces,
managed to fend off the combined armies of France and Spain
for the next four years.[10]

The Rif War signaled the onset of a series of colonial wars in
which increasingly numerous, increasingly well-armed nationalist insurgents took the field against European armies. However,
the only such conflict of that magnitude over the remaining
years of the inter-war period was the great anomaly of the genre,
the Italian conquest of Ethiopia in 1935–6. This was the only
sizeable colonial war of the epoch in which the indigenous forces
allowed themselves to be drawn into set-piece battles. This played
into the hands of the Fascist invaders, who were able to use
armour and aircraft (and poison gas) to good effect against the
lightly-armed Ethiopians.

The great explosion came in the aftermath of the Second
World War, from which the imperial powers emerged gravely
weakened, none more so than France, which almost immediately was forced to contend with risings across her empire, from
North Africa to Indo-China. The most serious of these conflicts
was, of course, the Indo-China War of 1946–54, in which a French
expeditionary force comprised of the cream of the country's
colonial armies, heavily supported by the USA, went down to
defeat at the hands of a Vietminh army led by the redoubtable
General Giap. Giap's great victory over the French at Dienbienphu
in May 1954 was one of the decisive battles of the twentieth
century. The French defeat underscores the point we have made
that manpower shortages constituted the prime weakness of the
European colonial armies during this period. Although the
French expeditionary force fought bravely and often skilfully,
its defeat was only a matter of time so long as the French government, wary of adverse public opinion, refused to send
conscripts to Indo-China.

Although manpower shortages rendered French defeat inevitable in Indo-China, some leading figures in the French army
preferred to believe that the expeditionary force had been vic-
tims of the Maoist strategy of revolutionary warfare, crafted during
the Chinese civil war of the 1930s and 1940s, and implemented
in Indo-China by the Vietminh. Veterans of Indo-China now

fashioned what they believed was an effective strategy of counter-revolutionary war and applied it in the next major round of French colonial warfare, in Algeria from 1954 to 1962. The strategists of counter-revolution believed that classic Maoist revolutionary warfare unfolded in five stages, moving from grass-roots agitation and propaganda through phases of gradually intensified popular mobilisation to a final full-scale offensive. They believed that revolutionary insurgency of this sort could be defeated by a counter-strategy which combined pre-emptive security force strikes and assassination of rebel leaders with a concerted campaign of 'psywar' and good works to conquer the hearts and minds of the indigenous population. Whatever can be said about the accuracy of the French analysis of Maoist revolutionary warfare strategy or the suitability of the French riposte to it, it must be conceded that the application of counter-revolutionary methods in Algeria, particularly during the 'Battle of Algiers' in 1957, met with success. Indeed, French forces clearly won the military battle of Algeria, having largely destroyed the rebel Army of National Liberation by 1958. What defeated the paras and legionaries of the French army in Algeria was support for an independent Algeria in international public opinion and the refusal of the French public to countenance the use of torture by French troops in implementing their counter-revolutionary strategy. A 1958 revolt of colonial army units, the perhaps unavoidable result of the traditional separation and alienation of the colonial forces from the rest of the French army, failed to win support from the large number of conscripts serving in Algeria. Its suppression and the accession to power of Charles de Gaulle, who believed that the liquidation of France's colonial empire was inevitable, sealed the fate of the French effort to retain its Algerian colony.

Britain fared somewhat better in facing up to her post-1945 imperial challenges. Though obliged to grant independence to India and to cut her losses in Palestine and Egypt, the British managed to achieve one of the more celebrated counter-insurgency triumphs in the Malayan Emergency of 1948-58. The British forces profited from a combination of skilful counter-guerrilla tactics and the fact that a large portion of the enemy force were ethnic Chinese, who were generally at odds with the Malay majority of the colony. Victory in Malaya was repeated in the Indonesian Confrontation of 1962–6, in which British troops, again with strong support from the indigenous population, managed to repel an Indonesian attempt to take over Borneo.

The Dutch had not been so lucky. Although even weaker in 1945 than the French, the Netherlands nonetheless managed to form an expeditionary force of Dutch soldiers and marines and, supported by its traditional indigenous allies, managed to regain control of most of the East Indies archipelago from nationalist rebels by 1948. A year later, however, the Netherlands was forced to bow to international pressure, led by the USA, to grant independence to Indonesia.

By 1960, less because of military defeat on the ground, major defeats such as Dienbienphu notwithstanding, than defeat before the court of domestic and world opinion, the European powers were obliged to grant independence to most of the colonies they had secured in the nineteenth century.

Western counterinsurgency

Militarily, imperial powers had found themselves especially hard-pressed to counter the advantages gained by colonial insurgents in their shift away from fighting pitched battles toward guerrilla warfare. The main problem for Western armies was the new manpower requirements. It was generally recognised that a 10-to-1 advantage in manpower was necessary to prevail against guerrillas. This was for the most part an impossible ratio for Western powers to achieve, given competing manpower needs and the general unpopularity of colonial-style wars among the public. One method which Western imperial armies employed to overcome this hurdle was to substitute firepower for manpower. Another was to try to achieve much greater battlefield mobility by using aircraft and motorised vehicles to transport troops and equipment. A related response was the creation of elite military units, which would possess both greater mobility than the enemy and the skills to fight him on his own terms. Finally, there were some counter-guerrilla strategists who believed that only a 'hearts-and-minds' approach, which aimed at weaning the peasant masses away from the insurgents by promoting better health care, education and perhaps even land reform, could produce final victory.

New weaponry

The imperial powers emerged from the First World War with an impressive array of new weapons. Most of them, however, proved to be of limited use in colonial warfare. The tank, for example, may have restored mobility to the European battlefield, but it was next to useless in the largely off-road venues of modern colonial-style warfare, such as the rain forests and rice paddies of Indo-China. Although British Colonial Secretary Winston Churchill strongly urged its use on the North-West Frontier of India in the 1920s, poison gas was only employed in colonial warfare by fascist Italy, in Ethiopia in 1935. Other weapons spawned by the trench warfare of 1914–18, such as flamethrowers and trench mortars, proved equally inappropriate for the expansion or maintenance of empire.

Nonetheless, the enormous increase in the overall firepower of Western armies as a result of the First World War had a significant impact on both the theory and practice of 'small wars' over the rest of the twentieth century. The predominance of automatic and semi-automatic weapons in European infantry warfare, and the emergence of heavy artillery as the 'King of Battles', encouraged both armchair strategists at home and officers in the field to see massive firepower as the solution to problems posed by the growing recourse of colonial peoples to guerrilla warfare. Of greatest importance, superior firepower would presumably enable Western armies to dispense with achieving the 10-to-1 manpower advantage considered necessary to defeat guerrillas.

The Second World War expanded the range of weaponry available to colonial armies, but, again, much of it proved to be of little use in combating guerrillas. Aircraft carriers, long-range, multi-engine bombers and nuclear bombs were patently irrelevant to the 'small wars' of the Third World. Other new weaponry, particularly amphibious landing craft, napalm, guided missiles and helicopters would be more useful. Also, the 1939–45 war heightened the belief among Western soldiers and statesmen in the ability of ever more devastating firepower to bring victory quickly and cheaply in terms of blood and treasure, always desirable qualities politically. These notions turned out to be largely illusory.

Battlefield mobility

While the new motorised vehicles often made little difference to colonial warfare, another weapon of First World War provenance, the military aircraft, did prove to be an important addition to the arsenal of the colonial powers. The Italians were first to use the aeroplane in colonial warfare, in Libya in 1912. In the interwar period, an economy-minded British government promoted the idea of imperial policing by aircraft, a notion strongly supported, of course, by the infant Royal Air Force, eager to find a mission to justify its existence in an era of cutbacks in military spending. RAF planes were most widely used for imperial policing in Iraq and on the Indian North-West Frontier, where they dropped leaflets to encourage loyalty and dropped bombs to punish disloyalty. These operations were most extensive in restive Iraq, where up to one-third of the RAF's aircraft were stationed during the interwar period.

The success of imperial policing by air was, however, much exaggerated. Once insurgents got used to the idea of punishment raining down on them from the sky, they took appropriate counter measures. Air operations were also much easier to mount over the plains and deserts of Iraq than over the mountains of the North-West Frontier. Later, the limitations of aircraft in colonial-type warfare would become even more apparent in the jungle fighting of Southeast Asia after 1945. Pilots' inability to locate targets amid heavy cloud cover and dense foliage led to the adoption of such counterproductive strategies as saturation bombing, which killed many civilians and propelled survivors into the arms of the enemy, and the use of toxic defoliants, which proved injurious to the health not only of local peasants but of 'friendly' soldiers as well.

Helicopters, however, first used in quelling the Malayan Insurgency in the 1950s, not only greatly enhanced battlefield mobility but also proved useful for evacuating sick and wounded troops. The machines were extensively used by the French in Algeria to ferry troops and supplies as well as weapons platforms for ground support. The US military would, of course, make the helicopter the workhorse of its airmobile divisions in Vietnam.

Special forces

Western governments did not, however, place all their eggs in the superior firepower basket. Most, particularly in the post-1945 era, began developing military units which were specially trained for counterinsurgency warfare. The British Royal Marines were largely converted into commandos during the 1939–45 war and continued to practise their new craft in the colonial wars of the postwar era, as in Malaya in 1948–58. The Special Air Service (SAS) was an even more highly-specialised Second World War creation that went on to play a role in colonial warfare, as a counter-terrorist force and practitioner of a 'hearts-and-minds' strategy to deny guerrillas popular support; their most successful effort took place during the 1962–6 Indonesian Confrontation in North Borneo.

France probably placed more reliance on specialist military formations than any other imperial power. To enhance mobility in counter-guerrilla operations, important elements of both her marine corps (*l'Armée Coloniale*) and Foreign Legion were transformed into parachute troops. The French also pioneered in setting up special naval forces for riverine operations in colonial wars, the so-called *Dinassault* units employed during the 1945–54 Indo-China war. They also were among the first to create deep-penetration units for jungle operations; these *Groupements Mixte d'Intervention* operated deep in the Vietnamese rain forests in the 1950s, often in close collaboration with dissident 'aboriginal' hill peoples such as the Montagnards or Meos.

'Hearts and minds'

Although they never received much in the way of a mandate from either politicians or generals, the advocates of 'soft' approaches to counterinsurgency did undertake some significant initiatives in the post-Second World War period. Scathingly derided by Graham Greene in *The Quiet American*, Edward G. Lansdale nonetheless did use psychological warfare and promises of reform to good effect in putting down the Hukbalahap insurgency in the Philippines in the 1950s. He was less successful in Vietnam a decade later. Britain's SAS contributed significantly to the success of counterinsurgency efforts in Borneo during the Indonesian Confrontation of 1962–6 by purveying propaganda and providing health care and technical assistance to the indigenous population. The French mounted major 'hearts and minds' strategies in the course of both the Indochina and Algerian wars. Although the efforts of the French SAS (Special Administrative Section) teams in Algeria, who resided in peasant villages and provided medical and technical assistance, showed some promise, they, like similar undertakings in Indochina, proved to be too little and too late.

Conclusion

It is worth pointing out, however, that the major factor in the French defeat in Algeria was not the failure of the SAS or the military superiority of the rebel Army of National Liberation, but the ultimate refusal of French public opinion to countenance the kind of 'dirty war', including the use of torture, the military seemed to think was necessary to secure victory. Not only the Algerian rebellion but colonial upheavals in general benefited from the declining moral authority, both at home and abroad, of the colonial powers. Whereas imperial conquest in the previous century had generally been greeted with more praise than scorn by the European public, particularly in the era of the 'New Imperialism' in the 1890s, support for empire eroded rapidly over the first half of the twentieth century, particularly in Britain. Among colonial peoples themselves the aura of Western military superiority had faded significantly amid the spectacle of mass and often senseless slaughter in two world wars.

Finally, European imperial rule suffered from a breakdown in the solidarity among Western nations that had served as a bulwark during the era of conquest in the nineteenth century. The Soviet Union created on the ruins of the Tsarist regime in Russia transformed a largely verbal support for Third World liberation in the 1920s and 1930s into large-scale material assistance to independence movements during the Cold War. The USA, although it had imperial holdings of its own, adopted a stance critical of European imperialism during the Second World War; while this position was gradually abandoned during the Cold War, it persisted long enough to add significantly to the pressure both on Britain to leave India and on the Netherlands to

give up Indonesia. Cold War rivalries enabled Third World liberation movements to play off the antagonists against each other
politically and gain massive material assistance, including modern weapons, in the process.

Finally, it is important not to underestimate the role of *will* in
the triumph of national liberation movements. We have already
noted how public opinion in many Western nations had lost
faith in empire or at least in the hard sacrifices required to
preserve it. The faith born of nationalism among the former
colonial peoples, on the other hand, supplied them with the
strength to persevere in the face of awesome applications of
Western armed might. This faith was reflected in Ho Chi Minh's
prophetic warning to French envoys in 1946: 'You can kill ten
of my men for every one I kill of yours. But even at those odds,
you will lose and I will win.'[11]

7. Naval Power and Warfare

LAWRENCE SONDHAUS

In the decades after the Napoleonic Wars, European navies took the lead in the transition from sail to steam propulsion (1815–60) and in the ensuing introduction of armour and the emergence of modern warship types (1860–90). Thereafter, the turn-of-the-century era of the battleship (1890–1922) overlapped at its close with the emergence of the submarine and aircraft carrier (1914–45), the latter era witnessing the relative decline of European navies with the emergence of the United States as the world's leading naval power. During the Cold War (1945–91) the British and other western European navies reduced the size of their fleets while the Soviet Union built Europe's largest naval force, of a size second only to that of the United States. The close of the twentieth century found the post-Communist Russian navy still Europe's largest but in a state of rapid decline, while the future of European navies in general remained uncertain.

FROM SAIL TO STEAM, 1815–60

During the years 1815–30 the wooden sailing ship still ruled the waves, but most navies acquired their first steamships and some visionaries prophesied a day in which the capital ships of a fleet would move by steam. The development of the first shell guns likewise led some to question the future viability of wooden warships, yet the wooden ship of the line remained the heart of the European battle fleet through the 1850s, its life extended briefly by the screw propeller.

Most navies purchased their first steamers from private British shipyards, then provided them with a nominal armament; for years those building their own steamships ordered engines from British firms. The Greek navy's 400-ton *Karteria*, a British-built paddle steamer commissioned in 1827 during the Greek War for Independence against the Turks, is generally accepted

172

to have been the first to engage in combat. Later that year, the destruction of the Turco–Egyptian fleet at the Battle of Navarino Bay (20 October 1827) by a fleet of British, French and Russian warships was the last major naval battle not to include steam-powered warships. The *Karteria* and three sister-ships suffered from chronic engine trouble and were no match for larger sailing warships. Nevertheless, they were important to the further development of steam warships, as several British officers serving in the Eastern Mediterranean became steamship proponents after observing them in action.[1]

After activating the paddle tug *Comet* in 1822, the British navy gradually made more use of paddle steamers and in 1830 commissioned its first purpose-built steam warship, the 900-ton paddle steamer *Dee*.[2] France's first successful steam warship, the 910-ton paddle steamer *Sphinx*, was built in 1828–9 and, like many early French steamers, equipped with imported British engines. It participated in the French invasion of Algiers in June 1830.[3] During the 1830s the introduction of increasing numbers of armed paddle steamers did nothing to change the balance of power among the leading navies, as Britain remained first, France second and Russia third.

The largest paddle steamer of the British navy, the *Terrible* (1845; 3190 tons), cost £94 650 to build – ten times more than the *Comet* of 1822 – and was expensive to operate, consuming unacceptable amounts of coal to reach its top speed of 11 knots. Like all paddle steamers, its paddle boxes took up much of the broadside and limited the number of guns mounted, in *Terrible*'s case to 19, in a ship larger than a 74-gun ship of the line.[4] In contrast, a steam engine driving a screw propeller could be installed in ships not differing dramatically in design from conventional sailing frigates and ships of the line. The elimination of side paddles made it possible to install a traditional broadside of guns, and the screw, unlike paddles, would not seriously hamper a ship's ability to move under sail. The British navy's first screw-propelled warship, the sloop *Rattler* (1843; 1110 tons), topped nine knots in its trials.[5] The French navy did not have a large screw warship until the converted sailing frigate *Pomone* (1845; 2010 tons), but in February 1848 France laid down the first screw ship of the line, the future *Napoléon*, a 5120-ton warship designed by Stanislas Dupuy de Lôme. The British

Admiralty responded by redesigning the sailing ship of the line *Agamemnon*, just laid down, as a 5080-ton screw liner. When completed, both ships were capable of 11–12 knots. After the revolution of 1848 slowed naval spending in France, Britain took an early lead in numbers of screw ships of the line, relying upon conversions of sailing ships as well as new construction. Meanwhile, the French navy remained far ahead of all but the British, as no other country began work on a screw ship of the line until 1852.[6]

The leading naval rivals became allies during the Crimean War (1853–6), as Britain and France aided the Ottoman Empire in its war against Russia. At the start of the conflict the Russian navy was the first to make decisive use of a French invention, the shell gun, which had evolved into a formidable weapon over the years since 1809, when artillerist Henri-Joseph Paixhans first experimented with the type. At Sinope (30 November 1853), the first major battle of the war, a Russian squadron of sailing ships of the line, its armament including heavy Paixhans shell guns, destroyed a Turco–Egyptian frigate squadron which had no shell guns.[7] The Russian navy, with no screw ships of the line in the theatre, did not venture out of Sevastopol once the Anglo–French fleet deployed in the Black Sea. Allied warships sustained significant damage in an indecisive bombardment of Sevastopol in October 1854 but returned in September 1855 to support the final, successful assault on the stronghold. In the bombardment of Kinburn (17 October 1855), the last Russian fortress on the Black Sea, the allied force included three 1575-ton armour-plated wooden floating batteries ordered by Napoleon III after Sinope and the initial bombardment of Sevastopol had exposed the vulnerability of wooden battleships. While historians continue to debate whether the floating batteries were decisive in the victory, at the time the French emperor thought they were, and his fact made Kinburn a milestone in the move toward armoured warships.[8]

After the Crimean War Britain and France resumed their naval rivalry, and during 1857 Dupuy de Lôme completed plans for an armoured frigate, the *Gloire*, laid down in March 1858.[9] By then France clearly had lost the race in screw ships of the line, in quality as well as quantity. Britain's 121-gun three-decker *Victoria* (1859; 6960 tons) was the largest and, at just over £150 000, the most expensive screw liner ever built. Counting conversions as well as new construction, by the time the last of the type were completed in 1861 Britain had 58, France 37, and Russia nine, with five smaller navies accounting for another nine.[10] One of the latter, Austria's *Kaiser*, was the only ship of the type ever to see action in battle against other warships, at Lissa (20 July 1866). By then, the ironclad revolution already had consigned most of these last wooden battleships to the inactive list, to live out their days as training vessels or receiving ships.

ARMOUR AND THE EMERGENCE OF MODERN WARSHIP TYPES, 1860–90

By the time the news of the American Civil War's Battle of Hampton Roads (8–9 March 1862) reached Europe, six European navies already had a total of 46 armoured broadside battery warships built or building, led by Britain and France with 16 apiece. Thus the USS *Monitor* and CSS *Virginia* did not start the ironclad revolution, but their battle silenced European critics of armoured warships. With the advent of armour, a country's industrial base became even more important to its naval power, and the sheer cost of larger armoured warships meant that only those aspiring to great power status would attempt to build them. By the early 1870s the list of naval powers for the first time was identical to the overall list of the great powers of Europe: Britain, France and Russia, joined by Italy, newly-united Germany and Austria–Hungary.

Dupuy de Lôme's *Gloire* was a three-masted broadside battery frigate with a wooden hull covered by 4.5 inches of wrought iron plate, displacing 5630 tons, roughly the same length and breadth as a screw liner. It carried most of its 36 guns (6.4-inch calibre) on the lone gun deck, in gunports barely six feet above the waterline. This feature, and coal bunkers capable of carrying less than 700 tons of coal, reflected its intended mission of line-of-battle service in European waters. The wooden hull was a compromise necessitated by the weakness of French industry. By 1861 France laid down another fifteen ironclads, of which only two had iron hulls. Most were virtual copies of the *Gloire*.[11] The first British armoured frigate, the *Warrior*, was laid down in

May 1859. Like the *Gloire* it was a three-masted broadside battery frigate with 4.5 inches of armour and 36 guns, but the similarities ended there, as the *Warrior* was made of iron and designed not as a line-of-battle ship but a large cruising frigate whose armour would enable it to stand in the line of battle. The 9140-ton *Warrior* was 125 feet longer than the *Gloire*, had bunkers holding almost 200 tons more coal, and could set twice as much canvas to the wind. Its engines were capable of over 14 knots, a knot faster than the *Gloire* and still a respectable speed two decades later. The smallest of the early British ironclads were similar in size to the largest of the French, leaving the British armoured fleet superior in size and firepower if not in numbers of ships. Considerable experimentation in design (culminating in the five-masted, 10 780-ton *Northumberland*) also left the fleet without the homogeneity of its French counterpart.[12]

European navies introduced various designs of 'monitors', low-freeboard turret ships modeled after the USS *Monitor*, but only Russia made a heavy investment in the type, ultimately building 16 of its first 26 ironclads as monitors. Meanwhile, the British navy pioneered the central-battery or casemate ship as a solution to the dilemma posed by the requirements of ever more powerful guns and ever-thicker armour. The design had a smaller battery of heavier guns concentrated in a heavily armoured casemate amidships, which also protected the ship's engines. Otherwise the ship was unarmoured except for a waterline belt. Most variations of the design provided for a recessed freeboard fore and aft of the casemate to allow the end guns to fire ahead and astern. Britain's *Bellerophon* (1866; 7550 tons), featuring belt and casemate armour 6 inches thick and a heavy battery of ten 9-inch guns in the casemate, was the first larger central battery warship.[13] By the 1870s every major European navy had at least one casemate ship.

The first naval battle between fleets of ironclad warships came during the War of 1866, which matched Austria against Prussia and Italy. At the Battle of Lissa (20 July 1866) an Austrian fleet under Rear Admiral Wilhelm von Tegetthoff, including seven ironclads, defeated an Italian fleet under Admiral Carlo Pellion di Persano, including 12 ironclads, and stopped an Italian bid to secure historically-Venetian territory in the eastern Adriatic littoral before an armistice ended the war. The chaotic mêlée opened with an Austrian line-abreast attack against the Italian line and closed four hours later with Tegetthoff's flagship *Erzherzog Ferdinand Max* ramming and sinking its counterpart *Re d'Italia*. A second Italian ironclad was also sunk.[14] Discounting Navarino in 1827, where the Turco–Egyptian fleet was destroyed at anchor, Lissa rates as the largest naval battle between Trafalgar (1805) and Tsushima (1905), and thus its 'lessons' affected both the design of warships and battle tactics. Tegetthoff's line abreast attack and ramming tactics were embraced by influential naval writers, including Britain's Vice Admiral Philip Colomb and France's Admiral Jurien de la Gravière.[15] For twenty years the line abreast remained the favoured battle formation, and into the twentieth century warships were built with pronounced ram bows.

The 1870s witnessed a clear division of fleets into armoured and unarmoured components, with the terms 'battleship' and 'cruiser' coming into use to describe the two groups of vessels. European battle fleets remained in home waters for the event of a war against another great power, while unarmoured fleets showed the flag worldwide in defence of colonial and trading interests. In the Russo–Turkish War of 1877–8 the wisdom of maintaining an armoured battle fleet first came under question. The Black Sea had been demilitarised under international law from 1856 to 1871 and Russia lacked a battle fleet there; the Ottoman Empire, in contrast, had an ironclad fleet of thirteen seagoing vessels and nine coastal or river warships. The hopelessly outnumbered Russian navy resorted to the use of torpedoes making the war the first in which the new technology played a significant role. The Russians converted fast merchant steamers into tenders for small steam launches, which they armed with spar torpedoes, towed torpedoes, and eventually self-propelled torpedoes, the latter pioneered by the Whitehead firm of Fiume (Rijeka), Austria–Hungary, in the late 1860s. In a Russian assault on the Turkish-held port of Batum on the night of 25–6 January 1878, the wooden screw gunboat *Intikbah* became the first warship sunk by self-propelled torpedoes. The Russian campaign actually sank few ships – two wooden screw gunboats, a small monitor and an armoured corvette – but it kept the vastly superior Turkish fleet on the defensive, fearful of torpedo attacks.[16]

By the late 1870s the limitations of wrought-iron armour led to experimentation first with 'sandwich' (iron-and-wood) armour, then compound (iron-and-steel) armour, amid rising doubts about the survivability of large armoured warships. Such skepticism, combined with the proven effectiveness of the self-propelled torpedo, created conditions under which Admiral Théophile Aube of the French navy developed the strategy of the Jeune École, deemphasising the battle fleet in favour of flotillas of torpedo boats and high seas commerce raiders. Members of the 'young school' pointed to the Russo–Turkish War to support their argument that torpedo boat flotillas could paralyse an enemy battle fleet, and thus were a far more effective deterrent than expensive and vulnerable battleships. While the concepts behind the Jeune École were French (specifically, anti-British), ironically the ship types most associated with it were developed in Britain. Armstrong launched the Chilean navy's *Esmeralda* (1883; 3000 tons), a modern steel cruiser with no sailing rig, armed with two 10-inch guns, six 6-inch guns, and three torpedo tubes. It had no side armour but two inches of deck armour, a feature which made it the first 'protected' cruiser.[17] Meanwhile, Thornycroft's *Lightning* (1876; 32 tons) provided the model for most torpedo boats. It was equipped with a forced draught boiler, designed to draw more steam from machinery restricted in size by the overall dimensions of the vessel. The efficiency of the forced draught system soon made it standard for all new warship boilers. During the early 1880s the French firm of Belleville developed a water-tube boiler technology which added further to the advantage in speed which torpedo boats and small cruisers enjoyed over battleships.[18] As the decade progressed, most navies built fewer battleships and many more modern steel cruisers and torpedo boats. 1887 was the only year between the onset of work on the *Gloire* in 1858 and the Washington Naval Treaty of 1922 in which no country laid down an armoured warship.

But by 1890 the brief era of the Jeune École had ended. Torpedo nets and electric searchlights were developed to make stationary battleships less vulnerable to torpedo attack, while improvements in propulsion systems and artillery pioneered aboard torpedo vessels or light cruisers were introduced to larger warships, giving them the speed and rapid medium-range firepower to counter the threat of the torpedo while underway. At the same time, Belleville boiler technology was introduced in larger warships, enabling them to benefit from the latest increases in speed.[19] The French also developed two other technologies which helped lead to the demise of their own Jeune École: 'smokeless' powder and armour-piercing chrome steel shells.[20] The latter gave new life to the big gun and to larger warships needed as platforms for such ordnance. When a revolution in armour production in 1890–2 resolved the problem of how to provide adequate protection for such vessels, the Jeune École lost what little life it had left.

THE ERA OF THE BATTLESHIP, 1890–1922

Strategic considerations joined the technical and technological factors that turned the leading navies back toward the battleship. It became generally accepted that an armoured battle fleet provided a better deterrent against attack and could defend home waters reliably regardless of the weather. Furthermore, most countries did not have a rival with a volume of overseas commerce sufficient to justify commerce-raiding as a primary strategy. Finally, from the United States, the writings of Alfred Thayer Mahan provided battle fleet proponents with historical arguments to support their points of view. Unarmoured cruisers and torpedo boats remained an important part of all navies, but no longer were considered a potential main striking force. Out of the confusion of 1860–90 there finally emerged a standard design of battleship, what would later be called the 'predreadnought'. Masts and yards, still in evidence on the casemate ships of the 1870s, finally disappeared. In the early 1890s compound armour gave way to nickel–steel plate, perfected by the German firm of Krupp. Increased protection without added weight facilitated a further increase in battleship size, paving the way for the dreadnought design after the turn of the century.

In addition to Britain and Russia, which had never suspended their battleship construction as a result of the Jeune École, Germany (from 1888), France (from 1889), Italy and Austria–Hungary (both from 1893) built ever-larger classes of battleships until the outbreak of the First World War. The Naval Defence Act (1889), funding a programme including eight 14 150-ton

battleships of the *Royal Sovereign* class, reaffirmed Britain's faith
in the primacy of the large armoured warship. A decade later
Admiral Alfred von Tirpitz secured the Reichstag's approval for
the First (1898) and Second (1900) Navy laws, establishing a
programme which eventually created the world's second-largest
battle fleet.[21] At the same time, Italy and Austria–Hungary –
ostensibly allies, with Germany, in the Triple Alliance – became
embroiled in their own Adriatic naval race, enhancing the size
and strength of their battle fleets.[22] France and Russia did not
keep pace, the former owing to the cost of keeping the French
army competitive with the German, the latter failing to recover
from its defeat at the hands of Japan in 1905.

The Russo–Japanese War (1904–5) produced no clear 'lessons' for the navies of the time, and in other naval conflicts
beyond Europe – the Sino–Japanese War (1894–5) and Spanish–
American War (1898) – cruisers rather than battleships played
the key role, yet nothing dimmed the enthusiasm of the battleship renaissance. Attention ultimately focused on the fact that
the medium calibre quick firing guns which inflicted the most
damage in the major battles of the Sino–Japanese and Spanish–
American wars were not a factor at the battles of the Yellow Sea
(10 August 1904) and Tsushima (27–8 May 1905), where the
12-inch guns of battleships and armoured cruisers had opened
fire at unprecedented distances. Even the Russians, not known
for their expertise in fire control, hit the Japanese flagship *Mikasa*
from 7000 metres in the opening exchange at Tsushima.[23]

Albeit quite by accident, Sir John Fisher's HMS *Dreadnought*
(1906; 18 110 tons) became the prototype of the twentieth-century
battleship, combining an unprecedented speed, protection and
all big-gun firepower soon imitated by other navies. If the 'lesson' presented in 1904–5 by long-range fire of unprecedented
accuracy helped accelerate the rush to build dreadnoughts, it
played no role in the actual genesis of the all big-gun battleship. In 1903 Vittorio Cuniberti, chief engineer of the Italian
navy, proposed an all big-gun design as an ideal battleship for
the British navy and Fisher himself likewise developed the idea
long before Tsushima, coming to the post of First Sea Lord in
1904 already convinced of the need for a new type of capital
ship dominated by a single calibre of gun.[24]

For decades naval historians, influenced by the works of Arthur

J. Marder, considered Fisher a visionary who foresaw the way of the future pointing inevitably toward the fast, all big-gun battleship. But in recent years Jon Tetsuro Sumida and his supporters have offered a more persuasive interpretation.[25] Fisher believed that Britain's long-term naval interests were global, not European; that the threats to British security at sea would come from France or the Franco–Russian combination; and that the conditions which had made the anti-British Jeune École plausible in the 1880s could, and probably would, return. When he became First Sea Lord, Fisher did, indeed, push for an entirely new type of capital ship, not a battleship but a 'fusion' of a battleship and armoured cruiser, eventually known as a battle cruiser.

Fisher's first programme of capital ships, laid down in 1905–6, included three battle cruisers (17 370 tons, 567 feet long, eight 12-inch guns, 6 inches of armour, with a speed of 25 knots) and, to placate battleship proponents, one battleship (18 110 tons, 527 feet long, ten 12-inch guns, 11 inches of armour, with a speed of 21 knots). The battleship (the *Dreadnought*) was laid down first, in October 1905, to serve as a test platform for the combination of unprecedented size, all big-gun armament, and Parsons turbine engines. The three battle cruisers (the *Invincible* class) were laid down early in 1906, to be completed late enough to incorporate any lessons derived from the sea trials of the *Dreadnought*. There is evidence that Fisher hoped the *Dreadnought* would be the last British battleship ever built, and that all subsequent capital ships would be battle cruisers. But in December 1905, when planning the programme for 1906–7, Fisher could find no support for his vision even among his own protégés, thanks to changes in the international arena during 1905 which invalidated his strategic premises. The Anglo–French entente of 1904 had survived the test of the Moroccan crisis, and the Russo–Japanese War had all but destroyed the Russian navy. The growing German navy now appeared to be the likely future adversary, and by 1907 a common fear of Germany would motivate an Anglo–Russian rapprochement, completing the Triple Entente. In these changed circumstances the battle cruiser, with its global reach for a war against France and Russia now unnecessary, lost out to the battleship, which would be needed for a future confrontation with Germany in the North Sea. Much to Fisher's dismay, the *Dreadnought* – which he had never intended to replicate – became the model capital ship rather than the *Invincible*.

After being completed in an unprecedented fourteen months, the *Dreadnought* impressed all critics during its trials. The success of the new design had an immediate impact on the shipbuilding programmes of every other significant navy in the world. Only eight pre-dreadnought battleships were begun after the completion of the *Dreadnought* (five by France, three by Austria–Hungary), and within seven years those countries and the other great powers of Europe – Germany, Russia and Italy – all had dreadnoughts in service or nearing completion. By 1913 even Spain had built a dreadnought, and Greece and Turkey had ordered dreadnoughts in foreign shipyards. Like nuclear weapons later in the twentieth century, possession of dreadnoughts meant that a country counted for something in global or regional balances of power, and the ability to build them from one's own domestic resources became the measure of true great power status.

Fisher failed to realise his dream of having the battle cruiser replace the battleship; instead, the emergence of the battle cruiser all but killed the armoured cruiser, a very popular ship type in the quarter-century preceding 1905. After the first of the *Invincibles* was laid down in February 1906, work began on just four armoured cruisers (one each for the navies of France, Germany, Italy, and Greece), the last of which was laid down in 1907. Construction of unarmoured or protected cruisers slowed as well; between 1905 and 1914 no navy laid down a ship of the type larger than 5500 tons, and few were built at all except by Britain and Germany. Meanwhile, the gap in tonnage between capital ships (dreadnoughts and battle cruisers) and other units continued to widen, and as their size grew so did their cost. The 18 110-ton *Dreadnought* had been built for £1.73 million, while the 27 500-ton *Queen Elizabeth*, laid down in 1912, cost £2.68 million.[26]

Britain entered the First World War with 45 of the new capital ships built or building, compared to 26 for Germany, 12 for France, 11 for Russia, 6 for Italy, 4 for Austria–Hungary, and 3 for Spain. Between 1914 and 1918 there were no fleet-scale actions aside from the Battle of Jutland (31 May – 1 June 1916), where Admiral John Jellicoe commanded a British fleet including 37 dreadnoughts and battle cruisers against Vice Admiral

Reinhard Scheer's German fleet, including 21. By that stage guns and gunnery had improved to the point where it became suicidal for heavy units to close within less than 10 000 metres of one another. The Germans inflicted more damage than they suffered, sinking the *Invincible* and two other battle cruisers while losing one pre-dreadnought and one battle cruiser of their own, but afterward left the British still in command of the North Sea.[27] Anchored at Wilhelmshaven once again, they shared the fate of most of Europe's dreadnought fleets, spending much of the war at anchor while smaller units shouldered the burden of the conflict at sea.

Even though capital ships saw little action during the war, the widely acknowledged role of the naval race in the origins of the war led to the Washington Naval Treaty (1922), an international agreement to scrap all but the newest capital ships and suspend new construction for ten years. The London Naval Treaty (1930) further extended the construction holiday until 1936. Among the European powers Britain emerged with a capital ship tonnage quota equal to that of the United States, while France and Italy had quotas 35 per cent as large.[28] For the three, the total number of dreadnoughts and battle cruisers laid down between the world wars (Britain nine, France five, Italy four) approximated that of a single robust year of pre-1914 construction. Because the 1922 treaty limited warships other than capital ships to 10 000 tons and 8-inch guns, in the inter-war years navies once again built armoured and protected cruisers, so-called 'treaty cruisers' with tonnage and armament at or just below the new limits. Britain wanted to extend the capital ship quotas to cruisers as well, but in the 1930 treaty secured only an agreement to limit the calibre of cruiser guns to 6 inches.[29]

SUBMARINES AND AIRCRAFT CARRIERS, 1914–45

During the First World War Germany used U-boats to sink 11.9 million tons of allied shipping, in the process losing 178 of its 335 submarines and 4474 submariners.[30] Yet submarines were not limited under the Washington Naval Treaty, despite the fact that the war had demonstrated their lethal power and the post-war Treaty of Versailles had prohibited Germany from operating them. The undersea raiders made life miserable for the British but did not revolutionise naval warfare or even vindicate the earlier concepts of the Jeune École, as the survival of Britain's superior surface fleet ensured its national security and naval preeminence. Nevertheless, Britain – which in 1914 had more submarines than any other naval power – pushed for their abolition at the Washington conference and later at the London conference, both times to no avail, failing largely because of opposition from France. The French navy, an early pioneer in submarine design, commissioned ten former German U-boats, and between 1922 and 1929 built 42 new submarines compared to 28 for Italy and just 14 for Britain.[31]

To shore up the collapsing regime of naval arms limitations, Britain concluded bilateral naval treaties with Germany in 1935 and the Soviet Union in 1937. The Third Reich was conceded a fleet equal to those of France and Italy under the 1922 quotas, with a submarine force 45 per cent the size of Britain's. Adolf Hitler did not formally abrogate the agreement until April 1939 but disregarded these limits in his subsequent naval buildup. Even though he considered the Tirpitz plan to have been a great mistake, he authorised construction of the 45 950-ton *Bismarck* and *Tirpitz*, along with other giant battleships never completed. Joseph Stalin likewise harboured maritime ambitions never fulfilled, in the late 1930s approving construction of the 59 150-ton *Sovetkii Soyuz* class of battleships, none of which was ever completed.[32] Ultimately both the German and Soviet navies of the Second World War invested most heavily in submarines, although the Germans entered the war in 1939 with just 57. The Soviets entered the war in 1941 with 130.[33]

Naval aviation grew from a modest beginning in 1913–14, when the British and French navies converted ships into the first seaplane tenders. During the First World War, most navies operated airplanes from coastal air stations or seaplanes from naval harbours, without dramatic effect. Britain laid down its first purpose-built aircraft carrier (HMS *Hermes*) early in 1918 and commissioned a converted liner as the first operational flush-deck carrier (HMS *Argus*) just weeks before the Armistice. The Washington Naval Treaty allowed the conversion to aircraft carriers of capital ships which otherwise would have had to be scrapped; in the 1920s Britain completed several conversions and in the 1930s laid down six larger carriers which formed the backbone of its fleet in the Second World War. France's *Béarn*, a converted dreadnought, was interwar Europe's only non-British aircraft carrier. The carriers reinforced Britain's superiority in capital ships over other European navies (as of 1939, Britain had 19 battleships and battle cruisers built and building compared to nine for France, six each for Italy and Germany and three for the Soviet Union).[34]

During the Second World War the *Béarn* (interned at Martinique in 1942 and eventually operated by the Free French) retained the distinction of being Europe's only non-British carrier, as the Italian, German and Soviet navies placed none in service. While British battleships and cruisers did most of the work in the disabling of Vichy French capital ships at Oran (3 July 1940), carrier-based British aircraft delivered the decisive blows in the sinking of Italian battleships at Taranto (11 November 1940) and the destruction of the *Bismarck* in the Atlantic (27 May 1941), in the latter case avenging the *Bismarck*'s sinking of the *Hood* (1920; 42 670 tons), interwar Britain's largest capital ship.[35] The Vichy French navy ceased to exist in November 1942, when Germany occupied all of France in response to the allied landings in French North Africa. The Italian navy likewise was eliminated in September 1943, when Italy left the war. The Battle of North Cape (26 December 1943), during which the British sank the battleship *Scharnhorst*, was the last engagement involving larger German surface units.[36] As in the First World War the U-boats bore the brunt of Germany's war at sea, but the allied convoy system and improvements in intelligence and antisubmarine warfare made the U-boat campaign of 1939–45 relatively less successful than that of 1914–18. Just 22 per cent more allied shipping was sunk (14.6 million tons) in a war that lasted 30 per cent longer, while four times more U-boats were lost (a staggering 754 of 863 in commission) and six times more submariners killed (27 491, with 5000 taken prisoner).[37] German submarines inflicted serious damage to British and allied shipping but not of the catastrophic sort that would have followed the loss of the British surface fleet, opening the way to the invasion and defeat of Britain.

At the end of the Second World War Britain still had the world's second-largest navy, a fleet significantly larger than it had been in 1919, with personnel numbering 863 500 and a navy list of just over 1000 warships, including 11 aircraft carriers, 41 escort carriers, and 131 submarines.[38] Owing to the destruction or surrender of the navies of Germany, Italy and the lesser maritime states, by 1945 the modest Free French and Soviet forces were the only other significant European navies.

Roughly half of the battleships and battle cruisers sunk in the Second World War fell victim to carrier-based aircraft, reflecting the emergence of the carrier as the capital ship of the second half of the 20th century. To some degree air power (if not exclusively carrier-based air power) also trumped the undersea threat, as more German submarines were sunk by allied aircraft than by allied surface vessels.[39] Yet of the four British carriers lost in the European theatre of the war, three fell victim to U-boats.[40]

EUROPEAN NAVIES IN THE ERA OF THE COLD WAR, 1945–91

In league with the United States under the North Atlantic Treaty Organisation (established 1949), the postwar navies of Britain and France were reduced in size and reconfigured for regional roles within the alliance. Italy and, after 1955, West Germany, likewise had modest naval forces with specific missions in NATO. As late as 1961 British sea power facilitated the defence of Kuwait from Iraqi invasion, but the end of Britain's 'east of Suez' commitments, announced in 1968, left the navy with little to do outside of NATO's North Sea and North Atlantic sphere.[41] Underscoring the further reduction of British responsibilities, after 1976 British warships were not regularly assigned to NATO duties in the Mediterranean.[42]

Battleships built before the Second World War were scrapped shortly after 1945, followed by many of those completed during the conflict. The only new European battleship commissioned after the war, Britain's *Vanguard* (1946; 44 500 tons), served just ten years and was sold for scrap in 1960. France's *Jean Bart* (recommissioned 1949; 46 500 tons) was the last European battleship to fire a shot in anger, during the Suez Crisis of 1956. When the last battleships passed out of service, carriers were left as the largest British and French warships. The British navy was responsible for such postwar innovations as the angled flight deck and the steam catapult for launching aircraft. Meanwhile, the French navy always kept at least one carrier in commission. The *Béarn* (finally retired in 1967) and two other French carriers operated off Vietnam during the 1946–54 war, while the British carrier *Triumph* saw action in the Korean War. The Anglo–French naval force involved in the Suez crisis of 1956 included two French and five British carriers. The Suez operation, a fiasco from the military–naval perspective, nevertheless provided the first evidence of the potential of carrier-based helicopter operations. In 1960 the British introduced the first carrier-based vertical/short takeoff and landing (V/STOL) aircraft, and the performance of such planes along with the promise shown by helicopters prompted the British government to cancel CVA-01, a projected 53 000-ton carrier, in 1966. France did not abandon the larger carrier type with its conventional jet aircraft, commissioning the *Foch* (1963; 32 780 tons), but from the late 1970s Britain's carrier force consisted exclusively of smaller vessels carrying V/STOL aircraft and helicopters, equipped with another innovation, the 'ski-jump' bow ramp. The Dutch navy also operated a carrier during the 1960s and in the 1980s Italy and Spain each commissioned a small V/STOL carrier.[43]

During the Cold War the British and French navies strained their budgets to maintain their own submarine-based nuclear deterrents. Britain's first nuclear-powered submarine, the *Dreadnought* (1963; 4000 tons submerged), cost £18.5 million, the four boats of the *Resolution* class (1967–9; 8400 tons submerged) roughly £40 million apiece. The *Resolution*s, armed with Polaris missiles, remained in service until replaced in the 1990s by the Trident missile submarines of the *Vanguard* class.[44] Meanwhile, France commissioned six ballistic missile submarines of the *Redoutable* class (9000 tons submerged) between 1969 and 1985, the largest French submarines until the *Triomphant* class of the late 1990s.[45]

Despite having been redesigned for a NATO role in the North Sea and North Atlantic, Britain's dramatically downsized navy performed well in the Falklands War (April–June 1982). Two carriers, the aging *Hermes* (1959; 23 900 tons) and the newer but smaller *Invincible* (1980; 16 000 tons), spearheaded a force of 35 warships and 22 auxiliary vessels facilitating the reconquest of the South Atlantic islands from Argentina. The Argentinian navy offered little resistance after the cruiser *General Belgrano* (ex-USS *Phoenix*, 1938; 10 800 tons), was torpedoed and sunk on 2 May by the submarine *Conqueror*. Exocet missiles fired by Argentinian aircraft and by ground forces on the islands posed the greatest threat to British vessels. Argentinian missiles and bombs ultimately claimed two destroyers, one frigate, one supply ship and one landing ship.[46]

The reemergence of Russian sea power ranks as the most dramatic development of post-1945 European naval history. A Cold War buildup, accelerating after 1956 under the direction of Admiral Sergei Gorshkov, gave the Soviet Union a navy second only to that of the United States, ultimately with a global presence, designed not to achieve command of the sea but to deny it to the US navy. Concern for access to the open seas prompted Gorshkov to redeploy his forces, elevating the Northern fleet (based in the Arctic, on the Kola Peninsula and White Sea) from the smallest of the four Soviet fleets to the largest. Nikita Khrushchev's preferences dictated a heavy emphasis on submarines, but the Soviet capitulation in the Cuban Missile Crisis (1962) in the face of a US naval blockade of Cuba strengthened the hand of Gorshkov in his quest for a 'balanced' fleet including significant surface units. The Soviet fleet made impressive showings during the next two Arab–Israeli wars, sending 70 warships to the Eastern Mediterranean in 1967 and 96 in 1973, in the latter case a force considerably larger than the US Sixth Fleet. Leonid Brezhnev authorised a modest carrier programme, starting with the 15 500-ton helicopter carriers *Moskva* and *Leningrad*, and continuing during the 1970s with the three 36 000-ton *Kiev* class carriers and the slightly larger *Admiral Gorshkov* (ex-*Baku*), platforms for both helicopters and V/STOL aircraft. A 65 000-ton aircraft carrier, laid down in 1983 as the *Leonid Brezhnev*, entered service in 1990 as the *Admiral Kuznetsov*.[47] Among other Soviet surface units the largest were the four 24 300-ton missile cruisers of the *Kirov* class, laid down between 1973 and 1986, the largest warships other than carriers built by any navy since the Second World War.[48] Coinciding with the build up in surface units, a programme of submarine construction continued and by the mid-1970s the Soviet fleet included 409 submarines, of which 95 were nuclear powered. In 1980 the Soviets

launched the first of six Typhoon-class ballistic missile submarines, the largest ever built by any navy. These giant vessels
surpassed the dreadnought in size (561 feet long, 18 500 tons
surfaced displacement) and speed (25 knots submerged).[49]

After coming to power in 1985, Mikhail Gorbachev forced
Gorshkov to retire. His successor as commanding admiral, former
submariner V. N. Chernavin, cooperated fully with Gorbachev's
policies, including reductions in the fleet. At the time of the
Soviet Union's demise in 1991, its navy list included 63 ballistic
and guided missile submarines and 147 other nuclear powered
submarines. In comparison, the US navy had 34 ballistic and
guided missile submarines and 80 other nuclear powered submarines. The Soviet navy also had larger numbers of frigates
and corvettes, but the US navy included many more carriers
(thirteen to five) and helicopter carriers or assault ships (thirteen to two), and also had more guided missile cruisers and
destroyers. While most American carriers were nuclear powered,
the largest nuclear powered warships in the Soviet navy were
the *Kirov* class missile cruisers.[50] In both personnel and number
of warships the Soviet navy of 1991 was slightly larger than the
next four European navies (the British, French, German and
Italian) combined.

THE PRESENT AND FUTURE OF EUROPEAN NAVIES

The fleet of post-communist Russia hoisted the flags of pre-
1917 Imperial Russia and reintroduced many warship names
from the old tsarist fleet, but the country's severe internal problems made the 1990s a decade of deterioration rather than
revitalisation for Russian sea power. The territorial breakup of
the Soviet Union affected only the Black Sea fleet, which became a pawn between Russia and Ukraine. Years of acrimonious
negotiations left the Black Sea installations in Ukrainian hands
while almost all of the warships remained Russian. Ukraine received three frigates, one obsolete submarine and several patrol
boats, and in 1999 announced its intention to complete the
11 490-ton cruiser *Ukrayina* (ex-*Admiral Lobov*), laid down in 1985
and inherited along with the Nikolaiev shipyard.[51]

The loss of Nikolaiev, the only former Soviet shipyard capable of servicing the *Admiral Kuznetsov*, posed serious problems for the long-term maintenance of Russia's largest warship. The *Admiral Kuznetsov* spent the 1990s with the Northern Fleet except for a brief Mediterranean deployment in 1995–6. All other Russian carriers were decommissioned during the 1990s. Of the remaining larger surface combatants, the missile cruiser *Admiral Ushakov* (ex-*Kirov*) and a sister ship were inactive throughout the decade for want of repairs, leaving just two units of the class in operation. Budget problems plagued the last ship of the class, the *Petr Veliki* (ex-*Yuri Andropov*). Laid down in 1986, it was finally completed in 1995 but did not enter service until 1998. For surface vessels as well as submarines, new construction all but ceased. During the 1990s two-thirds of Russian nuclear submarines (including three of the six Typhoons) were decommissioned or became inoperable, and by 2000 just 37 ballistic and guided missile submarines and 33 other nuclear submarines remained in service.[52] The accidental loss of the guided missile submarine *Kursk* in August 2000 raised serious questions about the combat readiness of units which, because of financial restrictions, rarely left port.[53]

Following the end of the Cold War, the European NATO navies proceeded with ambitious projects already underway and, in some cases, committed resources to new ones. France's 41 000-ton nuclear-powered carrier *Charles de Gaulle*, laid down in 1989, finally entered service late in 2000. Aside from the *Admiral Kuznetsov*, it was the largest new warship commissioned by any European navy since 1946. In 1998 Britain announced plans to build two 40 000-ton carriers to replace the three V/STOL carriers of the *Invincible* class, with contracts to be let in 2004. Further reflecting their commitment to maintain respectable sea power, Britain and France continued to build and operate large nuclear-powered ballistic missile submarines. In the British navy the four Trident submarines of the *Vanguard* class (1993–9; 15 900 tons submerged) replaced the old *Resolution* class, while the French navy commissioned the first two of a projected four units of the *Triomphant* class (1997–9; 14 120 tons submerged). Meanwhile, in 2000 Germany completed its largest naval vessel since the Second World War, the 20 400-ton deployment group support ship *Berlin*, and Italy ordered the 20 800-ton V/STOL carrier *Luigi Einaudi*.[54]

As the only European NATO navies with any sort of long-range power-projection capabilities, the British and French fleets contributed warships to the allied effort in the Persian Gulf War against Iraq in 1991 and against Yugoslavia during the Kosovo crisis of 1999. During the latter campaign the French navy deployed a battle group in the Adriatic led by the aging carrier *Foch* (destined for sale to Brazil upon the commissioning of the *Charles de Gaulle*), while the British sent the small carrier *Invincible*. Other British naval units engaged included the nuclear submarine *Splendid,* which fired some two dozen Tomahawk land-attack missiles (TLAMs) at targets in Kosovo.[55]

More important than their role as allies in such naval actions, at the turn of the century European countries were responsible for many more naval technological innovations than the United States. Constructing smaller ships in smaller classes, European navies and shipyards took the lead in the development of medium-sized amphibious vessels and in the application of stealth technology to frigates and corvettes. The 620-ton corvette *Visby*, completed in 2000 by Karlskronavarnet for the Swedish navy, had a hull made of plastic reinforced with carbon fiber, a low-weight, high-strength combination with the added benefit of a low magnetic signature. The *Visby*'s no-right-angles design also provided a model in signature reduction certainly of relevance to the design of larger surface combatants in the early twenty-first century, such as the US navy's DD-21 land-attack destroyer.[56] At the same time, the Azipod System of marine propulsion, developed in the 1990s by a subsidiary of Kvaerner Masa of Finland for icebreakers and cruise liners, appeared likely to be applied to warships early in the twenty-first century.[57] European builders also remained world leaders in the construction of small submarines, many of which were exported to the Third World, an important outlet at a time when the future size and role of European navies remained uncertain.

8. The Transformation of War in Europe 1945–2000

WARREN CHIN

Over the past four centuries Europe has been at the centre of five fundamental revolutionary changes in the art and conduct of war. This essay examines the latest of these revolutions within the context of the war in Bosnia (1992–5). This war is significant because it is the first major regional conflict to erupt within Europe since the end of the Second World War (1939–45). As such it was an area of concern for all of the major European powers and at certain times threatened to escalate from a local conflict into a general European war. Of equal importance is the fact that Bosnia demonstrates the essential characteristics of an evolution in war that has been described as postmodern war, new war and even neo-medieval war.[1] The aim of this analysis is to highlight why and how both the nature and conduct of war has changed. In addition, it also explores the possibility that existing military forces are ill prepared to meet the challenges posed by this new type of conflict and, as a result, are in danger of becoming obsolete.

Of necessity this discussion begins with a synopsis of the major changes that have affected the development of war over the preceding 400 years. The first significant watershed followed the Thirty Years War (1618–48) and saw the parallel development of the creation of permanent, professional armies and the emergence of the modern state – the origins of which stemmed from the need to create and maintain professional armed forces. The state achieved a legitimate monopoly on the use of violence and war was used to prosecute the interests of the state.[2] The second important development was the French Revolution and the Napoleonic Wars (1789–1815) that followed this political upheaval. Here the most important development was the emergence of democracy and nationalism, the creation of the nation in arms and the appearance of mass armies that had an

important impact on strategy and tactics.[3] The third of these
military revolutions was caused by the industrial revolution. Starting from about the mid-1850s, industrialists began to transfer
their skills in technology and mass production to the realm of
armaments manufacture. The application of these new techniques
resulted in a fundamental change in the material conditions of
the military realm. Mass production and the development of
new forms of transport ensured that states were able to create
armies of unprecedented size, and equip and supply them indefinitely in the field.[4] The result of these new processes was
the protracted mass industrialised slaughter of the First World
War (1914–18). This phenomenon was to reach its apotheosis
during the Second World War. Such was the destruction of this
war that in Europe alone the death toll was over 27 million
civilians and perhaps as many as 25 million military personnel.[5]

The period after 1945 did not witness the creation of a meaningful peace, but instead the onset of a new kind of war: the
Cold War. Between 1945–89, Europe was to be the frontline in
this new conflict. What made this conflict so different from earlier wars was the development of the atomic bomb. The creation
of this devastating weapon, and the fact that there was no meaningful defence against it – other than to possess such weapons
and threaten to use them if attacked – resulted in the fourth
transformation of war in Europe. During this time the purpose
of the military was not to fight wars, but to prevent them by
making the cost of any aggression so high that a rational state
would only launch an attack if it believed its very existence was
in danger. As a result of this new strategic imperative – embodied
within the doctrine of deterrence – Europe became the centre
of the largest concentration of military power the world had
ever seen. Divided into two rival military alliances (the North
Atlantic Treaty Organisation and the Warsaw Pact) the outcome
was the creation of a military stalemate that endured till the
unification of Germany in 1990. The one significant benefit of
this revolution was that it prevented the outbreak of a major war
between the great powers, an unparalleled development in the
history of the international system.[6]

THE FIFTH REVOLUTION; EXPLAINING THE
CO-EXISTENCE OF WAR AND PEACE IN EUROPE

During the Cold War a great deal of energy was invested in developing new weapons and new methods of war fighting. Such was the quality of innovation, in terms of both technology and doctrine, that by the 1980s the Soviets believed that another military technical revolution was taking place, this time based on the development of new information technologies. This technology allowed the development of long-range precision-guided munitions and the provision of real time surveillance of the battlefield. With this capability the killing zone now extended back from the forward edge of the battlefield to a depth of perhaps several hundred kilometres into enemy territory.[7] The potency of this new capability was demonstrated during the Gulf War (1990–1) and played a central role in allowing the US-led Coalition to defeat the Iraqi Army so decisively in 1991.

Of profound importance was the way in which civilian industries utilised and improved these defence technologies for the consumer market. Because of the size of this market and the rate of consumption within it civilian high-tech industries were able to embark upon a process of innovation that far exceeded the capabilities of the military industrial complex. The effects of this symbiosis between defence and industry were important because it provided a considerable impetus to the creation of the 'information revolution'. This in turn had important consequences for military research and development. More important, however, was the way in which the information revolution affected the political and economic development of contemporary society and the operation of the international system.

These changes have had a significant impact on our attitudes towards war and when it is permissible to use force. In general there is a greater reluctance to resort to war today than at any other time in Europe s history. This can be attributed to a variety of factors: the legacy of nuclear weapons, and changes in society brought about by the media. It is also important to note that, in the case of the advanced industrialised states of the West, wealth creation is no longer dependent upon the acquisition of living space or other resources to the extent that it was in the past. The application of scientific and technical knowledge has resulted in a significant increase in productivity and this has offered a safer path to prosperity than military conquest abroad.[8]

These developments, when combined with the spread of democratic government within Europe, have made it more difficult for modern states to go to war. As Mandelbaum explains, although it was the imperative of war that helped give rise to the modern state, its function today is to create the right economic conditions for wealth creation and to provide adequate welfare for the electorate. Ultimately its competence and that of the elected government will depend on how well it performs on these two domestic fronts and not on how much it has achieved through conquest and military glory.[9]

Within the context of the international system, the information revolution has increased the opportunities for states, organisations and individuals to communicate with each other. In economic terms this has increased the level of trade and the degree of interdependence between states. It is believed that this technological phenomenon is resulting in the homogenisation of the world and is consequently eroding the potential for strife and conflict between states.[10] The greater political and economic interdependence of the world caused by the information revolution has been termed globalisation.

And yet it is clear that Europe has not been blessed by the establishment of a universal peace. Small wars have raged on the periphery of the European mainland in the former Yugoslavia since the end of the Cold War. The problem is how to explain this anomaly. The traditional explanation of why the Yugoslavian state collapsed into civil war rests upon the idea of old and irreconcilable hatreds.[11] However, this merely begs another question: why did Yugoslavia not disintegrate into civil war before 1991?

THE NEW CAUSES OF WAR: THE CHANGING STRATEGIC ENVIRONMENT

It has been suggested that the answers to these questions are due to the unique circumstances that affected Yugoslavia's internal political development. This argument stresses the importance of the impact of Ottoman rule in the region. An important consequence of Turkish rule was that it short circuited state formation in the Balkans and blocked the exposure of this area to the Western liberal tradition. The result was the creation of a series of competing and exclusivist nationalisms. Communist rule served, in the long term, to exacerbate this competition because the largest ethnic group within Yugoslavia (the Serbs) believed that other minorities were being allowed to maximise their interests at the expense of the Serb majority. Whilst Tito was alive he was able to hold the Serbs in check. However, his death in 1980 allowed the Serbs to make a concerted effort to re-establish their dominance and this led to a series of actions that culminated in the demise of Yugoslavia.[12]

This is not a satisfactory explanation. As Ignatieff points out, there was considerable evidence of national cohesion in Yugoslavia in the 1980s and early 1990s. Intermarriage between different ethnic groups was quite frequent and a large minority of people (25 per cent of the population) described themselves as Yugoslavian rather than Serb, Croat or Muslim. Furthermore, although there were strong memories of the persecution of the Serbs by the Croats during the Second World War, many of that wartime generation were dead by 1990 and so even that event was fading into the past. What is also interesting is that other Eastern and Central European states that had also recently thrown off the yoke of Communism and were also faced by the problem of a mixed ethnic population did not collapse into civil war.[13] Burg and Shoup also question the rationale that old hatreds explain the civil war in Yugoslavia. They point out that ethnic strife in states such as Canada and Switzerland are not described in terms of 'age old hatreds'. Analysis of these conflicts focus instead on issues of power and interest and the nature of the political systems in these states.[14]

Lake and Rothchild also reject the idea that ethnic conflict is caused by 'ancient hatreds and centuries-old feuds'. They also reject the idea that ethnic passions were released with the demise of repressive Communist regimes at the end of the Cold War. In their view, ethnic conflict is caused when groups begin to fear for their safety. The cause of this heightened fear focuses on the weakness of the state to arbitrate between different groups and provide a sense of security. In essence, state weakness is a precondition for ethnic conflict. The main cause of conflict between different ethnic groups within the state lies in the scarcity of economic resources. In states such as Yugoslavia where ethnicity was an important basis for identity, competition often formed along ethnic lines. An important consequence of this economic austerity was the fact that it undermined the ability of the state to manage and resolve these conflicts.

How does this development relate to the information revolution and the outbreak of war in Europe? Huntington[15], Barber[16] and Kaplan[17] have all sought to demonstrate how the information revolution has had a direct impact on state collapse and civil war. However, the most explicit attempt to apply these ideas to the particular circumstances of Yugoslavia has been made by Kaldor in her study *New and Old Wars*. The main contention of this study is that globalisation is directly responsible for the collapse of the former Yugoslavia into a state of war.

In her view, globalisation undermines the basic building block of stability in the international system: the nation–state. This process of erosion is working at two levels and affects some states more than others; however, what is important is that both dimensions of this process have exerted an important impact on warfare in Europe. The most obvious illustration of this has been what Kaldor describes as the transnationalisation of military forces caused by the transnational connections between armed forces that developed during the Cold War, culminating in the emergence of two military blocs: NATO and the Warsaw Pact.[18] This integration has imposed significant constraints on the sovereignty of nations in terms of when and how they might seek to use force to achieve their aims. It also ensures that when military action is undertaken it is usually a collective effort involving either the United Nations or some other regional security system. As a result even the most local wars are likely to have a strong international dimension.

The second and more pernicious dimension of this erosion of state sovereignty stems from the domestic political situation within the state itself. Globalisation, whilst promoting wealth creation amongst certain states, has exacerbated economic decline in others. The consequences of this have been to promote corruption and crime, and intensify rivalries between various groups. Most importantly, declining tax revenues weaken the ability of the state to provide security for its people. This decline in power is paralleled by the emergence of internal armed factions. As a

result, the state's monopoly on violence is broken and it de-
scends into a spiral of increasing domestic violence and ultimately
civil war.[19] In essence, technology has generated new sources of
instability and conflict within the international system.

THE MEDIA AND MILITARY INTERVENTION

It is the international dimension of the war in the former Yugoslavia that makes it so distinctive from previous conflicts. Of
particular importance is the way in which the major military
powers became involved in their efforts to resolve this conflict.
Although the concept of military intervention is not new the
difference in the case of the war in Yugoslavia was that intervention took place within a recognised nation–state. As Bellamy
explains, this was an extremely important development in the
international system. One of the most basic points of international law and custom that grew out of the Treaty of Westphalia
in 1648 was the principle of non-intervention in the internal
affairs of nation–states. Occasionally this principle was breached,
as in 1961 in the Congo and again 1991 in Iraq, but these were
exceptions and when the UN was established in 1945 its char-
ter recognised the sanctity of the nation-state to conduct its
internal affairs as it saw fit.[20] Even a decade after the end of the
Cold War intervention in civil wars remains a controversial issue
that divides the international community. However, there is no
doubt that this practice is becoming more common and it is
also clear that the war in Yugoslavia played an important part in
establishing this change in the norms of both governments and
supranational organisations like the UN.

The impetus to intervene was again driven by the effects of
the information revolution. In this case it was the global media
network, which, as a result of developments in technology, was
able to provide real time pictures of the worst excesses of these
wars to millions of ordinary citizens living in the West. Inevitably the media posed the question why nothing was being done
to stop the slaughter in places like Croatia and Bosnia and this
in turn stirred the liberal and humanitarian consciences of West
European electorates who then demanded that their national
governments do something to end these genocidal wars. This

phenomenon is known as the CNN effect and describes a situation in which policy makers lose their sovereignty to act and are forced instead to react to the demands of the media. Just how powerful the CNN effect is remains open to question and indeed there are those who believe that its potency has been exaggerated. However, there are circumstances, for example when there is a policy vacuum, where the media has been able to influence government policy.[21] Television has also been used by private charities and pressure groups such as Oxfam, Christian Aid, Save the Children and Amnesty International as a way of mobilising worldwide support for their respective causes.[22]

In the case of Yugoslavia there was a distinct reluctance on the part of European governments to become directly involved in the war. However, as a result of the media's coverage of the death and destruction in Bosnia in 1992, Hudson and Stainer believe that national governments were forced to act:

> The catalyst which finally compelled the world to react was the combined force of the world s press and television. Probably never before had the influence of the media been more powerfully felt by governments of the world in the ensuing months and years of the war in Bosnia.[23]

In their view the decision made by Prime Minister John Major to commit 1800 troops to Bosnia in August 1992 was forced upon the British Government by the media. Moreover, they contest the view of Douglas Hurd, who was then Foreign Secretary, that the decision to commit troops had nothing to do with the media, but was seen as the best way of containing the conflict. As they point out the deployment of 1800 British troops to Bosnia could not achieve this mission.[24]

The media coverage of the war in Bosnia created a number of problems for both politicians and military commanders and exerted a profound impact on the conduct of operations. The first and most pronounced problem – and a feature of many military operations today – was the absence of any real material interest in the conflict. This was not a war of necessity but a war of choice.[25] As result, the governments that committed forces to Bosnia were only prepared to make the minimal investment of resources. The impression gained was that the object of the exercise was simply to demonstrate that the government was doing something. The issue of whether the force could play a meaningful role in the crisis was sometimes an issue of secondary importance. Freedman called this type of action 'symbolic security politics'[26] and there was much evidence of this in the early phases of the crisis in Bosnia. Badsey points to the example of the deployment of a European Community and NATO naval force to the Adriatic in July 1992. For the first four months of its operation it was only allowed to observe the slaughter that was taking place in the region.[27]

The second and related problem was the fear that, because there were no national interests at stake, it was vital that there should be no casualties. It was feared that if military personnel were lost, the media and public opinion might turn against the government. This imposed severe constraints on what the military could do and the need to avoid casualties had to be foremost in the minds of military planners when contemplating a particular course of action. Of equal importance was the need to ensure that, when military force was used by the intervening power, it should not result in the deaths of the civilian population. Not only would such an act contravene the laws of war but it also undermined the very reason for the intervention: to save lives. As a result the media came to dominate this conflict and it is expected that they will continue to do so in the future. As Badsey explains:

> Certainly, at the end of the 20th century the role of the media in military affairs cannot any longer be treated as a side-issue, except by wilful ignorance. From a military perspective, the 'media war' is beginning to rank in importance with the war fought on the ground or in the air, and in many cases the behaviour of the media will help determine military success or failure.[28]

THE NEW OPERATIONAL ENVIRONMENT OF WAR

According to Kaldor the conflict in Bosnia represented a new evolution in the development of war. The principal difference between this and previous wars was that this conflict was dominated by privately owned armed hordes whose main goal was to torture, terrorise and plunder those elements of the civilian population that were not part of their ethnic group. This marked a radical break with established methods of war fighting that relied on professional soldiers adhering to a strict code that proscribed attacks against the civilian population and where the goal of campaign was the destruction of the enemy force through battle.[29] One of the principal characteristics of this war was the ratio between civilian and military casualties. Kaldor estimates that at least eight civilians were killed for every military fatality.[30] To some extent this argument is overstated. The brutality inflicted on the civilian population between 1992–5 was very similar to the kinds of violence and atrocities committed in the region during the Second World War.[31] Moreover, one of the distinguishing characteristics of most wars since 1945 has been the fact that more civilians than soldiers have been killed.[32]

There is also a marked similarity between this war and civil wars that have taken place in other parts of the world since 1945. A good illustration of this was the civil war in Lebanon. It is apparent that the military also saw certain parallels between the war in Bosnia and previous civil wars. For example, the Americans often compared the war in Bosnia to their own experience in the Vietnam War. Like the Vietnam War they feared that military intervention would prove to be at best costly and at worst a complete failure. Bosnia also seemed to provide proof that the military analyst Martin van Creveld's book, THE TRANSFORMATION OF WAR, published in 1990, was correct. The future of war was going to be dominated by intra-state conflicts. Unfortunately, this was the one type of war that the professional military establishments of the West were unable to deal with. A cursory glance at British, French and American counterinsurgency operations against third world opponents in the period 1945–89 demonstrated the impotence of modern high tech forces. Even the Israeli Army foundered in Lebanon and within its own borders its military power proved impotent in dealing with the Intifada (1987–). Western military establishments relied too much on technology, had too many of their personal in the support arms and not enough men in the front line.[33]

EXPLAINING THE FAILURE OF UNPROFOR

Military intervention in the war in Bosnia was carried out under a United Nations mandate that came into effect in June 1992. The military contingent, called the United Nations Peacekeeping Force (UNPROFOR), was to remain in Bosnia until the Dayton Peace Accords were signed in November 1995. The general perception of UNPROFOR's performance during this time was that it was a failure. The fact that UNPROFOR was unable to prevent the deaths of over 200 000 people was seen as sufficient evidence of its impotence. It might also be possible to extrapolate from this that this failure proves van Creveld's argument concerning the ineffectiveness of Western military power in intrastate conflicts. However, both viewpoints are too simplistic and miss an important isssue: the intervening governments and their military commanders learned important lessons about how to use force in this strange new conflict environment and by 1995 military power played a critical role in bringing the war to an end.

Mistakes were made in Bosnia. Perhaps the most important of these was the way in which preconceived models of how force should be used were applied to a conflict environment where they were not appropriate. The most obvious example of this was the UN's slavish adherence to its traditional practice of peacekeeping.[34] This model required that UN forces should be deployed only when an effective ceasefire had been agreed between the warring parties and that the UN peacekeepers should have the consent of the belligerents to deploy. It was also important that they should maintain that consent by remaining impartial and using force only in self-defence. This worked very well in the context of interstate conflicts where the UN was dealing with recognised national governments that had agreed to a ceasefire that they could impose without question.

In Bosnia, however, there was no meaningful peace to keep because the political leadership of the warring factions either lied or as unable to impose their will on all their local commanders. Equally important the belligerents did not perceive the UN as being impartial. In the eyes of the Serbs, feeding the starving Bosnian Muslims was providing aid to their enemies. Consequently the UN lost its claim to be impartial. At the same time the UN found itself unable to use force except in circumstances where the lives of UN peacekeepers were threatened. As result, UN peacekeepers were forced to stand by as observers whilst the warring factions killed each other and innocent civilians. This failure to act caused the Bosnian Muslims, who suffered the lion's share of the casualties in this conflict, to conclude that the UN was also failing to be impartial. As result both sides increasingly viewed UNPROFOR as merely another faction.

The need to maintain consent and impartiality made it vitally important that the intervening force should not be provocative in terms of its size or even the equipment it used. A good illustration of how sensitive the UN was about the issue of equipment was its attempt to restrict the number of armoured personnel carriers (APCs) that the French and Canadian contingents were allowed to bring into Bosnia in September 1992. They were supposed to have no more than fifteen in each battalion. Luckily both contingents ignored this restriction and brought eighty APCs each. According to General MacKenzie, commanding officer of the Canadian contingent guarding Sarajevo airport, the APCs were to prove invaluable in keeping the Serbs in check.[35] The vulnerability of this force was increased further because it was necessary to distribute peacekeeping units over a wide area to protect the main targets of this war: the civilian population.

The UN was aware of the problems a UN peacekeeping force was likely to experience in Bosnia. It is interesting to note the UN rejected an appeal made by the Bosnian Muslim Government in March 1992 to deploy UN peacekeepers because there was no effective ceasefire in place and therefore no peace to keep. However, the failure of the European Community to broker an effective ceasefire in 1992 and the unwillingness of individual European states or the United States to become directly involved in the war only left the option of the UN. The pressure to intervene increased as the scale of the humanitarian disaster became clearer.

One of the fundamental reasons why major powers such as the United States refused to intervene militarily in this war was because it did not allow them to apply their model of war fighting. In general, Western professional military establishments require that their governments provide them with a clear and

achievable aim, a generous supply of resources and total autonomy in how they plan and conduct operations. However, as Luttwak
points out, this mode of thinking precludes any form of intervention in the kinds of conflicts that are taking place today and
is more reminiscent of a form of warfare that characterised
nineteenth-century Europe than the twenty-first century. Certainly when applied to the war in Bosnia it played a critical role
in stopping the United States from becoming involved.[36]

The sense of crisis generated by the media coverage of the
war dictated that something must be done and resulted in the
major powers literally dumping the problem in the hands of
the UN. Thus in the summer of 1992, it was estimated that
there were already over 750 000 refugees in Bosnia, 16 per cent
of the population. By this stage of the war it was also feared that
over 50 000 people had been killed and the media began to
report on Serb atrocities against Bosnian Muslim civilians. If
nothing were done it was believed that 40 000 people would
die of starvation and cold during the next winter.[37] Confronted
by this potential disaster the UN agreed to deploy military forces
to Bosnia in June 1992.[38]

Once on the ground it was clear that there was a significant
gap between what UNPROFOR was expected to do and what it
was actually capable of doing. Once again the response of the
international community was to play the game of symbolic security
politics. UNPROFOR was given greater freedom to resort to the
use of force in a range of circumstances that went beyond the
principle of self-defence. Thus, in September 1992, because
the Serbs stopped the delivery of aid to besieged Muslim towns
and villages, the Security Council authorised UNPROFOR to
protect aid convoys. In October 1992, the UN created a no-fly
zone over Bosnia in an effort to stop the Serbs using their air
force bombing Serb villages. The right to use force was extended
further when in 1993 the Security Council decided to make a
number of besieged Bosnian cities safe areas. This allowed the
UN commander to use force to protect the safe areas if attacked
by the Serbs.

There were a number of problems with this expansion of the
mission. First, many of the units in UNPROFOR did not really
have the capability to fight their way through to the starving
civilians and consequently the Serbs continued to block the

movement of humanitarian convoys. Second, UNPROFOR was too small to carry out these additional tasks. By 1994, there were only 23 000 UN troops in Bosnia. This lack of resources was made very apparent in the case of the safe areas. The UN Secretary General called for an additional 34 000 troops to be deployed to provide security for these UN protectorates. The UN Security Council reduced this to a force of 7500 troops and a year later only 5000 of this force were in place in Bosnia.[39] The enforcement of the no-fly zone also proved less than comprehensive because only a limited number of fighters were available to police the skies above Bosnia. As a result, the Serbs were able to violate the no-fly zone.

Air power was also used as a substitute for UN troops to protect the safe areas from Serb attack. However, such attacks were not particularly effective in deterring the Serbs. Air strikes were used for the first time to prevent the Serbs from seizing the Muslim town of Gorazde in April 1994. Three attacks were launched between the 10 and 15 April 1994. However, these air strikes were described as being pinpricks because they were so small and ineffective and had no discernible effect on Serb behaviour. More effective was the Serb response, which entailed seizing 200 UN personnel and holding them as hostages. They also began deploying surface-to-air missile (SAMs) defences to protect their forces. This made the UN think very carefully about using air strikes. It forced NATO air forces to remain at altitudes that made effective air strikes against ground targets very difficult. In addition it also resulted in fighters being taken off patrol and concentrating instead on providing support to fighters authorised to conduct air strikes. When required, this supporting package could be used to suppress Serb SAM defences. However, because no additional resources were available aircraft had to be taken off patrol to conduct this additional mission. Consequently, NATO's control of the skies was less than complete and the Serbs found it possible to use their air power to move their forces around, and to bomb Bihac in November 1994.[40]

FROM PEACEKEEPING TO WAR

In 1995 the war in Bosnia was effectively brought to a stop by the UN and NATO agreeing to use military power to coerce the Serbs to accept a negotiated settlement that divided Bosnia, on the basis of ethnicity, into a number of independent republics. What this action demonstrated was that it was possible to use the 'baroque'[41] military power of the West effectively in the midst of a complex civil war and that technology could be a source of strength rather than weakness in conflicts of this type.

The impotence of UNPROFOR reflected a lack of political will on the part of the international community to adopt a more robust response to this crisis. It was this failure, rather than any intrinsic weakness of conventional military power, that was the cause of the futile display of UNPROFOR. Consequently, it was the changing views of the international community that was of fundamental importance in releasing the constraints on the use of force.

The principal cause of this transformation was the fact that by May 1995 UNPROFOR was on the verge of collapse. After a four-month ceasefire the war broke out with renewed ferocity in March 1995. The Bosnian Muslims launched the first of a series of major offensives against the Serbs. The Serb response to this action was to attack the UN safe areas. In addition the Serbs also began bombarding Sarajevo. One such attack on 9 May resulted in many civilian casualties. The response of the UN to this attack merely confirmed how vulnerable UNPROFOR was. In an attempt to stop Serb artillery strikes against Sarajevo the UN ordered the Serbs to withdraw their heavy weapons from the exclusion zone around the city. The failure of the Serbs to comply resulted in air strikes against an ammunition dump in Pale. Undeterred, the Serbs escalated the crisis by shelling Tuzla, killing 71 civilians. This prompted a second air strike. The response of the Serbs on this occasion was to hold hostage 350 UN peacekeepers. Many of these were used as 'human shields' to protect other potential targets from NATO air strikes. The hostages were released in June after the UN had given guarantees that UNPROFOR would function as a traditional peacekeeping force.

Throughout the months of June and July the fortunes of the UN continued to decline. The UN's refusal to sanction the use of further force and its inability to force the Serbs to allow it to deliver desperately needed aid to either Sarajevo or the safe areas alienated the Muslims and the Croats. The release of the UN hostages in June merely provided confirmation in the minds of the Croats and the Muslims that UNPROFOR was sympathetic to the Serbs and that it had struck a deal with them in order to secure the release of the hostages. As a result both the Croats and Muslims also began obstructing the UN's efforts to deliver aid. These actions when combined with Serb intransigence effectively paralysed UNPROFOR.

The weakness of the UN was demonstrated again in July when the UN safe area of Srebenica was overrun. Tragically, the population of 40 000 Muslims was ethnically cleansed. This happened in spite of the presence of UN peacekeepers. More sinister was the suspected execution of over 7000 Bosnian Muslim men by the victorious Serbs. NATO tried to stop the fall of Srebenica through air strikes, but these had little effect on operations on the ground or in forcing a change in the behaviour of the Serb leadership. The fall of Srebenica and the massacre that followed it created a storm of protest by the media and the public. The pressure to take action against the Serbs was overwhelming. In response to the crisis created by the fall of Srebenica, and the danger that Gorazde, Tuzla and Bihac might go the same way, the British summoned a conference in London on 21 July 1995. After prolonged discussions it was agreed that in the event of a Serb attack against Gorazde NATO would launch widespread air attacks against Serb targets. Most important was the decision to withdraw remaining UN forces from the politically controversial safe areas. This action ensured that, in the event of further NATO air strikes, the Serbs would not be able to take UN soldiers hostage. On 23 July US, British and French air force generals met with the Bosnian Serb commander General Mladic and warned him that an extensive air campaign would be launched in response to an attack on Gorazde. NATO approved the proposed air plan on 25 July and the following week it was decided to extend the threat of air strikes to cover attacks against the remaining safe areas: Sarajevo, Tuzla and Bihac.

In addition, efforts were also made in May to increase the size of UNPROFOR and to give it more aggressive rules of engagement. Of particular importance was the decision to deploy a heavily armed force to support UNPROFOR. On the 28 May 1995 the British Government decided to deploy an air-mobile brigade to Bosnia to provide greater protection for the peace-keepers. In an extreme situation it could also assist in the withdrawal of UNPROFOR should that become necessary. On 3 June it was agreed that this force would be incorporated with French and Dutch troops into a multinational force titled the Rapid Reaction Force (RRF). Although there seemed to be no clear idea of what role this force of 15 000 troops should play in Bosnia there is no doubt that, once deployed, it created an effective deterrent that inhibited neither Serb nor Muslim attacks against UNPROFOR.

OPERATION DELIBERATE FORCE

The decisive use of force by NATO was not exercised in response to the impending collapse of Gorazde, but as a result of a mortar attack on the market place in Sarajevo on 28 August 1995 in which 38 people were killed and over 80 were wounded. It was decided that this action provided the justification for initiating Deliberate Force. Operation Deliberate Force represented a concerted effort to use force to end the war and is generally credited for forcing the Serbs to accept a ceasefire that finally culminated in the Dayton Accords. However, as Oudrat has pointed out, if the Bosnian Serb leaders had already agreed to the basic peace deal then on offer, why then did NATO find it necessary to use force?[42] Burg and Shoup believe that there was still considerable uncertainty about the final territorial settlement and the Bosnian Serbs were still entrenched around Sarajevo. In addition, air power was used to alter the military balance on the ground by helping Muslim and Croat offensives against the Bosnian Serbs that were underway during August and September 1995.[43]

According to the UN Commander of UNPROFOR, Lieutenant General Rupert Smith, Operation Deliberate Force was designed to deter the Serbs from attacking the designated safe areas. However, it was also intended to destroy the Serbs military offensive capability and hopefully bring them to the negotiating table. As such it envisaged the use of air strikes to provide immediate close air support to defend the safe areas. Most important, in terms of coercing the Serbs, was the proposal to attack targets away from the battlefield. This required large-scale systematic attacks against key targets. As a result, the air campaign was also designed to disrupt the logistical, command and control of the Bosnian Serb Army (BSA) throughout the theatre of operations.[44] The aim of military action was not to bring about the direct defeat of the Serbs, but to 'promote conditions which will facilitate the peace process, without sparking a wider Balkans conflict'.[45]

The actual campaign operated within clearly defined limits that were designed to prevent the war getting out of control. The targets selected for the first batch of air strikes really focused on attacking the BSA in the safe areas, ammunition dumps and their lines of communication and supply. NATO was not authorised to attack strategic targets such as power stations, industrial targets and the political infrastructure within the Bosnian Serb Republic. Escalation of this kind required the authorisation of national governments. It was also decided to keep air strikes away from the border between the Yugoslavia and the Serb state in Bosnia so that this did not provoke intervention by the Yugoslavian Army.

A principal constraint on the proposed campaign was the issue of casualties. This was NATO's and the UN's critical concern and if the mission was to be successful then it was vitally important that no pilots should be lost. This in turn meant that the air campaign had to be conducted in sequence. The first of these sequences was the suppression of the enemy's air defence system. Once this was achieved then it was a matter of hitting targets set out in the target list.

Concern over civilian and even Serb military casualties also imposed important constraints on the proposed air campaign. Of the 155 targets identified it was decided to sanction attacks against 87 targets. An important cause in the reduction of this target list was the need to reduce the chances of civilian casualties. Similar concerns resulted in the decision to cancel planned air strikes against the barracks of four BSA brigades.[46] In an effort to minimise the chances of fighter aircraft being attacked by Serb surface to air missiles it was decided that pilots should remain above 10 000 when conducting their attacks.

In spite of these restrictions Operation Deliberate Force represented a significant escalation of the war. It began with more than 60 aircraft bombing BSA positions around Sarajevo. Added to this *crescendo* of firepower was the artillery of the Rapid Reaction Force deployed around Sarajevo. This was the largest military action by NATO. Over two weeks of bombing NATO conducted over 3500 sorties and fired nearly 100 cruise missiles against nearly 400 Serb targets.

In the first instance the air campaign was not connected with wider diplomatic moves to end the war. The initial aim was more modest: air strikes would stop if the BSA ended their attacks on the safe areas, withdrew all heavy weapons from Sarajevo and agreed to a ceasefire throughout Bosnia. However, Richard Holbrooke, the US representative responsible for negotiating a settlement with the Serbs, was in close contact with NATO both before and during the actual campaign. It is also clear that Holbrooke used both the threat of air strikes, as well as threatening further escalation once the campaign began, as a way to coerce the BSA to accept proposals to partition Bosnia between the Muslims and Croats, and the Serbs.

After two days of bombing, the Bosnian Serb Army commander, Mladic, offered to meet the UN Commander to discuss the terms but insisted that the bombing should stop. It was decided to accommodate this request and the bombing was suspended on 1 September. The decision to suspend the bombing also helped Holbrooke's diplomatic mission in Yugoslavia and there were suspicions that the bombing halt was initiated primarily to help US diplomatic efforts in Belgrade. It is clear that Holbrooke was in close contact with the UN in Bosnia and briefed them on the current state of negotiations between the US and Yugoslavia. According to one of Holbrooke's advisors, Slobodan Milosevic asked for a halt to the bombing and Holbrooke promised to see what he could do. It seems that Holbrooke did in fact discuss the possibility of a bombing halt with the NATO commanders and this may have had some influence on their decision to agree to the temporary cessation of air strikes.

The resumption of the air campaign was driven by a combination of factors. Holbrooke wanted to put the Serbs under pressure again and in a meeting with NATO on 2 September urged them to resume the bombing campaign. It was also becoming increasingly clear that the BSA were stalling for time and were not complying with the UN's demands that they withdraw their heavy weapons from Sarajevo. Faced with mounting political pressure from above, and increasing evidence of the mendacity of the Serbs from below, the UN and NATO military commanders decided to begin bombing again on 5 September.

There was a noticeable shift in the nature and character of the renewed bombing campaign in that there was a greater emphasis on inflicting pain as a means of coercing the Bosnian Serbs to comply with the UN's demands. General Smith's target priorities moved from destroying Serb artillery and air defences to dismantling the systemic organisation of the BSA. This meant attacking the transport infrastructure, the BSA's communications network, its logistics, ammunition dumps and its reserve forces. This shift in targeting reflected his belief that in order to make Mladic change his mind it was important to frighten him and what frightened Mladic more than anything was losing control of his forces.[47] As a result of this decision the bombing expanded to cover wider areas of territory controlled by the BSA. However, after a further nine days of bombing the Serbs seemed no closer to 'throwing in the towel'. More worrying was the fact that by 14 September NATO had run out of targets to hit. All that was left were strategic targets and this required the authorisation of national governments. However, it was unlikely that permission would be granted for these attacks because it went beyond the UN mandate.

It is the view of Ripley that the US Government decided to pre-empt the possibility that the air campaign might fail, simply because it burned itself out through a lack of targets, by sending Holbrooke back to Belgrade with a less ambitious set of proposals. In essence, NATO promised to stop the bombing if the Serbs lifted their siege of Sarajevo and removed their heavy weaponry from the area. On the night of 13–14 September, and to the surprise of many, the Bosnian Serbs agreed to unilaterally cease offensive operations around Sarajevo. This resulted in the suspension of air operations for a period of 72 hours. This was then extended indefinitely leading to the establishment of a ceasefire between the warring factions in October 1995 which culminated in the Dayton Accords a month later.

Deliberate Force demonstrated the potency of modern high

tech forces fighting in the midst of a complex humanitarian emergency in which it was, initially at least, very unclear how force was to be used. However, it is important to recognise that other factors also played a critical role in bringing the Serbs to the negotiating table. The most important of these was the string of successful joint offensives launched by the Bosnian Muslims and Croats between August and October 1995. In early August, the Croats and the Bosnian Muslims combined to launch the first of attacks against the Serbs. The ostensible aim of this action was to save the safe area of Bihac from imminent collapse. According to Ripley these offensives were the largest military operations since World War II and involved more than 200 000 troops supported by thousands of artillery pieces and hundreds of armoured vehicles.[48] This suggests that the war in Bosnia had evolved beyond a collection of armed gangs and that Kaldor was premature in seeing this phenomenon as a permanent characteristic of 'new war'.

US military analysts were stunned by the success of the Croats and the speed with which they overran the Serb-occupied province of Krajina in Operation Storm. The collapse of Krajina left a big gap in the defences of the Bosnian Serbs In theory 50 000 Krajina Serbs were available to join the BSA in a new defence. However, this force had lost most of its equipment. In addition, the majority of the Serb Krajina Army were demoralised and many of them deserted.

This success was matched by further offensives in September with the Bosnian Muslims holding large elements of the BSA in place whilst the Croats pushed through the weakened defences of the Serbs in the western half of Bosnia. These attacks resulted in over 40 000 Serbs fleeing from their homes and, more importantly, exposed the Serb city of Banja Luka to Croat forces. The fear that this city, with its population of 400 000 Serbs, might fall to Croats also made the Bosnian Serbs willing to accept the UN's terms.

It is also important to recognise that the Bosnian Serbs were undermined by the failure of Slobadan Milosevic to throw the Yugoslavian Army in to support them in their hour of need. This failure to support the BSA has been attributed to Milosevic's desire to have economic sanctions lifted against Yugoslavia. To achieve this goal it became necessary to cooperate with the United

States by placing pressure on the Bosnian Serb leadership to accept a ceasefire and NATO's peace plan. Thus, on the 4 August, Milosevic broke off formal economic links with the Bosnian Serb Republic because of the refusal of its leaders to agree to the Contact Group's proposed partition of Bosnia.

THE ROLE OF THE UNITED STATES: DIPLOMACY AND WAR

An alternative view of these events would be to see them as part of a series of linked, although not always coordinated, processes orchestrated by the United States in an effort to resolve the conflict. Most important was the role of the US in ending the fighting between the Croats and Muslims in 1994. These diplomatic efforts resulted in a ceasefire in February 1994 and the creation of the Bosnian–Croat Federation in March of that year. Through this action both the Muslims and the Croats could now concentrate their forces on the Serbs.

The United States also provided funding, equipment and training for Croat forces. It is believed that Croat military success was due, in part, to the training given by a private US military consultancy based in Washington. There is also a rumour that senior US Army officers assessed the feasibility of the planned Croat offensive that resulted in the liberation of Krajina in August 1995. There is also strong evidence that the United States supplied arms and equipment to the Bosnian Muslims and that they facilitated the movement of money and arms from Islamic states that were sympathetic to the cause of the Bosnian Muslims. Without American backing it is questionable whether either the Muslims or the Croats would have been in a position to go on the offensive in 1995. Equally important in the resolution of this conflict was the way in which the United States was able to de-couple Yugoslavia from the Bosnian Serbs with the promise of ending sanctions if they cooperated in persuading the Bosnian Serbs to end the fighting.

In essence, by 1995 the Clinton Administration created the conditions within which external military force could be used effectively. Equally important, it made good use of local proxy forces, in the form of the Croats and the Bosnian Muslims, to fight the Serbs on the ground and thus reduced the need for US ground forces. The military success of Croat and Muslim operations on the ground created the right political conditions for the imposition of a ceasefire and ultimately a political settlement in the form of the Dayton Accords.

The bombing campaign also had a direct bearing on the outcome of the Croat–Muslim offensive that helped to change the military balance on the ground in their favour. The most obvious example of this was the destruction of the BSA Krajina Corps' command and control systems in the area of Banja Luka. On 10 September British and French aircraft severed the telephone links between Mladic's Headquarters and units at the front, making it all but impossible to coordinate BSA defences across western Bosnia. Serb commanders were very dependent on the telephone system because of the limited range of radios in the mountainous terrain and so found it impossible to organise themselves in the face of a fast-moving Croat offensive. It is also interesting that once Deliberate Force was suspended the Croat advance slowed considerably in the face of stronger Serb resistance until it ground to a halt outside Banja Luka. With the end of the air war it became possible for the Serbs to move their forces to where they were needed. As a result, the Serbs were able to stabilise their front line in western Bosnia by the time of the October ceasefire.[49]

It was also the Americans who eventually made a conscious effort to link military action, both in the air and on the ground, to the diplomatic process that resulted in the cessation of hostilities in October 1995. Deliberate Force was not part of some cunning political master plan to end the war. It was pure coincidence that the campaign coincided with the US Assistant Secretary, of State's shuttle diplomacy in the Balkans. As Holbrooke points out it was the Serb shelling of the market place in Sarajevo that dictated the timing of the air campaign, not the United States.[50]

However, Holbrooke made good use of Deliberate Force and Croatian and Muslim offensives against the Serbs to coerce them to accept the terms and conditions of the proposed peace plan. It is important to remember that the Croats consulted the Americans before launching their offensive in Krajina and wanted their blessing before proceeding. From the perspective of the Americans it was vital that the imbalance in terms of territorial ownership between the warring factions should be redressed in favour of the Croats and the Muslims and they believed that military action was the only way to achieve this goal. Holbrooke was also prepared to support the first halt in the bombing campaign because Milosevic promised to secure an end to the siege, of Sarajevo. Once it was clear that the Serbs were not willing to end the siege, Holbrooke was one of the strongest supporters of resuming the air war.[51] He was to make good use of the bombing campaign in his negotiations with the Serbs on 13–14 September. Although the bombing campaign was running out of targets, Holbrooke did not seize upon Serb offers of a ceasefire. At this time he wanted to give the Muslims and the Croats more time in the land war and so continued to bluff, insisting first on the termination of the siege of Sarajevo.[52] Even when the ceasefire was agreed its continuation depended upon the Serbs fulfilling a number of conditions. Holbrooke also made good use of the Croat offensives in September and October to pressure the Serb leadership to make further concessions. Was this a new hybrid: war in peace?

The war in Bosnia confronted the most powerful military alliance in the world (NATO) with a new military strategic and operational environment that was so challenging that it seemed to prove the assertion made by van Creveld and others that orthodox military power was impotent in fighting what are today termed postmodern wars. An important question asked by General Rose was whether military power could have been applied more effectively at the very start of the conflict in 1992. The answer he believes is no. Bosnia was a learning experience for the members of NATO. At the start of the conflict European armed forces such as the British Army were equipped and trained to deter, and if that failed, fight a massive conventional and nuclear war against the Warsaw Pact. It took three years to learn new ways of how to use force within the highly volatile and complex environment of a humanitarian disaster happening within the context of a protracted civil war.[53] The application of traditional models of military action proved ineffective. Clearly it was inappropriate to fight a war, but at the same time it was also very clear that principles of traditional peacekeeping could not be made to work. According to Bellamy, a new approach was needed, in essence a new form of war fighting.[54] As a result of their experiences in Bosnia the British began to develop a new doctrine that was designed to ensure that military power could be used effectively when applied to complex, humanitarian emergencies epitomised by the war in Bosnia. The essential problem was how to use force whilst at the same time preserving the principles of impartiality and consent for the operation amongst the warring parties and the local population. Such is the complexity of this dilemma that the British found it necessary to issue two doctrine publications on how to conduct peacekeeping operations in 1995–9.[55]

The general conclusion of these analyses is that in conflicts such as Bosnia military intervention should possess a range of capabilities so that it has sufficient power to deter attack, but if it is attacked or it cannot carry out its mission, it can resort to the use of force. In essence, the distinction between peace and war has become blurred and is perceived more as spectrum that moves from peace to war with humanitarian warfare somewhere in the middle as a shade of grey. Currently it is envisaged that military intervention will be able to move along this spectrum from peace to war and back again according to circumstances. It is important to note that war in this environment is not designed to secure military victory through the destruction of the enemy's forces. Instead it is intended that it should support the process of political bargaining.[56]

Another noticeable development in the war in Bosnia was the increasing reliance placed on air power and missile power to achieve the aims of intervening powers. Because of the perceived sensitivity of public attitudes towards casualties, governments found it almost impossible to use ground forces to impose a ceasefire on the Serbs. Air power has become the preferred way of fighting wars of this kind. The war against Kosovo was a perfect illustration of this practice. In military terms the most effective way of stopping the Serbs from ethnically cleansing the province would have been to intervene on the ground, rather than delivering punishing strikes from the air, but the political cost of such action was too great. Ironically, such action is more reminiscent of the way in which force was used in the eighteenth century. As Luttwak explains:

> Before the French Revolution, most wars were fought for much less than imperative purposes that rarely evoked popular

enthusiasm, with prudent strategies and tactics to conserve expensive professional forces. While no great purposes at hand could motivate the entire nation in war, there is much justification for some eighteenth-century warfare of our own, with our modest purposes and casualty avoidance as the controlling norm.[57]

Through the use of technology as a way of reducing the exposure of personnel to the dangers of war, and by applying a strategy more reminiscent of siege warfare in which political and economic sanctions were combined with a strategy of attrition and pain the West was, in the end, able to impose a solution in the Balkans not just in 1995, but also in Kosovo in 1999.

Notes and References

INTRODUCTION *Jeremy Black*

1. B. J. Fischer, *Albania at War 1939–1945* (London, 1999), p. 24.
2. J. Bourke, *An Intimate History of Killing: Face-to-Face Killing in Twentieth-Century Warfare* (London, 1999).
3. Kings College London, Liddell Hart Centre for Military Archives (hereafter LH), Hamilton papers (hereafter Hamilton), 4/2/3, p. 27.
4. T. Travers, *How the War Was Won: Command and Technology in the British Army on the Western Front, 1917–1918* (London, 1992); P. Griffith, *Battle Tactics of the Western Front: The British Army's Art of Attack* (New Haven, 1994); J. Bailey, *The First World War and the Birth of the Modern Style of Warfare* (Camberley, 1996); S. B. Schreiber, *Shock Army of the British Empire: The Canadian Corps in the Last 100 Days of the Great War* (Westport, 1997); J. P. Harris, *Amiens to the Armistice: The BEF in the Hundred Days' Campaign, 8 August – 11 November 1918* (London, 1998).
5. R. Hall, *The Balkan Wars 1912–1913. Prelude to the First World War* (London, 2000), p. 134.
6. V. G. Liulevicius, *War Land on the Eastern Front. Culture, National Identity, and German Occupation in World War I* (Cambridge, 2000), pp. 47, 81.
7. Several prominent works on the Eastern Front have been written by British authors who lack Russian.
8. D. Glantz, *Zhukov's Greatest Defeat. The Red Army's Epic Disaster in Operation Mars, 1942* (Lawrence, Kansas, 1999).
9. Pound to Admiral Layton, 9 February 1943, London, British Library, Department of Manuscripts, Additional Manuscripts, vol. 74796.
10. Roberts, 'Memorandum on the Defences of the Indian Ports', LH. Hamilton 1/3/3, p. 275.
11. LH. Montgomery-Massingberd 9/5/7, quotes pp. 9–10, 21, Milne Box 3, quote p. 3.
12. Chetwode to Montgomery-Massingberd, 20 July 1921, LH. Montgomery-Massingberd 8/22.
13. cf. 6 September 1921.
14. Rawlinson to Montgomery-Massingberd, 23 October 1922, LH. Montgomery-Massingberd 8/27.
15. Milne, 'The Role of the Air Force in Relation to the Army', undated. Catalogue says [1925–6], but document contains reference to a document of March 1930, LH. Milne Box 3.
16. LH. Montgomery-Massingberd 10/6.
17. G. Swain, *Russia's Civil War* (Stroud, 2000), p. 150.
18. Chetwode to Montgomery-Massingberd, 1 July 1921, LH. Montgomery-Massingberd 8/22.

19. H. Strachan, *The Politics of the British Army* (Oxford, 1997).

20. M. Knox, '1 October 1942: Adolf Hitler, Wehrmacht Officer Policy, and Social Revolution', *Historical Journal*, 43 (2000), pp. 801–25, especially 823–4. See, more generally, his *Common Destiny. Dictatorship, Foreign Policy, and War in Fascist Italy and Nazi Germany* (Cambridge, 2000).

21. Montgomery-Massingberd to Chetwode, 18 January 1929, LH. Montgomery-Massingberd 10/2.

22. LH. Hamilton 4/2/3, pp. 3, 17, 26.

23. R. J. Overy, *The Air War 1939–1945* (1987); H. Boog (ed.), *The Conduct of the Air War in the Second World War: an International Comparison* (New York, 1992); J. Buckley, *Air Power in the Age of Total War* (1999).

24. M. J. Neufield, *The Rocket and the Reich. Peenemünde and the Coming of the Ballistic Missile Era* (Washington, 1995).

25. LH. Hamilton 1/2/7/2.

26. B. Heuser, *NATO, Britain, France and the FRG: Nuclear Strategies and Forces for Europe, 1949–2000* (London, 1997).

27. Glantz, *Soviet Military Operational Art: In Pursuit of Deep Battle* (Totowa, New Jersey, 1991); J. A. English, *Marching Through Chaos. The Descent of Armies in Theory and Practice* (Westport, Connecticut, 1996), p. 154.

28. J. L. Romjue, 'The Evolution of American Army Doctrine', in J. Gooch (ed.), *The Origins of Contemporary Doctrine* (Camberley, 1997), pp. 70–3.

29. Rawlinson to Montgomery-Massingbered, 13 March 1922, LH. Montgomery-Massingberd 8/27.

1. EUROPE'S WAY OF WAR 1815–1864 *Dennis Showalter*

1. H. Winton, D. Mets (eds) *The Challenge of War: Military Institutions and New Realities, 1918–1941* (Lincoln, Nebraska, 2000) offers a set of comparative case studies in the process.

2. Norman Dixon, *On the Psychology of Military Incompetence* (London, 1984).

3. The standard – and the best – version of this approach is still Michael Howard, *The Franco-Prussian War* (London, 1961), pp. 1–39. A modified version of it appears in a more recent, and excellent general work by Brian Holden-Reid, *The American Civil War and the Wars of the Industrial Revolution* (London, 1999).

4. Geoffrey Wawro, 'Inside the Whale: The Tangled Finances of the Austrian Army, 1848–1866', *War in History* 3 (1996), 42–65.

5. Geoffrey Wawro, *Warfare and Society in Europe, 1792–1914* (London, 2000). It is a tribute to the credibility of the model that it influences a work of high quality by one of the best of the new generation of military historians.

6. Cf. Robert M. Schwartz, *Policing the Poor in Eighteenth-Century*

France (Chapel Hills, NC, 1988); and Jacques Lorgnier's massive *Marechaussée: histoire d' une révolution judiciaire et administrative,* 2 vols (Paris, 1994).

7. Jeremy Black, *Culloden and the 45* (London, 1990).

8. Cf. Helmuth Fechner, 'Westpreussen unter Friderizianischen Verwaltung', In *Deutschland und Polen,* ed. H. Fechner (Wuerzburg, 1964), pp. 30–46; and Walther Hubatsch, 'Friedrich der Grosse und Westpreussen', *Westpreussische Jahrbuch* 22 (1972), 5–14.

9. Still best on the dynamics of this process are George Rudé, *The Crowd in the French Revolution* (Oxford, 1959); and Richard Cobb, *The Police and the People: French Popular Protest, 1789–1820* (Oxford, 1972).

10. Useful case studies of the problem include Don Alexander, *Rod of Iron: French Counterinsurgency Policy in Aragon during the Peninsular War* (Wilmington, Delaware, 1985); Jean-L. Reynaud, *Contre-guerilla en Espagne (1808–1814)*; *Suchet pacifie l'Aragon* (Paris, 1992), and Milton Finley, *The Most Monstrous of Wars: The Napoleonic Guerrilla War in Southern Italy, 1806–1811* (Columbia, SC, 1994).

11. Cf. *inter alia* Stanley Palmer, *Police and Protest in England and Ireland, 1750–1850* (Cambridge, 1989); Gregory T. Smith, 'The State and the Culture of Violence in London, 1760–1840', Dissertation, University of Toronto, 1999; Alf Luedtke, *Police and State in Prussia, 1815–1850,* tr. P. Burgess (Cambridge, 1989); Roger Price, 'The Techniques of Repression: The Control of Popular Protest in Mid-Nineteenth Century France,' *Historical Journal* 25 (1982), 859–87; and, of course, Michel Foucault, *Discipline and Punish: The Birth of the Prison,* tr. A. Sheridan (New York, 1977).

12. Scott Hughes Myerly, *British Military Spectacle From the Napoleonic Wars Through the Crimea* (Cambridge, Mass., 1996) is a pathbreaking study of this phenomenon.

13. The three-year-old Prince Imperial was so disturbed by the sight of the wounded from 1859 that he had to be removed. Matthew Truesdell, *Spectacular Politics: Louis-Napoleon Bonaparte and the Fête Imperiale, 1848–1870* (Oxford, 1997), pp. 153–5.

14. The British garrison of Ireland was divided into almost 2000 separate detachments, based on 441 separate stations. The Marquess of Anglesey, *A History of the British Cavalry,* Vol. I, *1816–1850* (Hamden, CT, 1973), pp. 75–6.

15. Sabrina Mueller, *Soldaten in der deutschen Revolution von 1848/49* (Paderborn, 1999).

16. Douglas Porch, *Army and Revolution: France 1815–1848* (London, 1974), pp. 75–92.

17. See as a case study Lawrence Sondhaus, *In the Service of the Emperor: Italians in the Austrian Armed Forces, 1814–1918* (Boulder, Colorado, 1990).

18. Burkhard Koester, *Militaer und Eisenbahn in der Habsburgermonarchie 1825–1859* (Munich, 1999) is an excellent overview.

19. Frederick W. Kagan, *The Military Reforms of Nicholas I: The Origins*

of the Modern Russian Army (New York, 1999) is a major contribution to our understanding of that complex issue. See as well William C. Fuller, *Strategy and Power in Russia, 1600–1914* (New York, 1992), pp. 220–40.

20. Paul W. Schroeder, *The Transformation of European Politics, 1763–1848* (Oxford, 1994), and *The Concert of Europe and the Crimean War* (New York, 1972) make the best case for this position, which fits the dispatch of troops better than the exercise of diplomacy.

21. Gerald S. Graham, *The Politics of Naval Supremacy* (Cambridge, 1965), pp. 69–71.

22. A comparison may profitably be drawn with Italy, which in the aftermath of unification did arguably structure its army along lines intended to secure domestic stability rather than maximize warfighting potential. See Brian Sullivan. 'The Strategy of the Decisive Weight: Italy 1882–1922', in W. Murray, M. Knox and A. Bernstein (eds) *The Making of Strategy: Rulers, States, and War* (New York, 1994), pp. 307–351.

23. This argument is developed from Gerald L. Prokpowicz, 'Tactical Stalemate', *North and South* 22 (September 1999), 10–27.

24. The Russian regiment at this period was officially divided into *artels*, company-sized cooperatives with no direct military functions that provided social and economic stability for their members.

25. Robert M. Epstein, *Napoleon's Last Victory and the Emergence of Modern War* (Lawrence, Kansas, 1994).

26. It should be noted that continental regiments, unlike their single-battalion counterparts in the British and Union armies, consisted of three or four battalions, with a strength that ranged from 2500 to 4000. They were correspondingly large enough to attract full spectrums of loyalties. The same might be said, relatively speaking, of the Confederate brigades, usually four or five regiments from a single state, that formed the 'units of identity' in the Armies of Tennessee and Northern Virginia.

27. See for example Gary Hart, *The Minuteman; Restoring an Army of the People* (New York, 1998) and from quite a different perspective, Eliot Cohen, 'Why the Gap Matters', *National Interest*, 61 (Fall, 2000), 38–48.

28. Cf. *inter alia* Gary Cox, *The Halt in the Mud: French Strategic Planning from Waterloo to Sedan* (Boulder, Colorado, 1994), P. G. Griffith, *Military Thought in the French Army* (Manchester, 1989), and E. Carris, *La pensee militaire française* (Paris, 1960), pp. 226–62.

29. Joseph Monteilhet, *Les Institutions militaires de la France, 1814–1924* (Paris, 1932), pp. 12ff., remains a good overview of personnel policies, sharply critical of the limited-service principle. David M. Hopkin, '*La Ramée*, the Archetypical Soldier, as an Indicator of Popular Attitudes to the Army in Nineteenth-Century France', *French History* 14 (2000), 115–149.

30. Richard Holmes, *The Road to Sedan: The French Army, 1866–1870* (London, 1984), pp. 11–125, incorporates an excellent overview of the army's developing images and realities.

31. Rory Muir, *Tactics and the Experience of Battle in the Age of Napoleon* (New Haven, CT, 1998).

32. This was true even for the roughest and readiest field army on either side. A. R. B. Houghton, *Training, Tactics, and Leadership in the Confederate Army of Tennessee* (London, 2000). Perry D. Jamieson, 'The Development of Civil War Tactics', Dissertation, Wayne State University, 1979, remains worth consulting for the relationship of training, tactics and effectiveness.

33. Henri duc d'Aumale, *Les Zouaves et les chasseurs à pied* (Paris, 1855).

34. Thomas S. Abler, *Hinterland Warriors and Military Dress: European Empires and Exotic Uniforms* (New York, 1999), especially, pp. 100–110.

35. Cf. Geoffrey Wawro, 'An "Army of Pigs": The Technical, Social, and Political Bases of Austrian Shock Tactics, 1859–1866', *The Journal of Military History* 59 (1995), 407–434; and J. S. Curtiss, *The Russian Army under Nicholas I* (Durham, NC, 1965), pp. 113–30.

36. The following analysis is drawn from the author's monograph *The Wars of German Unification*, forthcoming in 2002.

37. On that subject see Gerd Stolz, *Die schleswig-holsteinisch Erhebung: Die nationale Auseiandersetzung in und um Schleswig-Holstein von 1848–51* (Husum, 1996).

38. C. I. Hamilton, *Anglo–French Naval Rivalry, 1840–1870* (Oxford, 1993), pp. 183–9.

39. James L. Morrison, 'The United States Military Academy, 1833–1866: Years of Progress and Turmoil', Dissertation, Columbia University, 1970.

40. W. S. Serman, *Les origines des officiers français, 1848–1870* (Paris, 1979), remains definitive for statistics and mentalities.

41. The quotation is paraphrased from Raoul Girardet, *La Société militare dans la France contemporaine, 1815–1939* (Paris,1953), p. 110.

42. Wawro, 'An "Army of Pigs"', *passim*; Istvan Deak, *Beyond Nationalism: A Social and Political History of the Habsburg Officer Corps, 1848–1918* (New York, 1990), pp. 99–110.

43. Cf. Ian Worthington, 'Antecedent Education and Officer Recruitment: The Origins and Early Development of the Public School-Army Relationship', *Military Affairs* 41 (1977), 183–9. Hew Strachan, *The Reform of the British Army, 1830–54* (Manchester, 1984), pp. 109–145. Strachan makes a point valid for all armies at this period and most others: much of the behavior that shocked settled elements of society was to be predicted in young men out from under supervision for the first time in their lives.

44. Azar Gat, *Military Thought: The Nineteenth Century* (Oxford, 1992), pp. 21–4, 45–8. Some indication of the bias against theory in this period is Gat's decision to begin his discussion, for practical purposes, with the emergence of Moltke. The previous forty years are treated as a kind of foreword.

45. A particular point of M. D. Welch, *Science and the British Officer: The Early Days of the Royal United Services Institute For Defence Studies (1829–1869)* (Weymouth, 1998).

46. Anatol Lieven, 'Nasty Little Wars', *The National Interest* 62 (Winter, 2000/01), 65–76.

47. Arden Bucholz, *Moltke, Schlieffen, and Prussian War Planning* (New York, 1991), pp. 25–7.

48. John Sweetman, *War and Administration: The Significance of the Crimean War for the British Army* (Edinburgh, 1984). Sir James Outram, *The Conquest of Scinde: A Commentary*, 2 vols in 1 (Edinburgh, 1846) demonstrates matters were no less complex when dealt with on the spot.

49. Geoffrey Wawro, 'Austria versus the Risorgimento: A New look at Austria's Italian Strategy in the 1860s', *European History Quarterly* 26 (1996), 7–29.

50. Roger Norman Buckley, *The British Army in the West Indies. Society and the Military in a Revolutionary Age* (Gainesville, Fla., 1998), pp. 19–23. The negative side of the post-Napoleonic period's emphasis on practical problem-solving in best indicated by a general neglect of medical matters that far surpassed anything seen in the armies of the late Napoleonic years. The consequences for the sick and wounded in the Crimea and Italy were only the most visible – not the most horrible.

51. The best analysis of the General Staff concept in its early stages remains Charles White, *The Enlightened Soldier: Scharnhorst and the Militaerische Gesellschaft in Berlin, 1801–1805* (New York, 1989). Volume II of Michael Leggiere, 'The Life, Letters, and Campaigns of Friedrich Wilhelm Graf von Dennewitz', Dissertation, Florida State University, 1997, incorporates an account of the unlikely and successful 'marriage' between Buelow and Hermann von Boyen, the leading reformer who acted as his chief of staff during the Wars of Liberation.

52. Showalter, *Wars of German Unification, passim.*

53. Cf. inter alia Eberhard Kessel, *Moltke* (Stuttgart, 1957) – still by a long way the best analysis of Moltke's work and career; and Eberhard Kolb, 'Helmuth von Moltke in seiner Zeit. Aspekte und Probleme', in R. Foerster (ed.) *Generalfeldmarschall von Moltke: Bedeutung and Wirkung*, (Oldenbourg, 1991), pp. 1–17.

54. Ellis Kimerling Wirtschafter, *From Serf to Russian Soldier* (Princeton, 1990).

55. This line of argument is heavily based on Kagan, *Military Reforms of Nicholas I.* For Russia's strategic problems see as well A. D. Lambert, *The Crimean War: British Grand Strategy against Russia* (Manchester, 1990).

56. Cf. Hamilton, *Anglo-French Naval Rivalry, passim*; and C. J. Bartlett, *Great Britain and Sea Power, 1815–1853* (Oxford, 1963).

57. Lawrence Sondhaus, *The Habsburg Empire and the Sea: Austrian Naval Policy, 1797–1866* (West Lafayette, Indiana, 1989), is a good case study of that process.

58. Jacob Kipp, 'Consequences of Defeat: Modernizing the Russian Navy, 1856–1863', *Jahrbuecher fuer die Geschichte Osteuropas*, 20 (1973), 210–25.

59. Dennis Showalter, 'Weapons, Technology, and the Military in Metternich's Germany: A Study In Stagnation?', *Australian Journal of Politics and History* 24 (1978), 227–38.

60. Dennis E. Showalter, 'Infantry Weapons, Infantry Tactics, and the Armies of Germany, 1849–64', *European Studies Review* 4 (1974), 119–140, remains a useful case study and overview.

61. Dennis E. Showalter, *Railroads and Rifles: Soldiers, Technology, and the Unification of Germany* (Hamden, CT, 1975), pp. 167–178.

62. Hew Strachan, *From Waterloo to Balaklava: Tactics, Technology, and the British Army, 1815–54* (Cambridge, 1985), incorporates the best overview of linear tactics; Holmes, *Road to Sedan*, 208–16; and Geoffrey Wawro, *The Austro-Prussian War* (New York, 1996), pp. 22–5 and 32–5, are best for the rest.

63. Carl von Clausewitz, *On War*, tr. O. J. Matthys Jolles (New York, 1943), p. 173.

64. 'It seems to me that we cannot afford to keep our troops awaiting possible movements of the enemy, but that our true policy is, as far as we can, so to employ our own forces, as to give occupation to his at points of our selection.' Robert E. Lee to Jefferson Davis, June 25, 1863, in C. Dowdey and L. Manarin (eds) *The Wartime Papers of R. E. Lee* (New York, 1961), p. 532. By that time the Army of Northern Virginia certainly met the European criteria for a 'professionalized strike force' if ever an army did.

65. Michael Duffy, *Soldiers, Sugar and Seapower: The British Expeditions to the West Indies and the War against Revolutionary France* (Oxford, 1987).

66. Christopher Hall, *British Strategy in the Napoleonic War, 1803–1815* (Manchester, 1992).

67. Strachan, *Reform of the British Army*, p. 270.

68. J. Y. Wong, 'The Limits of Naval Power: British Gunboat Diplomacy in China from the *Nemesis* to the *Amethyst*, 1839–1949', *War and Society* 18 (2000), 93–120.

69. Douglas M. Peers, *Between Mars and Mammon; Colonial Armies and the Garrison State in Early Nineteenth Century India* (London, 1995) discuses the changing status and missions of the Bengal Army. Lorenzo Crowell, 'The Madras Army in the Northern Circars, 1832–1833: Pacification and Professionalism', Dissertation, Duke University, 1982, is an excellent case study of the growing dissonance between internal security and field operations.

70. Lawrence James surveys the period's military dynamic in *Raj: The Making and Unmaking of British India* (New York, 1997), pp. 119–47. See as well D. George Boyce, 'From Assaye to the *Assaye*: Reflections on British Government, Force, and Moral Authority in India', *The Journal of Military History* 63 (1999), 643–68.

71. The *troupes de la marine* at this period should not be confused with the *fusiliers marins*, first organised in 1859 to perform the shipboard and landing-party duties frequently associated with marine forces.

Nor were they amphibious-warfare specialists like the US Marine Corps of the WWII/Cold War era. Ironically, their missions and self-image most closely resembled those of the contemporary US Marines: an elite fire brigade/power projection entity.

72. Pierre Montagnon, *La Conquête de l' Algérie, 1830–1871* (Paris, 1986) is a recent general history. A. T. Sullivan, *Thomas-Robert Bugeaud, France and Algeria: 1784–1849: Power, Politics, and the Good Society* (Hamden, CT, 1983) stresses the changing nature of operations. Worth noting as well was Algeria's role as a place of exile for revolutionaries and activists.

73. Stacey R. Davis, 'Transforming the Enemy: Algerian Colonization, Imperial Clemency, and the Rehabilitation of France's 1851 Republican Insurrectionaries', Dissertation, Yale University, 1999.

74. Anthony Clayton, *France, Soldiers, and Africa* (London, 1988), pp. 245–6.

2. EUROPEAN WARFARE 1864–1913 *Jeremy Black*

1. See also his 'Weapons, Technology and the Military in Metternich's Germany: A Study in Stagnation?' *Australian Journal of Politics and History*, 24 (1978), pp. 227–38 and F. W. Kagan, *The Military Reforms of Nicholas I: The Origins of the Modern Russian Army* (New York, 1999).

2. M. Howard, *The Franco-Prussian War* (1961); Showalter, *Railroads and Rifles: Soldiers, Technology and the Unification of Germany* (Hamden, Connecticut, 1975); A. Bucholz, *Moltke and the German Wars, 1864–1871* (2001).

3. Bucholz, *Moltke, Schlieffen, and Prussian War Planning* (1991); D. J. Hughes (ed.), *Moltke on the Art of War* (Novato, California, 1993).

4. P. M. Kennedy (ed.), *The War Plans of the Great Powers 1880–1914* (1979); G. Rothenberg, 'Moltke, Schlieffen and the Doctrine of Strategic Envelopment', in P. Paret (ed.), *Makers of Modern Strategy* (Princeton, 1986), pp. 296–325; S. E. Miller, S. M. Lynn-Jones and S. Van Evera (eds.), *Military Strategy and the Origins of the First World War* (2nd edn, Princeton, 1991); G. A. Tunstall, *Planning for War Against Russia and Serbia: Austro-Hungarian and German Military Strategies, 1871–1914* (Boulder, 1993).

5. G. Ritter, *The Schlieffen Plan: Critique of a Myth* (1958); T. Zuber, 'The Schlieffen Plan Reconsidered', *War in History*, 6 (1999), pp. 262–305; R. T. Foley (ed.), 'Schlieffen's Last Kriegsspiel', *War Studies Journal*, 3 (1998), pp. 117–33 and 4 (1999), pp. 97–116.

6. King's College London, Liddell Hart Archive, Hamilton papers (hereafter KCL. Hamilton), 4/2/9, quotes pp. 36–7, 28–9, 35, 11, 56a.

7. H. L. Wesseling, *Soldier and Warrior: French Attitudes toward the Army and War on the Eve of the First World War* (Westport, Connecticut, 2000).

8. Hamilton to Lt. Col. Charles à Court Repington, 27 February 1911, KCL. Hamilton 5/1/7.

9. A. Gat, *The Development of Military Thought: the Nineteenth Century* (Oxford, 1992), pp. 114–72; D. Porch, *The March to the Marne: The French Army, 1871–1914* (Cambridge, 1981); J. Snyder, *The Ideology of the Offensive: Military Decision Making and the Disasters of 1914* (Ithaca, New York, 1984); R. A. Prete, 'The Preparation of the French Army Prior to World War I: An Historiographical Reappraisal', *Canadian Journal of History*, 26 (1991), pp. 241–66.

10. London, Public Record Office (hereafter PRO), War Office 106/6187, p. 77.

11. PRO. 30/40/13, p. 62.

12. J. A. Grant, *Big Business in Russia: The Putilov Company in Late Imperial Russia, 1868–1917* (Pittsburgh, 1999).

13. K. Neilson, 'Russia', in K. Wilson (ed.), *Decisions for War, 1914* (1995), p. 102.

14. N. Ferguson, 'Germany and the Origins of the First World War: New Perspectives', *Historical Journal*, 35 (1992), p. 733.

15. K. D. Moll, *The Influence of History upon Seapower 1865–1914* (Stanford, 1968), pp. 37–40.

16. W. H. McNeill, *The Pursuit of Power. Technology, Armed Force, and Society since A.D. 1000* (Oxford, 1982), pp. 237–8, 265–7.

17. I. McCallum, *Blood Brothers: Hiram and Hudson Maxim – Pioneers of Modern Warfare* (1999).

18. KCL. Hamilton 1/3/3, p. 166.

19. D. E. Showalter, 'Marching in Step: Technology and *Mentalité* for Artillery, 1848–1914', in S. C. Chiabotti (ed.), *Tooling for War: Military Transformation in the Industrial Age* (Chicago, 1996), pp. 27–48.

20. J. Smith, *The Spanish–American War* (1994).

21. KCL. Hamilton 4/2/9, p. 10.

22. W. Nasson, *The South African War, 1899–1902* (1999).

23. Hamilton to Richard Haldane, Secretary of State for War, 1 Sept. 1909, KCL. Hamilton 4/2/6, p. 5.

24. KCL. Hamilton 4/2/3, p. 45.

25. KCL. Hamilton 4/2/9, p. 10.

26. Hamilton to Repington, 16 Nov. 1910, KCL. Hamilton 5/1/7.

27. Hamilton to Erskine Childers, 30 Oct. 1910, KCL. Hamilton 5/1/8.

28. G. C. Cox, 'Of Aphorisms, Lessons, and Paradigms: Comparing the British and German Official Histories of the Russo–Japanese War', *Journal of Military History*, 66 (1992), pp. 389–401; S. P. MacKenzie, 'Willpower or Firepower? The Unlearned Military Lessons of the Russo–Japanese War', in D. Wells and S. Wilson (eds), *The Russo–Japanese War in Cultural Perspective, 1904–05* (1999), pp. 36–7.

29. M. Hoard, 'Men Against Fire: The Doctrine of the Offensive in 1914', in P. Paret *et al.* (eds), *Makers of Modern Strategy from Machiavelli to the Nuclear Age* (Princeton, 1986), pp. 510–26.

30. D. Herrmann, *The Arming of Europe and the Making of the First World War* (Princeton, 1996); D. Stevenson, *Armaments and the Coming of War. Europe, 1904–1914* (Oxford, 1996).

31. J. M. B. Lyon, ' "A Peasant Mob": The Serbian Army on the Eve of the Great War', *Journal of Military History*, 61 (1997), p. 493.

32. P. Gatrell, *Government, Industry and Rearmament in Russia, 1900–1914: The Last Argument of Tsarism* (Cambridge, 1994). For a more positive view, B. W. Menning, *Bayonets Before Bullets: The Imperial Russian Army, 1861–1914* (Bloomington, Indiana, 1993).

33. R. Hall, *The Balkan Wars 1912–1913. Prelude to the First World War* (2000).

3. THE FIRST WORLD WAR *Spencer Tucker*

1. See David G. Herrmann, *The Arming of Europe and the Making of the First World War* (Princeton, NJ, 1996).

2. A number of recent studies address the nature of the social tensions. See Robert J. W. Evans and Hartmut Pogge von Strandmann, *The Coming of the First World War* (Oxford, 1988).

3. Bernadotte E. Schmitt and Harold C. Vedeler, *The World in the Crucible, 1914–1919* (New York, 1984), p. 28.

4. Herrmann, *The Arming of Europe*, pp. 195–6.

5. Gary P. Cox, 'Schlieffen Plan', *The European Powers in the First World War, An Encyclopedia.* Edited by Spencer C. Tucker (New York, 1996), pp. 633–5.

6. Gerhard Ritter, *The Schlieffen Plan: Critique of a Myth* (New York, 1958).

7. On the battle see Henri Isselin, *The Battle of the Marne* (Garden City, NY, 1966).

8. Dardanelles Commission, *Final Report* (London, 1919); Robert Rhodes James, *Gallipoli, The History of a Noble Blunder* (New York, 1965); and Alan Moorehead, *Gallipoli* (New York, 1956).

9. See Georges Blond, *Verdun* (London, 1976) and Alistair Horne, *The Price of Glory. Verdun, 1916* (New York, 1962); also William Hermanns, *The Holocaust. From a Survivor of Verdun* (New York, 1972).

10. Lyn Macdonald, *Somme* (London, 1983); Martin Middlebrook, *First Day on the Somme* (New York, 1972).

11. For a general survey of the war in the East see Norman Stone, *The Eastern Front, 1914–1917* (New York, 1975).

12. The best single-volume history of World War I at sea is Paul G. Halpern, *A Naval History of World War I* (Annapolis, MD, 1994).

13. See Geoffrey M. Bennett, *The Battle of Jutland* (Philadelphia, 1964).

14. Hubert C. Johnson, *Breakthrough! Tactics, Technology, and the Search for Victory on the Western Front in World War I* (Novato, CA, 1994),

p. 17; Peter Simkins, *World War I. The Western Front* (New York, 1991), pp. 87–8.

15. In the British Army the total was 58 per cent from artillery and mortar shells, and slightly less than 39 per cent from machine gun and rifle bullets. Simkins, *World War I*, p. 124.

16. Boyd Dastrup, *King of Battle: A Branch History of the US Army's Field Artillery* (Fort Monroe, VA, 1992), pp. 126–9.

17. Johnson, *Breakthrough!*, p. 4; Boyd Dastrup, *The Field Artillery: History and Sourcebook* (Westport, CT, 1994), pp. 44–5. See also Bruce I. Gudmundsson, *On Artillery* (Westport, CT, 1993).

18. Philip J. Haythornthwaite, *World War One Source Book* (London, 1992), p. 181; David T. Zabecki, *Steel Wind. Colonel Georg Bruchmüller and the Birth of Modern Artillery* (Westport, CT, 1995), pp. 7 and 10; Randal Gray, *Chronicle of the First World War* (New York, 1991), II: 284.

19. For a discussion of tactics and technology in the war see Johnson, *Breakthrough!*

20. Martin Van Creveld, *Supplying War: Logistics from Wallenstein to Patton* (London, 1977), p. 110.

21. Robert Gardiner (ed), *The Eclipse of the Big Gun. The Warship 1906–45* (Annapolis, MD, 1992), p. 15.

22. Ibid., pp. 15–17.

23. For discussion of early submarines see Spencer C. Tucker, *Handbook of 19th Century Naval Warfare* (Stroud, 2000), pp. 173–185.

24. Herrmann, *The Arming of Europe and the Making of the First World War*, pp. 70–4; Correlli Barnett, *The Great War* (New York, 1980), p. 133.

25. Robert Cowley, 'The Somme: The Last 140 Days,' *MHQ: The Quarterly Journal of Military History*, Vol. VII, No. 4, Summer 1995: 81; Winston S. Churchill, *The World Crisis*. 6 vols (New York, 1923–31), III: 185–7; A. J. Smithers, *Cambrai. The First Great Tank Battle 1917* (London, 1992), pp. 37–53.

26. John F. Votaw, 'Tanks', *The European Powers in the First World War*, pp. 684–5; Smithers, *Cambrai*, pp. 49–50; Prior and Wilson, *Command on the Western Front*, pp. 228–9.

27. Churchill, *The World Crisis*, III: 186.

28. Barnett, *The Great War*, p. 84.

29. Johnson, *Breakthrough!*, pp. 170–3.

30. Ibid., pp. 71, 119–21 and 124.

31. Gray, *Chronicle of the First World War*, II: 297.

32. Theodore Roscoe, *On the Seas and in the Skies. A History of the U. S. Navy's Air Power* (New York, 1970), pp. 27–31.

33. Anthony Livesey, *The Historical Atlas of World War I* (New York, 1994), p. 15.

34. Gray, *Chronicle of the First World War*, I: 284; II: 290.

35. Richard P. Hallion, *Rise of Fighter Aircraft 1914–1918* (Annapolis, MD, 1984), pp. 8–13.

36. Lee Kennett, *The First Air War, 1914–1918* (New York, 1991), pp. 94 and 170.

37. Ibid., pp. 50 and 219.

38. Ibid., pp. 48–53.

39. Earl H. Tilford, Jr, 'Air Warfare, Strategic Bombing', *The European Powers in the First World War*, p. 14.

40. Raymond H. Fredette, *The Sky on Fire. The First Battle of Britain 1917–1918 and the Birth of the Royal Air Force* (New York, 1976), pp. 157, 221–6.

41. R. D. Layman, *Naval Aviation in the First World War. Its Impact and Influence* (Annapolis, MD, 1996).

42. Stanley Sandler, 'Warships, Aircraft Carriers', *The European Powers in the First World War*, pp. 731–2.

43. Livesey, *The Historical Atlas of World War I*, p. 156.

44. William Moore, *Gas Attack: Chemical Warfare, 1915 to the Present Day* (London, 1987), p. 11.

45. William R. Griffiths, *The Great War* (Wayne, NJ, 1986), p. 67.

46. Moore, *Gas Attack*, pp. 1–2; 23–5; Griffiths, *The Great War*, p. 67.

47. Moore, *Gas Attack*, pp. 72–85.

48. Simkins, *World War I*, p. 68.

49. Augustin M. Prentiss, *Chemicals in War* (New York, 1937), pp. 661–2.

50. Gray, *Chronicle of the First World War I*, I: 287.

51. Bohon, 'Brusilov Offensive', *The European Powers in the First World War*, pp. 145–7; Brusilov, *A Soldier's Note-Book*, pp. 218–43.

52. A misnomer. Actually one of the first to propose abandoning linear tactics was French Captain André Laffarague who wrote a pamphlet on the subject in 1915. They should more properly be called 'infiltration tactics' or 'storm troop tactics'. See Zabecki, *Steel Wind*, p. 23, and Bruce I. Gudmundsson, *Stormtroop Tactics. Innovation in the German Army, 1914–1918* (Westport, CT, 1995).

53. See Erwin Rommel, *Infantry Attacks*. Trans. G. E. Kidde (Washington, 1944), pp. 168–207. Also Gudmundsson, *Stormtroop Tactics*.

54. Griffiths, *The Great War*, pp. 132–7.

55. On the latter see Arthur Mendel, 'On Interpreting the Fate of Imperial Russia', in Theofanis George Stavrou (ed.), *Russia Under the Last Tsar* (Minneapolis, 1969).

4. The European civil war: reds versus whites in Russia and Spain, 1917–1939 *Francisco J. Romero Salvadó*

1. As will be explained throughout this paper these conflicts were complex phenomena that went far beyond a mere struggle of 'Reds' versus 'Whites'.

2. For the narrative of Russian events the old Julian Calendar, thirteen days behind that in the West, will be used until 31 January 1918 (14 February) when the Soviet government switched to the European calendar.

3. O. Figes, *A People's Tragedy* (London, 1996), pp. 408–19.

4. J. Bradley, *Civil War in Russia, 1917–20* (London, 1975), pp. 22–3.

5. Events narrated by John Reed, *Ten Days that Shook the World* (New York, 1986), pp. 181–218, 252.

6. It was the so-called 'war by railways', E. Mawsdley, *The Russian Civil War* (London, 1987), pp. 16–30.

7. Bradley, *op.cit.*, pp. 37–9.

8. J. D. White, *The Russian Revolution, 1917–21* (London, 1994), pp. 179–80.

9. W. H. Chamberlin, *The Russian Revolution, 1917–21*, 2 vols (Oxford, 1987), Vol. 1, p. 403.

10. O. Figes, *Peasant Russia, Civil War. The Volga Countryside in the Revolution, 1917–21* (Oxford, 1989), p. 4.

11. R. Pipes, *Russia under the Bolshevik Regime, 1919–24* (London, 1994), pp. 10–11.

12. J. Smele, *Civil War in Siberia. The Anti-Bolshevik Government of Admiral Kolchak, 1918–20* (Cambridge, 1996).

13. Chamberlin, *op.cit.*, Vol. 2, pp. 134–48, 242–65, 320–33. For the military outcome from the Whites' angle see Denikin's memoirs, *The White Army* (Cambridge, 1992).

14. Mawdsley, *op.cit.*, pp. 196–200.

15. Smele, *op.cit.*, pp. 234–5.

16. Ibid, p. 677.

17. Bradley, *op.cit.*, p. 166.

18. Figes, *Peasant Russia*, pp. 162–5; Smele, *op.cit.*, pp. 195–8.

19. C. Read, *From Tsar to Soviets. The Russian People and their Revolution, 1917–21* (London, 1996), p. 196;

20. The appearance of a few tanks in Iudenich's march on Petrograd sent the Red defenders into panic. A handful of British tanks also had a stupefying effect at the start of Denikin's offensive in May 1919. This seems to indicate the vital role they might have played if used in large numbers.

21. Britain offered more consistent aid, although from a diplomatic standpoint and due to her past economic interests and political alliance, France was most implacable in her hostility to the Soviet Union. Most British military aid was sent to Kolchak between October 1918 and October 1919, amounting to 97 000 tons of supplies, including 600 000 rifles, 6381 machine-guns, 192 field guns, 346 million rounds of small-arms ammunition and over 200 000 uniforms. Denikin received in the course of 1919, 198 000 rifles, 6200 machine guns and 500 000 rounds of small-arms ammunition. Some aircraft and tanks were provided including British crews. Pipes, *op.cit.*, pp. 66–79; Mawdsley, *op.cit.*, pp. 144, 167.

22. Smele, *op.cit.*, p. 192.

23. Pipes, *op.cit.*, pp. 9–10.

24. Bradley, *op.cit.*, pp. 167–8, 181–2.

25. O. Figes, 'The Red Army and Mass Mobilization during the Russian Civil War', *Past and Present*, no. 129 (November 1990), pp. 168–211.

26. Chamberlin, *op.cit.*, Vol. 2, pp. 19, 238.

27. Mawdsley, *op.cit.*, pp. 181, 274–5.

28. Some of the most important rural uprisings took place at the end of the civil war. The peasants felt that they should no longer put up with wartime requisitions. Over 118 separate rebellions took place in February 1921. However, badly armed and uncoordinated, the majority were put down in a short time. Read, *op.cit.*, pp. 266–72.

29. K. Mc. Dermott and J. Agnew, *The Comintern* (London, 1996), pp. 14–18; D. Geary, *European Labour Protest, 1848–1939* (London, 1984), pp. 134–5.

30. H. Graham and P. Preston (eds), *The Popular Front in Europe* (London, 1987), p. 1.

31. The Dictatorship aggravated tensions and rivalries within the armed forces. Sections of the army were incensed by Primo's plan to transform his provisional military government into permanent rule, cut down the military budget, reduce the inflated officer corps and deal with the promotion system. From 1926 the regime was plagued by military conspiracies and plots.

32. H. Thomas, *The Spanish Civil War*, 3rd edn (Harmondsworth, 1986), pp. 215–57.

33. P. Preston, *Franco* (London, 1993), pp. 178–84.

34. P. Preston, *A Concise History of the Spanish Civil War* (London, 1996), pp. 145, 153.

35. M. Richards, *A Time of Silence. Civil War and the Culture of Repression in Franco's Spain, 1936–1945* (Cambridge, 1994), p. 7; Preston, *Concise*, p. 160.

36. M. Alpert, 'Soldiers, Politics and War', in P. Preston (ed.), *Revolution and War in Spain, 1931–1939* (London, 1984), pp. 210–11.

37. F. J. Romero Salvadó, *Twentieth Century Spain* (London, 1999), p. 114.

38. H. Graham, 'Against the State: A Genealogy of the Barcelona May Days (1937)', *European History Quarterly*, Vol. 29, No. 4 (1999), pp. 485–542.

39. Alpert, 'Soldiers', p. 212.

40. M. Alpert, *A New International History of the Spanish Civil War* (London, 1996), p. 53.

41. R. H. Whealey, *Hitler and the Spanish Civil War, 1936–39* (Lexington, 1989), pp. 28–9

42. P. Preston, 'Mussolini's Spanish Adventure: From Limited Risk to War', in P. Preston and A. L. Mackenzie, *The Republic Besieged. Civil War in Spain* (Edinburgh, 1996), pp. 42–3.

43. Whealey, *op.cit.*, p. 14.

44. J. Lacouture, *Léon Blum* (New York, 1982), pp. 305–7; J. Avilés Farré, *Pasión y farsa. Franceses y Británicos ante la Guerra Civil Española* (Madrid, 1994), pp. 2–10.

45. See the following works by E. Moradiellos: 'The Origins of British Non-Intervention in the Spanish Civil War: Anglo-Spanish Relations in Early 1936', *European History Quarterly*, Vol. 21 (1991), pp.

339–61; 'The Gentle General: The Official British Perception of General Franco during the Spanish Civil War' in Preston and Mackenzie, *The Republic Besieged*, pp. 2–9.

46. G. Howson, *Arms for Spain. The Untold Story of the Spanish Civil War* (London, 1998), pp. 55–6.

47. Moradiellos, 'The Origins', p. 360.

48. T. G. Powell, *Mexico and the Spanish Civil War* (Albuquerque, 1981), p. 71.

49. D. Smyth, 'We Are with You: Solidarity and Self-Interest in Soviet Policy towards Republican Spain, 1936–1939' in Preston and Mackenzie, *The Republic Besieged*, pp. 88–100.

50. H. Thomas, *op.cit.*, p. 463.

51. H. Graham, 'War, Modernity and Reform: The Premiership of Juan Negrín', in Preston and Mckenzie (eds), *The Republic Besieged*, p. 193.

52. Howson, *op.cit.*, pp. 130–1, 142.

53. Thomas, *op.cit.*, p. 982.

54. Howson, *op.cit.*, p. 74.

55. P. Preston, 'Italy and Spain in Civil War and World War', in P. Preston and S. Balfour, *Spain and the Great Powers* (London, 1999), p. 173.

56. Whealey, *op.cit.*, pp. 101–2.

57. Howson, *op.cit.*, pp. 107–13, 138–40, 146–52.

58. Lacouture, *op.cit.*, pp. 346–9.

59. E. Moradiellos, *La perfidia de Albión. El gobierno británico y la guerra civil española* (Madrid, 1996), pp. 272–81.

60. Thomas, *op.cit.*, pp. 852–5.

61. Avilés, *op.cit.*, p. 177.

5. THE SECOND WORLD WAR   *S. P. Mackenzie*

The scholarly literature on the Second World War in English alone is enormous. Space limitations therefore dictate that the books cited – chosen in part because of their comparatively recent vintage – are illustrative rather than a comprehensive in scale.

1. See A. R. Millett and W. Murray (eds), *Military Effectiveness*, ii, *The Interwar Period* (Boston, 1988).

2. For the *Wehrmacht* in this successful period see Research Institute for Military History, *Germany and the Second World War*, ii–iv (Oxford, 1991–8). For comparisons with the armed forces of other powers at war see the relevant portions of the chapter on each state in A. R. Millett and W. Murray (eds), *Military Effectiveness*, iii, *The Second World War* (Boston, 1988).

3. L. Grenkevich, *The Soviet Partisan Movement, 1941–1944*, D. Glantz (ed.) (London, 1999); M. R. D. Foot, *SOE: An Outline History of the Special Operations Executive, 1940–1946* (London, 1984); G. Chalou, *The*

Secrets War: The Office of Strategic Services in World War II (Washington, DC, 1992).

4. R. Shaffer, *Wings of Judgment: American Bombing in World War II* (New York, 1985); C. C. Crane, *Bombs, Cities and Civilians: American Airpower Strategy in World War II* (Lawrence, 1993); D. Richards, *The Hardest Victory: RAF Bomber Command in the Second World War* (London, 1994); S. A. Garrett, *Ethics and Air Power in World War II: The British Bombing of German Cities* (New York, 1993).

5. A. W. Vincent, *The Illusion of Victory: Fascist Propaganda and the Second World War* (New York, 1998); R. Herzstein, *The War that Hitler Won: Goebbels and the Nazi News Media Campaign* (New York, 1997); R. Mackay, *The Test of War: Inside Britain, 1939–45* (New York, 1998); J. Barber, *The Soviet Home Front, 1941–1945* (New York, 1991).

6. See, for example, O. Bartov, *Hitler's Army: Soldiers, Nazis, and War in the Third Reich* (New York, 1991); J. A. Crang, *The British Army and the People's War* (Manchester, 2000).

7. On the conditions under which soldiers switched sides see, for example, A. Beevor, *Stalingrad* (London, 1998). On the political uses to which senior turncoats were put see H. Shukman (ed.), *Stalin's Generals* (London, 1993), chapter 23.

8. For instance, C. D. Laurie, *The Propaganda Warriors: America's Crusade against Nazi Germany* (Lawrence, KS, 1996).

9. See D. M. Glantz, *The Role of Intelligence in Soviet Military Strategy in World War II* (Novato, CA, 1990); *British Intelligence in the Second World War* (Cambridge, 1993); Chalou, op.cit.

10. See M. Harrison (ed.), *The Economies of World War II: Six Great Powers in International Comparison* (New York, 1998); G. T. Millet and H. Rockoff (eds), *The Sinews of War: Essays on the Economic History of World War II* (Ames, IA, 1993); Mackay, *op.cit.*, R. Overy, *War and Economy in the Third Reich* (Oxford, 1994); H. Vatter, *The US Economy in World War II* (New York, 1985).

11. See A. F. Wilt, *War From the Top: German and British Decision Making during World War II* (Bloomington, IN, 1990); A. Bullock, *Hitler and Stalin* (London, 1991), chapters 15–18; Barnett, *Hitler's Generals, passim*; B. Mueller-Hillebrand, *Germany and Its Allies in World War II: A Record of Axis Collaboration Problems* (Frederick, MY, 1980).

12. Wilt, *op.cit.*; K. Sainsbury, *Churchill and Roosevelt at War* (New York, 1994).

13. Bullock, *op.cit.*; A. Seaton, *Stalin as Military Commander* (New York, 1975).

14. See, for instance, D. French, *Raising Churchill's Army: The British Army and the War against Germany, 1919–1945* (Oxford, 2000); M. D. Doubler, *Closing with the Enemy: How GIs Fought the War in Europe, 1944–1945* (Lawrence, KS, 1994); I. Gooderson, *Air Power at the Battlefront: Allied Close Air Support in Europe, 1943–45* (London, 1998); D. M. Glantz and J. House, *When Titans Clashed: How the Red Army Stopped Hitler* (Lawrence, KS, 1995), chapters 9–17.

15. See Shukman, *Stalin's Generals, passim*; J. Keegan (ed.), *Churchill's Generals* (London, 1991); C. D'Este, *Patton: A Genius for War* (New York, 1995).

16. See R. Overy, *Why the Allies Won* (London, 1995).

6. COLONIAL WARS 1815–1960 *Bruce Vandervort*

1. P. D. Curtin, *Disease and Empire: The Health of European Troops in the Conquest of Africa* (Cambridge, 1998), pp. xii, 159.

2. Ibid., p. 177.

3. Galliéni, *Deux campagnes au Soudan français, 1886–1888* (Paris, 1891), p. 626.

4. Herron (compiler), *Colonial Army Systems of the Netherlands, Great Britain, France, Germany, Portugal, Italy, and Belgium* (Washington, DC, 1901), p. 44.

5. M. C. Gillett, *The [US] Army Medical Department, 1865–1917*, Army Historical Series (Washington, DC, 1995), p. 67.

6. R. W. Slatta, ' "Civilization" Battles "Barbarism": The Limits of Argentine Indian Frontier Strategies', in James C. Bradford (ed.), *Soldiers at the Interface: The Military and Conflict Between Cultures* (College Station, Texas, 1997), p. 144.

7. Killingray, 'Colonial warfare in West Africa, 1870–1914', in J. A. DeMoor and H. L. Wesseling (eds), *Imperialism and War: Essays on Colonial War in Asia and Africa* (Leiden, 1989), p. 146.

8. Quoted in J.-C. Jauffret, *Parlement, gouvernement, commandement: l'armée de métier sous la 3e République, 1871–1914*, vol. 2 (Vincennes, 1987), p. 1141.

9. Grosser Generalstabs, *Die Kaempfe der deutschen Truppen in Suedwestafrika auf Grund amlichten Materials bearbeitet von der Kriegsgeschichtlichen Abteilung I des grossen Generalstabs*, vol. 2 (Berlin, 1907), p. 300.

10. J. E. Alvarez, 'Between Gallipoli and D-Day: Alhucemas 1925', *Journal of Military History* 63, 1 (January 1999): 81 n. 15.

11. Quoted in Stanley Karnow, *Vietnam, A History: The First Complete Account of Vietnam at War* (New York, 1983), p. 169.

7. NAVAL POWER AND WARFARE *Lawrence Sondhaus*

1. Andrew J. Lambert, 'Introduction of Steam', in *Steam, Steel and Shellfire: The Steam Warship 1815–1905*, ed. Robert Gardiner (London, 1992), pp. 19–20; Douglas Dakin, *British and American Philhellenes during the War of Greek Independence, 1821–33* (Thessaloniki, 1955), 124–6, 137.

2. Lambert, 'Introduction of Steam', pp. 17–23, 29; Denis Griffiths, 'Warship Machinery', in *Steam, Steel and Shellfire: The Steam Warship 1815–1905*, ed. Robert Gardiner (London, 1992), p. 170.

3. Lambert, 'Introduction of Steam', p. 19; Maurice Dupont and Étienne Taillemite, *Les guerres navales françaises: du Moyen Age à la guerre du Golfe* (Paris, 1995), pp. 227–33.

4. Andrew J. Lambert, *Battleships in Transition: The Creation of the Steam Battlefleet, 1815–1860* (Annapolis, Maryland, 1984), p. 19; idem, 'Introduction of Steam', pp. 23–4; David K. Brown, *Paddle Warships: The Earliest Steam Powered Fighting Ships, 1815–1850* (London, 1993), p. 79; Griffiths, 'Warship Machinery', p. 170.

5. Andrew J. Lambert, 'The Screw Propeller Warship', in *Steam, Steel and Shellfire: The Steam Warship 1815–1905*, ed. Robert Gardiner (London, 1992), pp. 35, 43; Brown, *Paddle Warships*, p. 48.

6. C. I. Hamilton, *Anglo-French Naval Rivalry, 1840–1870* (Oxford, 1993), pp. 37, 42–3, 51–3; Andrew J. Lambert, *The Last Sailing Battlefleet: Maintaining Naval Mastery, 1815–1850* (London, 1991), p. 90; idem, 'The Screw Propeller Warship', 36–40, 46; idem, *Battleships in Transition*, pp. 124, 138, 140.

7. Anthony J. Watts, *The Imperial Russian Navy* (London, 1990), pp. 12–13; F. N. Gromov (ed.), *Tri Veka Rossiiskogo Flota* (St. Petersburg, 1996), vol. 1, pp. 191–2; Bernd Langensiepen and Ahmet Güleryüz, *The Ottoman Steam Navy, 1828–1923*, ed. and trans. James Cooper (Annapolis, Maryland, 1995), pp. 4, 193. Andrew J. Lambert, *The Crimean War: British Grand Strategy against Russia, 1853–56* (Manchester, 1991), p. 60, and idem, *Battleships in Transition*, p. 92, argues that competent gunnery using solid shot alone would have achieved the same outcome at Sinope, citing the fact that it took six hours for the Russians to destroy the Turco–Egyptian squadron.

8. Andrew J. Lambert, 'Iron Hulls and Armour Plate', in *Steam, Steel and Shellfire: The Steam Warship 1815–1905*, ed. Robert Gardiner (London, 1992), p. 52, considers the performance of the batteries to have been 'much exaggerated'. See also James Phinney Baxter, *The Introduction of the Ironclad Warship* (Cambridge, Massachusetts, 1933), pp. 78–86; Watts, *The Imperial Russian Navy*, p. 13.

9. Lambert, 'Iron Hulls and Armour Plate', p. 53.

10. Lambert, 'The Screw Propeller Warship', pp. 41, 46; idem, *Battleships in Transition*, pp. 65, 122–47.

11. Lambert, *Battleships in Transition*, pp. 101, 122–43; idem, Iron Hulls and Armour Plate', pp. 53–4; *Conway's All the World's Fighting Ships, 1860–1905* (London, 1979), pp. 286–7.

12. David K. Brown, *Warrior to Dreadnought: Warship Development, 1860–1905* (London, 1997), pp. 12–13; Lambert, 'Iron Hulls and Armour Plate', pp. 55–8; *Conway, 1860–1905*, pp. 7–13.

13. David K. Brown, 'The Era of Uncertainty, 1863–1878', in *Steam, Steel and Shellfire: The Steam Warship 1815–1905*, ed. Robert Gardiner (London, 1992), pp. 76–8; *Conway, 1860–1905*, pp. 4–5, 12–18.

236 *Notes and References*

14. Lawrence Sondhaus, *The Habsburg Empire and the Sea: Austrian Naval Policy, 1797–1866* (West Lafayette, Indiana, 1989), pp. 255–6.

15. James J. Tritten, 'Doctrine and Fleet Tactics in the Royal Navy', in *A Doctrine Reader: The Navies of the United States, Great Britain, France, Italy, and Spain*, ed. James J. Tritten and Luigi Donolo (Newport, RI, 1995), p. 21; *idem*, 'Navy and Military Doctrine in France', p. 54.

16. Langensiepen and Güleryüz, *The Ottoman Steam Navy*, pp. 5–7, 162; Gromov, *Tri Veka Rossiiskogo Flota*, 1:252–3; Watts, *The Imperial Russian Navy*, pp. 15–16. On the Whitehead firm see Antonio Casali and Marina Cattaruzza, *Sotto i mari del mondo: La Whitehead, 1875–1990* (Rome, 1990).

17. John Roberts, 'Warships of Steel, 1879–1889', in *Steam, Steel and Shellfire: The Steam Warship 1815–1905*, ed. Robert Gardiner (London, 1992), p. 107.

18. Griffiths, 'Warship Machinery', pp. 176–7.

19. John Campbell, 'Naval Armaments and Armour', in *Steam, Steel and Shellfire: The Steam Warship 1815–1905*, (ed.) Robert Gardiner (London, 1992), p. 163; Griffiths, 'Warship Machinery', p. 177.

20. John Roberts, 'The Pre-Dreadnought Age, 1890–1905', in *Steam, Steel and Shellfire: The Steam Warship 1815–1905*, ed. Robert Gardiner (London, 1992), p. 113.

21. Lawrence Sondhaus, *Preparing for Weltpolitik: German Sea Power before the Tirpitz Era* (Annapolis, Maryland, 1997), pp. 221–5.

22. Lawrence Sondhaus, *The Naval Policy of Austria–Hungary, 1867–1918: Navalism, Industrial Development, and the Politics of Dualism* (West Lafayette, Indiana, 1994), pp. 170–86.

23. Watts, *The Imperial Russian Navy*, pp. 22–3; David C. Evans and Mark R. Peattie, *Kaigun: Strategy, Tactics, and Technology in the Imperial Japanese Navy, 1887–1941* (Annapolis, Maryland, 1997), pp. 119–24.

24. Charles H. Fairbanks Jr, 'The Origins of the *Dreadnought* Revolution: A Historiographical Essay', *International History Review*, xiii (1991), p. 262.

25. Unless otherwise noted, sources for the next several paragraphs are Nicholas Lambert, 'Admiral Sir John Fisher and the Concept of Flotilla Defence, 1904–1909', *Journal of Military History*, lix (1995), pp. 641–60; Jon Tetsuro Sumida, *In Defence of Naval Supremacy: Finance, Technology and British Naval Policy, 1889–1914* (Boston, 1989), pp. 50–61; *idem*, 'Sir John Fisher and the *Dreadnought*: The Sources of Naval Mythology', *Journal of Military History*, lix (1995), p. 620 and *passim*; Campbell, 'Naval Armaments and Armour', p. 165; Griffiths, 'Warship Machinery', p. 178.

26. Sumida, *In Defence of Naval Supremacy*, p. 358.

27. The most recent of many English accounts on the battle is Keith Yates, *Flawed Victory: Jutland 1916* (London, 2000). On the German perspective see Holger H. Herwig, *'Luxury' Fleet: The Imperial German Navy, 1888–1918*, revised ed. (Atlantic Highlands, NJ, 1987), pp. 178–89.

28. See Erik Goldstein and John H. Maurer, *The Washington Naval Conference: Naval Rivalry, East Asian Stability, and the Road to Pearl Harbor* (Illford, 1994).

29. Joseph A. Maiolo, *The Royal Navy and Nazi Germany, 1933–39: A Study in Appeasement and the Origins of the Second World War* (London, 1998), pp. 12, 15; Ernest Andrade Jr, The Cruiser Controversy in Naval Limitations Negotiations, 1922–1936', *Military Affairs*, xlviii (1984), pp. 113–20.

30. Herwig, *'Luxury' Fleet*, pp. 247, 291.

31. Richard Dean Burns, 'Regulating Submarine Warfare, 1921–41: A Case Study in Arms Control and Limited War', *Military Affairs*, xxxv (1971), pp. 57–8; Henri Legohérel, *Histoire de la Marine française* (Paris, 1999), pp. 105–6.

32. See Maiolo, *The Royal Navy and Nazi Germany*, passim; Tobias R. Philbin III, *The Lure of Neptune: German Soviet Naval Collaboration and Ambitions, 1919–1941* (Columbia, SC, 1994), pp. 23–37.

33. German figure from James L. George, *History of Warships: From Ancient Times to the Twenty-first Century* (Annapolis, Maryland, 1998), p. 164; Soviet figure from I. V. Kasatonov, (ed.), *Tri Veka Rossiiskogo Flota* (St. Petersburg, 1996), vol. 3, 12.

34. Arthur J. Marder, *From the Dardanelles to Oran: Studies of the Royal Navy in War and Peace, 1915–1940* (London, 1974), pp. 180–2; Soviet figure from Kasatonov, *Tri Veka Rossiiskogo Flota*, 3:12.

35. Marder, *From the Dardanelles to Oran*, pp. 253–8; James J. Sadkovich, *The Italian Navy in World War II* (Westport, CT, 1994), pp. 90–5; Graham Rhys-Jones, *The Loss of the Bismarck: An Avoidable Disaster* (London, 1999), *passim*.

36. George, *History of Warships*, p. 145.

37. Michael Gannon, *Operation Drumbeat* (New York, 1990), xxi, p. 417.

38. Paul M. Kennedy, *The Rise and Fall of British Naval Mastery* (London, 1976), pp. 302, 333. 39. Ibid., p. 303.

40. George, *History of Warships*, pp. 184–5; Sadkovich, *Italian Navy*, pp. 290–1.

41. Eric Grove and Geoffrey Till, 'Anglo-American Maritime Strategy in the Era of Massive Retaliation, 1945–60', in *Maritime Strategy and Balance of Power: Britain and America in the Twentieth Century*, ed. John B. Hattendorf and Robert S. Jordan (New York, 1989), pp. 286–99.

42. Joel J. Sokolsky, 'Anglo–American Maritime Strategy in the Era of Flexible Response, 1960–80', in *Maritime Strategy and Balance of Power: Britain and America in the Twentieth Century*, ed. John B. Hattendorf and Robert S. Jordan (New York, 1989), pp. 311–2, 317.

43. George, *History of Warships*, pp. 181, 189–94; Legohérel, *Histoire de la Marine française*, pp. 119–21; Hugh Thomas, *Suez* (New York, 1966), pp. 123–49; Grove and Till, 'Anglo-American Maritime Strategy, 1945–60', pp. 296, 299.

44. 'Submarines of the Royal Navy', www. argonet. co. uk, accessed 28 October 2000.

45. 'World Navies Today', www. hazegray. org/worldnav/europe/france. htm, accessed 28 October 2000.

46. David K. Brown, *The Royal Navy and the Falklands War* (London, 1987).

47. George E. Hudson, 'Soviet Naval Doctrine and Soviet Politics, 1953–1975', *World Politics*, xxix (1976), pp. 90–113; Norman Polmar, *The Naval Institute Guide to the Soviet Navy*, 5th (ed.) (Annapolis, Maryland, 1991), pp. 16, 39–40, 135–45.

48. Polmar, *The Naval Institute Guide to the Soviet Navy*, pp. 148–9, calls the *Kirovs* 'battle cruisers'.

49. Kennedy, *Rise and Fall of British Naval Mastery*, p. 333; Polmar, *The Naval Institute Guide to the Soviet Navy*, pp. 96–7.

50. Polmar, *The Naval Institute Guide to the Soviet Navy*, pp. 2–4.

51. A. D. Baker III, 'World Navies in Review', US Naval Institute *Proceedings*, cxxvi/3 (March 2000), p. 35; 'World Navies Today', www.hazegray.org/worldnav/europe/ukraine.htm, accessed 28 October 2000.

52. Figures from 'World Navies Today', www.hazegray.org/worldnav/russia/, accessed 28 October 2000.

53. Russian naval officials initially alleged that the *Kursk* collided with a foreign (US) submarine shadowing it. See Norman Friedman, 'What Happened to the *Kursk*?', US Naval Institute *Proceedings*, cxxvi/10 (October 2000), pp. 4–6.

54. Baker, 'World Navies in Review', pp. 34–7; 'Submarines of the Royal Navy', www.argonet.co.uk, accessed 28 October 2000.

55. Richard Cobbold, 'Kosovo: What the Navies Did', US Naval Institute *Proceedings*, cxxv/10 (October 1999), p. 87.

56. Thomas E. Engevall, 'Swedish Navy Mixes Evolution and Revolution to Launch Stealth Multimission Corvette', US Naval Institute *Proceedings*, cxxv/3 (March 1999), pp. 60–2.

57. Kit Bonner, 'Naval Propulsion for the 21st Century: The Azipod System', US Naval Institute *Proceedings*, cxxv/8 (August 1999), pp. 74–6.

8. THE TRANSFORMATION OF WAR IN EUROPE 1945–2000 *Warren Chin*

1. See M. Kaldor, *New and Old Wars. Organised Violence in the Global Era* (Cambridge, 1999); C. Hables Gray, *Postmodern War: The New Politics of Conflict* (London, 1997); S. Woodward, 'Failed States: Warlordism and Tribal Warfare', *Naval War College Review*, vol. LII, no. 2, spring 1999); Mark Duffield, 'Post-Modern Conflict: Warlords Post Adjustment States and Private Protection', *Civil Wars*, vol. 1, no. 1, (Spring 1998).

2. G. Parker, *The Military Revolution: Military Innovation and the Rise of the West, 1500–1800* (Cambridge, 1988).

3. H. Strachan, *European Armies and the Conduct of War* (London, 1983), pp. 38–90.

4. S. Naveh, *In Pursuit of Military Excellence: The Evolution of Operational Theory* (London, 1997), pp. 30–61.

5. N. Davies, *Europe. A History* (London, 1997), p. 1005.

6. K. J. Holsti, *Peace and War: armed conflicts and international order 1648–1989* (Cambridge, 1991), pp. 285–9.

7. M. Gareev, *If War Comes Tomorrow: The Contours of Future Armed Conflict* (London, 1998).

8. J. Ce, 'The Utility of Force in a World of Scarcity', *International Security*, vol. 22, no. 3 (Winter 1997/98), p. 143.

9. M. Mandelbaum, 'Is Major War Obsolete?' *Survival*, vol. 40, no. 4, Winter 1998–9, pp. 24–5.

10. F. Fukyama, *The End of History and the Last Man* (London, 1992).

11. R. Kaplan, *Balkan Ghosts: A Journey Through History* (New York, 1993).

12. W. W. Hagen, 'The Balkans' Lethal Nationalisms', *Foreign Affairs* July/August 1999, pp. 52–64.

13. M. Ignatieff, *The Warrior's Honour: Ethnic War and the Modern Conscience* (London, 1998), pp. 34–41.

14. S. L. Burg and P. S. Shoup, *The War in Bosnia Herzegovina: Ethnic Conflict and International Intervention* (New York, 1999), p. 5.

15. S. Huntington, 'The Clash of Civilisations', *Foreign Affairs*, Vol. 71, No. 3, Summer 1993.

16. B. Barber, *Jihad versus McWorld* (New York, 1995).

17. R. Kaplan, *The Ends of the Earth: A Journey at the Dawn of the 21st Century* (New York, 1996).

18. M. Kaldor, *New and Old Wars* (London, 1999), p. 5.

19. Ibid., p. 5.

20. C. Bellamy, *Knights in White Armour: The New Art of War and Peace* (London, 1997), pp. 30–4.

21. W. P. Strobel, 'The Media and US Policies Toward Intervention: A Closer Look at the CNN Effect' in C. A. Croker *et al.*, *Managing Global Chaos: Sources and Responses to International Conflict.* (Washington, DC: US Institute of Peace Press, 1996), pp. 357–76. See also S. Badsey, 'The influence of the media on recent British military operations', in I. Stewart and S. Carrauthers, (eds.), *War Culture and the Media* Trowbridge, 1996), pp. 5–21.

22. M. Ignatieff, *The Warrior's Honor: Ethnic War and the Modern Conscience* (London, 1998), p. 21.

23. M. Hudson and J. Stainer, *War and the Media* (Bodmin, 1997), p. 279.

24. Ibid., p. 283.

25. For an in-depth discussion of this lack of US vital national interests in the conflict in Bosnia see B. D. Barkey, 'Bosnia: A Question of Intervention', *Strategic Review*, Autumn 1993, pp. 48–59.

26. *International Herlad Tribune*, 26 October 1992.
27. S. Badsey, 'The influence of the media on recent British military operations', in I. Stewart and S. Carruthers (eds), *War Culture and the Media* (Trowbridge, 1996), p. 3
28. S. Badsey, 'The influence of the media on recent British military operations', in I. Stewart and S. Carruthers (eds), *War Culture and the Media* (Trowbridge, 1996), p. 6.
29. M. Kaldor, *New and Old Wars* (1999), p. 5.
30. Ibid., p. 8.
31. S. L. Burg and P. S. Shoup, *The War in Bosnia* (1999), p. 39.
32. M. van Creveld, *The Transformation of War* (New York, 1991), pp. 20–1.
33. M. van Creveld, *The Transformation of War* (New York, 1991).
34. See A. Roberts, 'Crisis in UN Peacekeeping' and J. MacKinley, 'Improving Multifunctional Forces', *Survival*, vol. 36, Autumn 1994.
35. General Lewis MacKenzie, *Peacekeeper: The Road to Sarajevo* (Vancouver, 1993) p. 201.
36. E. Luttwak, 'Toward Post-Heroic Warfare', *Foreign Affairs*, Vol. 74, No. 3 May/June 1995, p. 114.
37. T. Moackaitis, *Peace Operations and Intrastate Conflicts: The Sword or the Olive Branch* (London, 1999) p. 90.
38. Ibid.
39. Ibid.
40. General Sir Michael Rose, *Fighting for Peace* (London, 1998), p. 200.
41. This term was used by M. Kaldor in the early 1980s to describe technically complex and expensive weapons that offered little in the way of a combat advantage. See the *Baroque Arsenal* (London, 1982).
42. C. de-Jonge Oudrat, 'Bosnia' in D. C. F. Daniel and B. Hayes, (eds), *Coercive Inducement and the Containment of International Crises* (Washington, DC, 1999), p. 71.
43. S. L. Burg and P. Shoup, *The War in Bosnia* (1999), p. 352.
44. T. Ripley, *Operation Deliberate Force: The Campaign in Bosnia 1995* (Lancaster, 1999) p. 167.
45. Ibid., p. 169.
46. Ibid., p. 207
47. T. Ripley, *Operation Deliberate Force* (Lancaster, 1999), p. 268.
48. Ibid., p. 21.
49. M. C. McLaughlin, 'Assessing the Effectiveness of Deliberate Force: Harnessing the Political–Military Connection', in Colonel Robert Owen (ed.), *Deliberate Force: A Case Study in Effective Air Campaigning* (Maxwell Air Force Base, Alabama, 2000), p. 193.
50. R. Holbrooke, *To End a War* (New York, 1999), p. 104.
51. Ibid., p. 119.
52. Ibid., p. 149.
53. General M. Rose, *Fighting For Peace* p. 240.

54. C. Bellamy, *Spiral Through Time: Beyond Conflict Intensity* SCSI Occasional Paper No. 35, August 1998, pp. 31–8.

55. Army Field Manual Vol. 5, Operations other than War Part 2, *Wider Peacekeeping* (London, 1995). See also Permanent Joint Head Quarters, *Peace Support Operations* Joint Warfare Publication 350, (Northwood, 1999).

56. PJHQ, *Peace Support Operations*, pp. 3–5 and 3–6.

57. E. Luttwak, 'Toward Post Heroic Warfare', *Foreign Affairs* Vol. 74, No. 3, May–June 1995, p. 110.

Notes on Contributors

Jeremy Black is Professor of History at Exeter University. His books include *War, Past, Present and Future, Western Warfare 1775–1882* and *War in the New Century*.

Warren Chin is currently a Lecturer at the British Joint Services Command and Staff College. From 1995–9 he was a Senior Lecturer in the War Studies Department, Royal Military Academy Sandhurst and from 1992–5 he taught politics and international politics at London Guildhall University. He completed his MA and PhD at the War Studies Department, King's College London. He has written on land warfare, the future of war, weapons acquisition and the defence industry. He is currently working on the history of the revolution in military affairs.

S. P. Mackenzie is Professor of History at the University of South Carolina and author of *The Home Guard: A Military and Political History, Politics and Military Morale: Current-Affairs and Citizenship Education in the British Army 1914–1950*, and *Revolutionary Armies in the Modern Era*.

Francisco J. Romero Salvadó is Senior Lecturer in European History at London Guildhall University and an expert on inter-war Spanish history.

Dennis Showalter is Professor of History at Colorado College, past president of the Society for Military History and joint editor of *War in History*. His publications include *Railroads and Rifles: Soldiers, Technology, and the Unification of Germany* and the forthcoming *Wars of German Unification*.

Lawrence Sondhaus is Associate Professor at the University of Indianapolis. His books include *Preparing for Weltpolitik: German Sea Power before the Tirpitz Era* and *Naval Warfare 1815–1941*.

Spencer Tucker holds the John Biggs Chair of Military History at the Virginia Military Institute. He is the author or editor of numerous books on military or naval history. His most recent book is *Who's Who in Twentieth-Century Warfare*.

Bruce Vandervort is Editor of the *Journal of Military History* and Associate Professor at the Virginia Military Institute. His works include *Wars of Imperial Conquest in Africa 1830–1914*.

Index

CPSIA information can be obtained
at www.ICGtesting.com
Printed in the USA
LVHW031702191220
674621LV00001B/68